DESIGN Of JOBS

DESIGN
Of
JOBS

Edited
By LOUIS E. DAVIS
JAMES C. TAYLOR

SECOND
EDITION

Goodyear Publishing Company, Inc.
Santa Monica, California

*"Without work
all life goes rotten—
but when work is soulless
life stifles and dies"*

Albert Camus

Library of Congress Cataloging in Publication Data

Davis, Louis E   comp.
  Design of jobs.

  Bibliography: p.
  1. Personal management—Addresses, essays, lectures.
2. Work design—Addresses, essays, lectures. 3. Job.
satisfaction—Addresses, essays, lectures.   I.   Taylor,
James C.,   joint comp. II. Title.
HF5549.D393   1979   658.3'06   78-23397
ISBN 0-87620-219-9

Current printing (last digit):

10 9 8 7 6 5 4 3 2 1

ISBN: 0-87620-219-9

Y-   2199-1

Printed in the United States of America

Cover: A. Marshall Licht

CONTENTS

Preface

Since publication of the first edition of *Design of Jobs* in 1972* developments in job and organization design, while positive on the whole, have been quite uneven. Most notably at the end of the 1960s, there burst upon the scene in advanced Western countries the explicit concern with the quality of working life as a social reform issue calling for public response. A focus quickly developed on the quality of life in the workplace and a variety of action programs have been stimulated to reform the organization of work and workers' relationships with organizations. Almost every Western country now either has a governmental agency devoted to enhancing the quality of working life, piecemeal or systematically, or has publicly supported private agencies similarly engaged. In a number of countries the quality of working life has been elevated to the status of a national economic necessity through coupling the quality of working life with productivity. The future of work reform is bright; scientific management and bureaucracy as conventionally practiced are under challenge and have uncertain futures.

Attempts in countries around the world to improve the quality of working life, although undertaken with different intensities, are producing a variety of new approaches to job design and work organization. Leading innovations are included in this edition. Some of the approaches are devoted to increasing participation by workers in the job design process itself. A third edition of *Design of Jobs* might well elaborate on these developments since there are too few complete reports at present.

---

*Davis, L.E. and Taylor, J.C., eds. (1972) *Design of Jobs,* London: Penguin Books.

In the face of the pressures to reform the organization of work in support of improving the quality of working life, we are disappointed at the imperceptibly slow advance in development of a solid theoretical base for the design of jobs. There are indications that future theoretical developments may shift from a focus on individual job design to the design of larger organizational units. Very disappointing is the failure to develop inclusive criteria and comprehensive measures of effectiveness by which different designs of jobs can be evaluated. This omission slows our rate of learning from the innovations being developed on the basis of field experience. Since the early work of Davis little has taken place to provide inclusive, comprehensive measures of cost effectiveness of job designs. Davis indicated then that not much progress would be made in the reform of job designs as long as the total costs of all outcomes of performing work were not considered in design. Although research on human asset accounting, useful in its own right, is taking place, it provides neither the stimulation for job reform nor the assistance the designer of jobs needs when making job design choices. Recent theoretical developments regarding the costs of some effects of different work organization hold promise for development of future measures which may be relevant for job design. Acknowledging that we have a serious gap in this edition, we reluctantly are obliged to omit readings on cost criteria for job design (Part 4 of the first edition) since existing writings are still only indicative and little new that overcomes the indicated shortcomings has become available since 1972.

The preparation of the papers contained in this book to provide a coherent and nonredundant set of readings was a considerable undertaking. We are indebted to Professor Gerald J. Wacker for the skill and effort he brought to this endeavor. To Eli Berniker we are indebted for the care and patience he gave to the final editing of the manuscript. We acknowledge with gratitude the support provided by the Ford Foundation, General Electric Foundation, and the Institute of Industrial Relations, University of California, Los Angeles. We are grateful to the authors and publishers of the papers in this volume for permitting us to edit and publish them in the form we have chosen. Lastly we are thankful to our colleagues at the Center for the Quality of Working Life for their advice and assitance. Of course none but ourselves are to be held responsible for the omissions or interpretations contained in this book.

Los Angeles, October 1978

Louis E. Davis
James C. Taylor

Overview

The major purpose of this book is to show that the concepts and requirements for the design of jobs have changed in recent years. The ways in which jobs are designed have become a central concern for highly developed societies. This concern becomes evident when we realize that most job designs are no longer socially evolved but are quite consciously created, at a particular time, and often by someone who will not perform the jobs. Georges Friedmann (1961), referring to the organization of work, said that we are now in *milieu technique* as distinct from the older *milieu naturel*. Hence we are faced with a new and serious responsibility for appropriately developing jobs and organizations, and linking them to the larger society. The requirement now is that, in a context having few external referents, organizations—with their technical and social systems, their roles and jobs—must be designed to satisfy a number of joint objectives. For the organization and its members the designs must allow for flexibility or adaptability in a social environment that is growing turbulent. For individuals the designs must provide meaningfulness; variety; connections to futures; as much autonomy or self-regulation as can be developed; a minimum of coercion; opportunities to learn, develop, and grow; choices and alternatives; and decision making in the work and its outcomes.

The readings included here start from the styles and models of job design in the industrial era. The remainder of the book emphasizes recent theoretical developments in the area of work roles as part of organization design rather than of job design, and the emerging empirical support for these new positions. Readings also emphasize that what we know about the nature of jobs and work is not enough to predict job design in the future—that we must also recognize the new forces in society at large, both their individual and combined effects.

The onset of the industrial revolution saw the disruption of a long historical evolution in the nature of jobs. The new train of development, whose beginnings were signalized by the work of Charles Babbage, moved from a natural or tradition-guided structure of jobs and role relationships to man-made, ordered, rationalized (in mechanical or economic terms) structures and relationships. At the height of this development (1890–1920), Frederick W. Taylor and Frank Gilbreth laid down the rule that any natural or tradition-guided development was to be viewed with suspicion, and that its existence was, in itself, reason enough to change it. We have been unequal to the task thus imposed on us of designing jobs and roles that appropriately relate man, with his needs and unique capabilities, to technology: to modify and design technology to permit effective social system design; to retain and support the social fabric in which work is done; and to meet man's needs as an individual and as a member of society. What we have seen is the rationalization of man, inappropriately called the rationalization of work, and in the 1960s, the rationalization of systems. Throughout the twentieth century the Taylor thesis was expanded into a pseudoscience of work and was dutifully taught to engineers, personnel managers, and business, industrial, and government managers. It was supported by an ideology and a positivist philosophy of American psychology, which can be epitomized as the robot model of man (von Bertalanffy, 1967, p. 7). All this was in accord with the social ideology of the industrial era and was enshrined as social policy in such governmentally issued pronouncements as the *U.S. Dictionary of Occupational Titles*.

TECHNOLOGY AND WORK: A DIFFERENCE BETWEEN JOBS AND WORK ROLES

Not so long ago tasks, jobs, and work were the blue-collar equivalent of occupations and professions. They were terms depicting workers' relationship to their labors. These terms could be thought of as static, well-delineated entities, differing only in the inclusiveness of their referents. The task was the basic molecular unit.* Tasks were the elements of jobs, and jobs were the components of work. But jobs and work, viewed in this way, include only the relationship between worker and product. Work in this sense may be said to include implicitly the workers' relationship to their tools and their relationships to other persons in the performance of work. However, explicit concern with the technical and social components of jobs and work is of more recent origin.

---

* Individual movements and motions, although smaller units than tasks, came in as specialized terms of time and motion study, and not as part of the common language.

In the early era of simple technology, the classical time and motion study did expressly include the workers' tools, but considered workers as machines— sometimes complicated, unreliable and recalcitrant machines. The more recent notion in mass production, that of workers as a physical extension of the machines they work with (or for), has perpetuated this particular man-machine relationship to the present day. But technology continues to develop, and now, in many settings of modern advanced (process) technology, the worker has ceased to be considered an extension of the machine and is instead thought to be its supervisor.

By technology we mean the complex or combination of techniques used to alter materials or information in some specified or anticipated way to achieve a desired end result. The term *modern advanced technology* has been used in at least two very different ways. One use refers to sophistication and newness in the production system or process; continuous process or its lesser form, automation, is the archetype here. Technology is applied to the specific requirements of a producing organization through the design of a technical system. The second use refers to sophistication and newness in the product, such as electronics. In popular usage both applications are correct. The new production process is new technology: A familiar product is created in a new way. A new product such as the computer is also a new technology if it in turn provides the technique for transforming something else in a new way. Strictly speaking, plastics, frequently referred to as a modern technology, are not a new technology, but are the *product* of a new technology—a new product of new methods.

Our definition of sophisticated or modern technology is confined to advances in the techniques of production rather than to the development of new products per se. Through technical system design the impact of technology on job design has always been strong. However, the implications of evolving sophisticated technology specifically for job design are considerable. More sophisticated production technologies have recently provided an entirely new definition of work and skills.

In sophisticated technologies, people's roles shift from the tool and its use or guidance to the system and its maintainance, regulation, and control. When a sophisticated technical system is combined with a social system design suited for simpler deterministic technologies, inappropriately small and simple jobs result. *Job,* here defined, is that portion of the employee's work role that consists of activities related to the transformation of objects or materials. Overly limited jobs increase costs both by requiring a larger and steeper organizational superstructure to coordinate and control work activities and by deadeningly affecting job holders. The integration of inappropriate social system designs with sophisticated technologies continues to be the dilemma of the 1970s and will be of the 1980s.

As technology has been defined, people use tools and techniques to effect change in some third object. From these three elements three technological relationships can be expressed: machine–product, man–product, and man–machine. In sophisticated or modern technology the first two of these three relationships completely define the *production* process. The first, the machine–product relationship, defines that portion of the process that is under automatic control. The second, the man–product relationship, defines that portion of the production process that the machine at present cannot perform; it is, in effect, the residuum of the first relationship. This second relationship defines the employee's job. The third, the man–machine relationship, describes primarily a *maintenance* function (*role-* rather than *job-*relevant). To the degree that advanced technology, as we define it, exists as sophistication of material and complexity of machines, the machine-product relationship predominates in the production process and the necessity for human intervention in machine operation is minimal or nonexistent. The intervention tends to shift to system level requiring system diagnosis and regulation. To the degree that sophistication of technology exists only in the control feedback process, there is continued, albeit diminished, inclusion of the man–product relationship. Even though operators need to continue to act on the more sophisticated feedback, their job, the man–product relationship, may change to that of monitoring, diagnosing, regulating, and responding to system deviations under more complex feedback systems. Operators need not wonder or wait under these conditions: The evaluative information comes quickly, unambiguously, correctly via a direct process in addition to their own senses.

It follows that the more sophisticated the machine-product dimension is, the more limited the man-product relationship will be. Since the man-product relationship has been traditionally thought of as the job, what happens to the worker under conditions of sophisticated technology, i.e. minimal man–product relationship? One option, of course, is that the worker's *role* (defined as a set of rules and expectations from the employee as well as the organization, which direct all his occupational or "at work" behavior) diminishes and disappears with the job—that is, the worker either is displaced, or continues working at the "nonjob" until a decision to retire or quit is made. Another option might be that the worker's *role* enlarges as the job diminishes—that is, the role enlarges vertically as the worker, coming into contact with more members of the organization to get things done, takes or is given responsibility for production supervision, quality control, and maintenance supervision. The role, then, becomes more complex, more demanding, as the job becomes simpler. This involvement via *role enlargement* is organically different from the kind of involvement included in *horizontal job enlargement,* in which the worker undertakes more, rather than fewer, of the man–product functions.

The notion of occupational role is a current rather than an historical concept. It explicitly includes an individual's *work related associations* with others on the job. Although in a formal sense these particular social relations have always been a part of work, they have been ignored in traditional job design theories. This is understandable for at least two reasons. First, man-as-machine theories of time and motion study had no reason to be concerned with the cooperation among workers when the emphasis was on the saving of time through efficient movement. Cooperation was an unneeded concept since the managerial hierarchy cemented individual man–task units together. Second, the nature of the technology between 1910 and 1950 reduced the need for coordination by workers since that coordination was built into the process of work flow, with the residuum being taken care of by management. The notion of *role* has, however, come into prominence and is displacing *job* as a central concept in the "at work" relationship. The concept of role has at least two sources. First is the general human relations concern in industrial study—a parallel but unrelated movement to job design, which has developed over the past fifty years. The second factor is the change in technology that has demanded closer coordination and cooperation among workers and has therefore brought the social component into prominence.

In the genealogy of work design, four conceptual trends are identified: task and job rationalization, job content, role content, and self-maintaining organizational units. Note that few of the readings included in this volume explicitly use the role concept and still fewer the even more recent concept of self-maintaining organizational units which builds on the role concept.

GENEALOGY OF WORK DESIGN

The origins of modern work design are presented here as a family tree (see pages xx - xxi) of significant intellectual and research innovations which have *directly* contributed to the present state of development. Obviously, it is not a history of each innovation nor of all the concepts, practices, or research that indirectly influenced the innovations that are of concern here. Such a comprehensive genealogy of ideas and practices would be most instructive but is quite beyond the scope of this book.

Task and Job Rationalization

The longest line of development commences with the economics of Adam Smith and the engineering of Charles Babbage at the time of the organization of the factory system, about 1800. *Scientific management* under Frederick W. Taylor and *motion study* under Frank Gilbreth, introduced about 1910, are an extension of the work of Babbage. *Work simplification,* introduced about 1935,† and *human engineering,* introduced about 1940,‡ are both derivatives of this line. The former development added human relations to motion study in seeking to overcome worker resistance to the mechanistic goals of scientific management. The latter, growing up around the man–machine interface, applies motion study, applied experimental psychology, and work-physiology to the operating of complex devices. These developments form the underlying foundations of the contemporary task and job rationalization approach to work design.

---

† Improvement management is a somewhat more comprehensive form of work simplification, retaining its objectives. For seminal papers describing these developments see Mogenson (1963) and Goodwin (1968).

‡ Ergonomics is a British development very similar to human engineering, but with a greater emphasis on work physiology. See Morgan et al. (1963) for human engineering, and Murrell (1965) for ergonomics.

—

The *human relations* development, starting about 1930, contributes passively to job rationalization through its use by work simplification practitioners.

Job Content

The active contribution of the human relations development was to rediscover man in formal organizations (Mayo, 1933); it stimulated worker *satisfaction research* (Hoppock, 1935), which followed shortly.§ However, this research excluded the content of the work itself. Other effects were also stimulated by Mayo's and Hoppock's work. Foremost among these was the interest, begun about 1950, in *intrinsic job satisfaction* at the University of Michigan's Institute for Social Research, which contributed the concept of *job enlargement* around 1955. In addition, the influence of Charles R. Walker's *nature-of-work* studies on the development of job enlargement is powerful and direct. The job enlargement development focused on providing more and varied tasks or duties as a means of countering the extreme fractionation of jobs promulgated by the job rationalization school of work design.

An unintended and independent effect of work satisfaction research brought Frederick Herzberg and others to the conclusion that the content and structure of jobs rather than the conditions surrounding them were the significant influences on performance, satisfaction and motivation. By 1960, Herzberg developed *job enrichment* which added planning, regulation, and control activities (named by him vertical enrichment) to the individual job.

About 1960, there developed a concern with sociocultural and psychological characteristics of work, which also evolved from job enlargement research. The concern centered on the characteristics of workers' upbringing, cultural exposure, and consequent need structure, which condition the workers' reactions to jobs, whether fractionated, enlarged, or enriched.

Role Content

The third cluster of developments includes *job design* (Davis and Canter, 1955) and *sociotechnical systems* (Emery and Trist, 1960). Job design, an American development, had its origins in the attempts at comprehensive work systems design including the social systems within which the work systems are embedded. Since the early 1960s, this development has been closely interacting with the sociotechnical systems developments of the Tavistock Institute in London, and now is inseparable from it.

Sociotechnical systems derived partly from the research on the *dynamics of small groups* by W. R. Bion (1955) and Kurt Lewin (1947), and from the work of Ludwig von Bertalanffy (1950) in developing *open systems theory from general systems theory*.

The pioneering work of Eric Trist and Fred Emery (1960), which concerned the interaction of technical systems with social systems and advanced the analytic concept of organizational variance coupled with open systems classification of

---

§ For key references concerning each development see list of Further Reading.

organization environments, laid the basis for present *sociotechnical practice*. Miller and Rice (1967) added to this the concept of *sentient boundary* to aid in further elucidating the units of organization. The contribution of *characteristics of job designs* by Louis E. Davis (1957, 1960), coupled with Fred Emery and Einar Thorsrud's (1969) contribution of psychological requirements of jobs, rounds out the sociotechnical developments. The addition of the values and concepts coming from the *democratization of the workplace* developments by Emery and Thorsrud (1969) has stimulated highly participative means of studying and changing jobs. Finally Davis (1971) stresses the need to refocus on technology because of the shifts in roles and the growth of role interdependence brought about by advanced technology.

The contributions of sociotechnical systems to work design are the concepts of *joint optimization of technical and social systems, work system boundaries,* and *psychological requirements of jobs.* The popular misconception of sociotechnical systems has been to see them as a single solution such as is offered by job enlargement and job enrichment rather than as a method of analysis and design based on an explicit set of values. The misconception has led to seeing sociotechnical systems as requiring "autonomous" work groups. Many analyses have indicated that the semiautonomous group structure is appropriate to a number of present organizational concerns—such as increasing technological complexity, high rates of change, and turbulence of social environments—calling for flexibility or adaptability. Semiautonomous groups are teams working together to accomplish the group's primary task as distinct from a collection of workers reporting to a supervisor. By definition, *occupational roles* are more central to the work process than are *jobs* in autonomous groups. The self-coordination and cooperation required among members, and the use of multiple (and even redundant) skills, as well as formation of composite teams, makes role content rather than job content the central concern of sociotechnical systems.

Self-Maintaining Organizational Units

The fourth strand is of very recent origin descending directly from sociotechnical systems developments and integrating with advances in the application of systems theories to organizations. Ackoff and Emery (1972) utilized the concept of *directive correlation* developed by Sommerhoff (1950) as an element of the conceptualization of work groups and organizations as *purposeful systems.* This view of organizations resulted in the broadening of sociotechnical systems emphases from job and role content to that of *organizational units.* Further developments arose out of the needs confronting the designer of new organizations and has continued to develop with the opportunities to design completely the new plant-organizations intended particularly for application of sophisticated technologies. Responding to these new-design needs rather than to the needs raised by change or redesign of existing organizations and jobs has been instrumental in developing the concept of the *self-maintaining organization unit.* Depending on requirements of the instance, there may or may not be specific or identifiable jobs as such; rather, there will be roles and organizational systems. The full impact of these developments for theory and practice in organization and job design, more properly role design, is not yet felt.

Despite the disappointingly slow rate of theoretical development, the articles considered advances are included in Part 3 (Recent Theoretical Trends). Perhaps the most important theoretical treatment for the future is provided by Emery in "The Assembly Line" (1975), and by Davis in "Job Design: Overview and Future Direction" (1977). Both indicate that the job, i.e., the man–task unit, is the inappropriate unit of organizational design; the job is not the fundamental building block of organizations. This position is contrary to the central precept of both scientific management and bureaucracy. Therefore, focusing on job revision, job enlargement, job enrichment, etc., will not fundamentally alter the organizational *system,* the *roles* of the organization's members and managers, the opportunity for *self-regulation,* or the *flexibility or adaptability* of the organization and its members. Emery and Davis indicate that issues ranging from individual motivation to organizational governance will likely be approached successfully when "one man and his task" as the unit of organization is abandoned and organizational units developed that are self-maintaining both organizationally and technically while permitting the social system to discharge its essential functions. In these instances, it is predicted that job design will become indistinguishable from organization design.

At present, the four strands of development described in this overview exist concurrently. Since we live in a society that is organized largely on industrial and only partly on postindustrial models, it is not inappropriate that all four strands should coexist. However, because of accelerating changes in technology and the social environment, the task and job rationalization strand probably probably will become increasingly dysfunctional and its application probably will diminish in the future. Disturbingly, while the trend toward postindustrial organization is growing, the job rationalization mode is being imported with untutored disregard into the white collar service sector—to that sector's and its participants' considerable peril.

It is one of the purposes of this volume to aid in clarifying the technological and societal matrix underlying the design of jobs, and to point out the relationships between the nature of the organization, its technical system, its supporting social system, and the mode of job design appropriate to it.

REFERENCES

Ackoff, R. L., and Emery, F. E. (1972) *On Purposeful Systems*. Chicago: Aldine Press.

Arygyris, C. (1957) *Personality and Organization*. New York: Harper & Row.

Bartley, S. H., and Chute, E. (1947) *Fatigue and Impairment in Man*. New York: McGraw-Hill.

Bion, W. R. (1955) "Group Dynamics: A Review." In M. Klein, P. Heimann, and R. E. Money-Kyrle, eds. *New Directions in Psycho-Analysis*. London: Tavistock.

Carroll, B. (1969) *Job Satisfaction*. Industrial and Labor-Relations Library, Cornell University, Key Issues Series, no. 3.

Davis, L. E. (1957) "Toward a Theory of Job Design." *Journal of Industrial Engineering,* vol. 8, no. 5, pp. 19-23

Davis, L. E. (1971) "The Coming Crisis for Production Management: Technology and Organization." *International Journal of Production Research,* vol. 9, pp. 65-82.

Davis, L. E. (1977) "Job Design: Overview and Future Direction." *Journal of Contemporary Business,* vol. 6, no. 2, pp. 85-102.

Davis, L. E., and Canter, R. R. (1955) "Job Design." *Journal of Industrial Engineering,* vol. 6, no. 1, p. 3.

Davis, L. E., and Cherns, A. B., eds. (1975) *The Quality of Working Life,* Vols. I and II. New York: Free Press.

Davis, L. E., and Werling, R. (1960) "Job Design Factors." *Occupational Psychology,* vol. 34, no. 2, pp. 109-132.

Emery, F. E., and Trist, E. L. (1960) "Socio-technical Systems." In C. W. Churchman and M. Verhulst, eds. *Management Sciences, Models, and Techniques,* vol. 2. London: Pergamon Press, pp. 83-97.

Emery, F. E., and Thorsrud, E. (1969) *Form and Content in Industrial Democracy.* London: Tavistock.

Emery, F. E. (1975) "The Assembly Line—Its Logic and Our Future." *National Labour Institute Bulletin,* vol. 1, no. 6.

Fitts, P. M., and Jones, R. E. (1947) *Psychological Aspects of Instrument Display.* Report TSEAA-694-12A, US Air Force Air Material Command.

Friedmann, G. (1961) *The Anatomy of Work.* London: Heinemann Educational Books (Reprinted, New York: Free Press, 1964).

Gilbreth, F. B. (1911) *Motion Study.* New York: Van Nostrand.

Goodwin, H. F. (1968) "Improvement Must Be Managed." *Journal of Industrial Engineering,* vol. 19, pp. 538-45.

Herzberg, F. (1966) *Work and the Nature of Man.* New York: Harcourt, Brace & World.

Hoppock, R. (1935) *Job Satisfaction.* New York: Harper and Row.

Hopwood, A. (1977) *Toward Assessing the Economic Costs and Benefits of New Forms of Work Organization.* Geneva: ILO.

Hulin, C. L., and Blood, M. R. (1968) "Job Enlargement, Individual Differences, and Worker Responses." *Psychological Bulletin,* vol. 69, February, pp. 44-55.

Kahn, R. L., and Morse, N. C. (1951) "The Relationship of Productivity to Morale." *Journal of Social Issues,* vol. 7, no. 3, pp. 8-17.

Lawler, E. E. (1969) "Job Design and Employee Motivation." *Personnel Psychology,* vol. 22, Winter, pp. 426-35.

Lehrer, R. N. (1957) *Work Simplification.* Englewood Cliffs, N.J.: Prentice-Hall.

Lewin, K. (1947) "Frontiers in Group Dynamics." *Human Relations,* vol. 1, pp. 5-41.

Likert, R. (1961) *New Patterns of Management.* New York: McGraw-Hill.

McGregor, D. (1960) *The Human Side of Enterprise.* New York: McGraw-Hill.

Marx, Karl (1967) *Economics and Philosophical Manuscripts of 1844.* Moscow: Foreign Languages Publishing House.

Mayo, E. (1933) *The Human Problems of an Industrial Civilization.* New York: Macmillan.

Miller, E. J., and Rice, A. K. (1967) *Systems of Organisation.* London: Tavistock.

Mogenson, A. H. (1963) "Work Simplification—A Program of Continuous Improvement." In H. B. Maynard, ed. *Industrial Engineering Handbook,* 2nd ed. New York: McGraw-Hill, pp. 10, 183-91.

Morgan, C. T., Cook, J. S., Chapanis, A., and Lund, M. W. (1963) *Human Engineering Guide for Equipment Design.* New York: McGraw-Hill.

Munsterberg, H. (1913) *The Psychology of Industrial Efficiency*. New York: Houghton Mifflin.

Murrell, K. F. H. (1965) *Ergonomics: Man and His Working Environment*. London: Chapman Hall.

Roethlisberger, F. J., and Dickson, W. J. (1939) *Management and the Worker*. Cambridge, Mass.: Harvard University Press.

Smith, Adam. (1970) *Wealth of Nations*. London: Penguin.

Sommerhoff, G. (1950) *Analytical Biology*. London: Oxford University Press.

Thorsrud, E., and Emery, F. E. (1969) *Moten Ny Bedriftsorganisasjon*. Oslo, Norway: Tanum Press.

Trist, E. L., and Bamforth, K. W. (1951) "Some Social and Psychological Consequences of the Long-wall Method of Coal Getting." *Human Relations,* vol. 4, pp. 3-38.

Turner, A. N., and Lawrence, R. R. (1965) *Industrial Jobs and the Worker*. Cambridge, Mass.: Harvard University Press.

U.S. Employment Service (1965) *Dictionary of Occupational Titles,* 3rd rev. ed. U.S. Department of Labor, Manpower Administration, Bureau of Employment Security.

Vernon, H. M. (1921) *Industrial Fatigue and Efficiency*. London: Routledge & Kegan Paul.

Von Bertalanffy, L. (1950) "The Theory of Open Systems in Physics and Biology." *Science,* vol. 3, pp. 23-8.

Von Bertalanffy, L. (1967) *Robots, Men and Minds*. New York: George Braziller.

Walker, C. R., and Guest, R. H. (1952) *The Man on the Assembly Line*. Cambridge, Mass.: Harvard University Press.

Weber, M. (1946) *Essays in Sociology*. Translated by H. H. Gerth and C. Wright Mills. Oxford, England: Oxford University Press.

Genealogy of Work Design

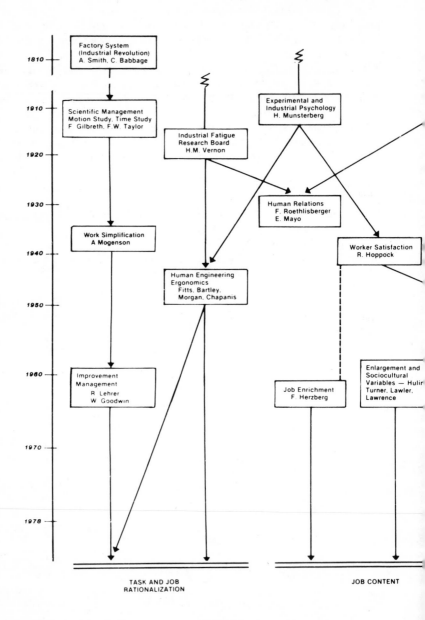

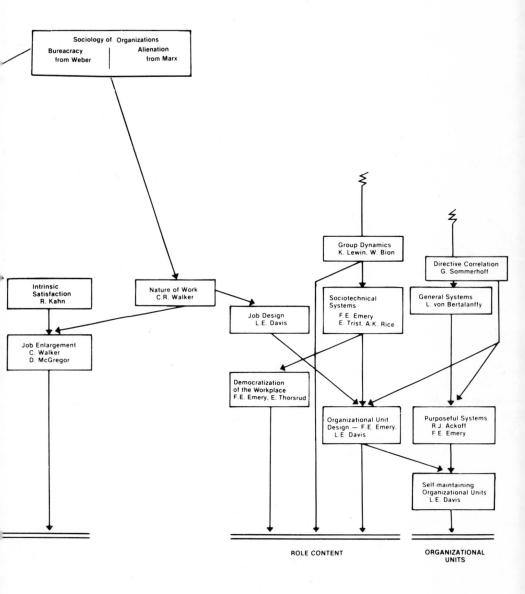

ROLE CONTENT   ORGANIZATIONAL
UNITS

xxi

Part 1

EVOLUTION OF JOB DESIGN IN INDUSTRIAL SOCIETY

Introduction

1. On the Economy of Machinery and Manufactures (1835)
—Charles Babbage

2. Allocation of Functions Between Man and Machines in Automated Systems (1963)
—Nehemiah Jordan

3. Operating Units (1965)
—Robert Boguslaw

4. History of Work Concepts (1975)
—Peter Warr and Toby Wall

5. Job Design: Historical Overview (1977)
—Louis E. Davis

INTRODUCTION

The concept of designing jobs is of relatively recent origin, beginning in the period of the Industrial Revolution. It was then that society accepted a new central relationship—that between the person and the machine, replacing the relationship of the previous era—that between the person and nature.

The concepts that determined job content and structure in the early industrial period require serious study, for they have left their historical residue in the present conventional wisdom about the world of work. The crucial early developments can be examined in terms of the societal values of the then-emerging industrial era. We wish to emphasize the often-neglected point that neither social and technological developments nor theoretical constructs can be understood without knowledge of the fundamental values underlying them.

The industrial era began with the catalytic discovery that machines are more than ancillary devices; they could be combined with particularly conceived tasks for people to create a powerful new social means for overcoming the historical specter of scarcity. This was clearly seen by Babbage. The history of jobs and their design evolved from this social technology set in the positivistic, optimistic ethos of technological determinism. The material consequences in overcoming scarcity were enormous. The social consequences, however, were work performed under social compulsion and regimentation, and work so organized that people became interchangeable spare parts.

A central question of the now-waning industrial era remains unanswered: How do we design or redesign organizations and work systems that can satisfy the needs of society, its organizations, and their members *without* dehumanizing work?

Charles Babbage (reading 1) identified the central premise of social technology in the industrial era. Frederick W. Taylor* operationalized it in the name of science, providing a powerful mechanistic philosophy of organization that reinforced the existing and expanding bureaucratic one. Taylor's machine model of organization remains the most pervasive dogma of the modern or industrial era, and is critiqued by Boguslaw (reading 3). The social values that supported the dogma have been made explicit by economists whose specious explanations of human motivation unfortunately still persist.

The technical systems designers, including practitioners of human engineering, human factors, ergonomics, applied experimental psychology, industrial engineering, and computer systems design, all carry into action the industrial era's conviction that people and machines are competitors. Consequently, only the mechanical qualities of men and women are considered when deciding what people are to do and what machines are to do. Jordan (reading 2) makes a plea for *complementarity* of men and machines, calling for recognition and utilization of people's unique capabilities.

Robert Boguslaw (reading 3) shows that the 1911 concepts of scientific management are not only carried into the present by Taylor's lineal descendants, the industrial engineers, but also by computer systems engineers. Both design and

---

*Frederick W. Taylor, (1911), *Scientific Management,* New York: Harper and Brothers.

operate production systems based on the concept of people as operating units who may be manipulated and adjusted to suit technical system needs as defined by the designers.

Peter Warr and Toby Wall (reading 4) review the central issue of motivation, the human aspect of job design. They take us through successive "theories" that have inspired work designers, touching on a question that ought to concern society's leaders: What if jobs were designed, but no one came? Even as these "theories" are reported, they are being replaced as Western society reaffirms the need to restore the autonomy and dignity of the individual.

Last, Louis E. Davis (reading 5) provides a historical overview of job design which may be taken to be a history of deliberate and systemic reform of work. That this history starts only twenty-five years ago is not surprising. However, along with other developments in advanced Western societies, it signals the waning of the industrial era and the emergence of the postindustrial era.

1
On the Economy of
Machinery and Manufactures
Charles Babbage

If the *maker* of an article wish to become a *manufacturer,* in the more extended sense of the term, he must attend to other principles besides those mechanical ones on which the successful execution of his work depends; and he must carefully arrange the whole system of his factory in such a manner, that the article he sells to the public may be produced at as small a cost as possible. Should he not be actuated at first by motives so remote, he will, in every highly civilized country, be compelled, by the powerful stimulus of competition, to attend to the principles of the domestic economy of manufactures.[. . .]

Perhaps the most important principle on which the economy of a manufacture depends, is the *division of labour* amongst the persons who perform the work. The first application of this principle must have been made in a very early stage of society; for it must soon have been apparent, that a larger number of comforts and conveniences could be acquired by each individual, if one man restricted his occupation to the art of making bows, another to that of building houses, a third

Excerpts from Charles Babbage. *On the Economy of Machinery and Manufacturers.* Charles Knight, fourth edition enlarged, 1835, Chapters 13 and 19, pp. 119-22, 172-90. *Reprints of Economic Classics,* Augustus M. Kelly, New York, 1965.

boats, and so on. This division of labour into trades was not, however, the result of an opinion that the general riches of the community would be increased by such an arrangement; but it must have arisen from the circumstance of each individual so employed discovering that he himself could thus make a greater profit of his labour than by pursuing more varied occupations. Society must have made considerable advances before this principle could have been carried into the workshop; for it is only in countries which have attained a high degree of civilization, and in articles in which there is a great competition amongst the producers, that the most perfect system of the division of labour is to be observed. The various principles on which the advantages of this system depend, have been much the subject of discussion amongst writers on Political Economy; but the relative importance of their influence does not appear, in all cases, to have been estimated with sufficient precision. It is my intention, in the first instance, to state shortly those principles, and then to point out what appears to me to have been omitted by those who have previously treated the subject.

Of the time required for learning. It will readily be admitted, that the portion of time occupied in the acquisition of any art will depend on the difficulty of its execution; and that the greater the number of distinct processes, the longer will be the time which the apprentice must employ in acquiring it.[. . .]

Of waste of materials in learning. A certain quantity of material will, in all cases, be consumed unprofitably, or spoiled by every person who learns an art; and as he applies himself to each new process, he will waste some of the raw material, or of the partly manufactured commodity. But if each man commit this waste in acquiring successively every process, the quantity of waste will be much greater than if each person confine his attention to one process; in this view of the subject, therefore, the division of labour will diminish the price of production.

Another advantage resulting from the division of labour is, *the saving of that portion of time which is always lost in changing from one occupation to another.* When the human hand, or the human head, has been for some time occupied in any kind of work, it cannot instantly change its employment with full effect.[. . .]

Change of tools. The employment of different tools in the successive processes is another cause of the loss of time in changing from one operation to another.[. . .]

Skill acquired by frequent repetition of the same processes. The constant repetition of the same process necessarily produces in the workman a degree of excellence and rapidity in his particular department, which is never possessed by a person who is obliged to execute many different processes. This rapidity is still further increased from the circumstance that most of the operation in factories, where the division of labour is carried to a considerable extent, are paid for as piece-work. It is difficult to estimate in numbers the effect of this cause upon production. In nail-making, Adam Smith has stated, that it is almost three to one; for, he observes, that a smith accustomed to make nails, but whose whole business has not been that of a nailer, can make only from eight hundred to a thousand per day; whilst a lad who had never exercised any other trade, can make upwards of two thousand three hundred a day.[. . .]

The division of labour suggests the contrivance of tools and machinery to execute its processes. When each process, by which any article is produced, is the sole occupation of one individual, his whole attention being devoted to a very limited and simple operation, improvements in the form of his tools, or in the mode of using them, are much more likely to occur in his mind, than if it were distracted by a greater variety of circumstances. Such an improvement in the tool is generally the first step towards a machine.[. . .]

When each process has been reduced to the use of some simple tool, the union of all these tools, actuated by one moving power, constitutes a machine.[. . .]

Such are the principles usually assigned as the causes of the advantages resulting from the division of labour. As in the view I have taken of the question, the most important and influential cause has been altogether unnoticed, I shall re-state those principles in the words of Adam Smith: "The great increase in the quantity of work, which, in consequence of the division of labour, the same number of people are capable of performing, is owing to three different circumstances: first, to the increase of dexterity in every particular workman; secondly, to the saving of time, which is commonly lost in passing from one species of work to another; and, lastly, to the invention of a great number of machines which facilitate and abridge labour, and enable one man to do the work of many." Now, although all these are important causes, and each has its influence on the result; yet it appears to me, than any explanation of the cheapness of manufactured articles, as consequent upon the division of labour, would be incomplete if the following principle were omitted to be stated.

That the master manufacturer, by dividing the work to be executed into different processes, each requiring different degrees of skill or of force, can purchase exactly the precise quantity of both which is necessary for each process; whereas, if the whole work were executed by one workman, that person must possess sufficient skill to perform the most difficult, and sufficient strength to execute the most laborious, of the operations into which the art is divided. *

---

*I have already stated that this principle presented itself to me after a personal examination of a number of manufactories and workshops devoted to different purposes; but I have since found that it had been distinctly pointed out, in the work of Gioja, *Nuovo Prospetto delle Scienze Economiche,* Milano, 1815, vol. 1, ch. 4.

2

Allocation of Functions Between Man and Machines in Automated Systems

Nehemiah Jordan

In a document entitled "Factors affecting degree of automation in test and checkout equipment" which, among other things, reviews the problems of allocation of functions, Swain and Wohl (1961) assert:

> A rather stark conclusion emerges: *There is no adequate systematic methodology in existence for allocating functions* (in this case, test and checkout functions) *between man and machine.* This lack, in fact, is probably the central problem in human factors engineering today. . . . It is interesting to note that ten years of research and applications experience have failed to bring us closer to our goal than did the landmark article by Fitts in 1951 (p. 9).

These two competent and experienced observers summarize ten years of hard and intensive labor as having basically failed. This is a serious problem. Why this failure?

We can attempt to seek a possible answer to the question by seeking a similar case in other fields of scientific endeavor and seeing what can be learned from it. And another case is easy to find; it is in fact a classical case. In their book *The Evolution of Physics,* Einstein and Infeld (1942) spend some time discussing the problems which beset pre-relativity physics in which they focus upon the concept of "ether." They point out that ether played a central role in physical thinking for over a century after having first been introduced as a necessary medium for propagating electromagnetic waves. But during all this time all attempts to build and expand upon this concept led to difficulties and contradictions. A century of research on ether turned out to be sterile in that no significant advance was made during that time. They conclude: "After such bad experiences, this is the moment to forget ether completely and try never to mention its name" (p. 184). And they do not mention the concept anymore in the book. The facts underlying the concept were not rejected, however, and it was by focusing upon the *facts* while rejecting the *concept* that Einstein could solve the problems which bedeviled the physics of his day.

The lesson to be learned from this momentous episode is that when a scientific discipline finds itself in a dead end, despite hard and diligent work, the dead end

Excerpts from Nehemiah Jordan. "Allocation of Functions Between Man and Machines in Automated Systems." *Journal of Applied Psychology,* vol. 47, 1963, pp. 161-165.

should probably not be attributed to a lack of knowledge of facts, but to the use of faulty concepts which do not enable the discipline to order the facts properly. The failure of human factor engineering to advance in the area of allocation of functions seems to be such a situation. Hence, in order to find an answer to the question "Why this failure?" it may be fruitful to examine the conceptual underpinnings of our contemporary attempts of allocating functions between men and machines. And this brings us back to the landmark article by Fitts (1951) mentioned earlier.

This article gave rise to what is now informally called the "Fitts list." This is a two-column list, one column headed by the word "man" and the other by the word "machine." It *compares* the functions for which man is superior to machines to the functions for which the machine is superior to man. Theoretically, this leads to an elegant solution to the allocation of functions. Given a complex man–machine system, identify the functions of the system and then, based on such a list which was expected to be refined with time and experience, choose machines for the functions they are best suited for and men for the functions they are best suited for. This is a clean engineering approach and it is not surprising that great hopes were placed upon it, in *1951*. The only gimmick is that it did not and does not work.

The facts to be found in all the existing versions of the Fitts list are all correct, just as the facts underlying the concept ether were all correct. Hence the inutility of these lists must be attributed to what we are told to do with these facts, to the instruction to compare man to the machine and choose the one who fits a function best. I question the *comparability* of men and machines. If men and machines are not comparable, then it is not surprising that we get nowhere when we try to compare them. Just as the concept of ether led to inutility, perhaps the concept of man–machine comparability does the same. Let us explore somewhat the background to the concept *comparability*.

The literature on the place of a man in man–machine systems converges to two posthumous articles by Craik (1947a; 1947b). These articles are recognized by almost all as being the basis upon which much that followed is built. Craik argues that in order to best be able to plan, design and operate a complex system, man functions and machine functions should be described in the same concepts, and, by the very nature of the case, these concepts have to be engineering terms. In other words, Craik recommends that we describe human functions in mathematical terms *comparable* to the terms used in describing mechanical functions.

In fairness to Craik's memory, it must be stressed that these two papers, published after his death, were notes for a discussion and probably not meant for publication. Hence he should not be blamed for failing to recognize the simple fact that anytime we can reduce a human function to a mathematical formula we can generally build a machine that can do it more efficiently than a man. In other words, to the extent that man becomes comparable to a machine we do not really need him any more since he can be replaced by a machine. This necessary consequence was actually reached but not recognized in a later paper, also a fundamental and significant paper in human factor engineering literature. Birmingham and Taylor (1954) in their paper, "A design philosophy for man–machine control systems," write: "Speaking mathematically, he (man) is best when doing least" (p. 1752). The conclusion is inescapable—design the man out of the system. If he does best when he does least, the least he can do is zero. But then the conclusion is also ridiculous. Birmingham and Taylor found themselves in the same paradoxical situation which Hume found himself some 200 years earlier where his logic showed him that he could not know anything while at the same time he knew he knew a lot.

This contradiction, so concisely formulated by Birmingham and Taylor yet not recognized by them or, it seems, by their readers, should have served as a warning that something was wrong with the conceptualization underlying the thinking in this area. But it did not.

Now we can see why the Fitts lists have been impotent. To the extent that we compare, numerically, human functions to machine functions we must reach the conclusion that wherever possible the machine should do the job. This may help to explain a curious aspect in designers' behavior which has annoyed some: an annoyance expressed trenchantly by a human factors engineer over a glass of beer thus: "Those designers, they act as if they get a brownie point every time they eliminate a man."

Let us return to the Fitts lists. They vary all over the place in length and in detail. But if we try to abstract the underlying commonalities in all of them we find that they really make one point and only one point. Men are flexible but cannot be depended upon to perform in a consistent manner, whereas machines can be depended upon to perform consistently but they have no flexibility whatsoever. This can be summarized simply and seemingly tritely by saying that men are good at doing that which machines are not good at doing and machines are good at doing that which men are not good at doing. Men and machines are not comparable, they are *complementary*. Gentlemen, I suggest that complementary is probably the correct concept to use in discussing the allocation of tasks to men and to machines. Rather than compare men and machines as to which is better for getting a task done, let us think about how we complement men by machines and vice versa to get a task done.

As soon as we start to think this way we find that we have to start thinking differently. The term "allocation of tasks to men and machine" becomes meaningless. Rather we are forced to think about a task that can be done by men *and* machines. The concept "task" ceases to be the smallest unit of analysis for designing man–machine systems though still remaining the basic unit in terms of which the analysis makes sense. The task now consists of actions, or better still activities, which have to be shared by men and machines. There is nothing strange about this. In industrial chemistry the molecule is the fundamental unit for many purposes and it does not disturb anybody that some of these molecules consist of hundreds, if not thousands of atoms. The analysis of man–machine systems should therefore consist of specifications of tasks and activities necessary to accomplish the tasks. Man and machine should complement each other in getting these activities done in order to accomplish the task.

It is possible that with a shift to emphasizing man–machine comparability new formats for system analysis and design will have to be developed, and these formats may pose a problem. I am convinced, however, that as soon as we begin thinking in proper units this problem will be solved with relative ease. Regardless of whether this is so, one can now already specify several general principles that may serve as basic guidelines for complementing men and machines.

Machines serve man in two ways: as tools and as production machines. A tool extends man's ability, both sensory and motor; production machines replace man in doing a job. The principle underlying the complementarity of tools is as follows: man functions best under conditions of optimum difficulty. If the job is too easy he gets bored, if it is too hard he gets fatigued. While it is generally silly to use machines to make a job more difficult, although this may be exactly what is called for in some control situations, tools have, since their inception as eoliths, served to make a difficult job easier and an impossible job possible. Hence tools should be used to bring the perceptual and motor requirements of a task to the optimum levels for human performance. We have a lot of experience with tools and they present few, if any, problems.

The problem is more complex with machines that do a job in place of man. Here we can return with benefit to the commonalities underlying the Fitts lists. To the extent that the task environment is predictable and a priori controllable, and to the extent that activities necessary for the task are iterative and demand consistent performance, a production machine is preferable to man. To the extent, however, that the environment is not predictable, or if predictable not controlled a priori, then man, aided by the proper tools, is required. It is in coping with contingencies that man is irreplaceable by machines. This is the essential meaning of human flexibility.

Production machines pose a problem rarely posed by tools, since they replace men in doing a job. They are not perfect and tend to break down. When they break down they do not do the job. One must always then take into account the criticality of the job for the system. If the job is critical, the system should so be designed that man can serve as a manual backup to the machine. Although he will then not do it as well as the machine, he still can do it well enough to pass muster. This is another aspect of human flexibility—the ability for graceful degradation. Machines can either do the job as specified or they botch up; man degrades gracefully. This is another example of complementarity.

Planning for feasible manual backup is a difficult job in the contemporary complex systems that we are constructing. It has generally been neglected. In most simple systems explicit planning is not necessary since man's flexibility is generally adequate enough to improvise when the relatively simple machines break down. But this changes with growing system complexity.

It is here that "automation" should be mentioned. Some of you may have been bothered by the fact that automation is in the title of this paper but has, as yet, still to be introduced. The reason is rather simple. Although automation represents a significant technological breakthrough which has generated many specific problems, the allocation of tasks to men and machines being one of them, conceptually, an automated machine is just another machine, albeit radically different in its efficiency and performance characteristics. The problems that were generally latent or not too critical in the older, simpler man–machine systems became both manifest and critical, however, with its introduction. One of the most critical areas is manual backup.

We customarily design automated systems by allocating to man those functions which were either difficult or too expensive to mechanize, and the rest to machines. As many articles in the literature indicate, we have looked upon man as a *link* in the system and have consequently given him only the information and means to do a job assigned to him as a link. When the system breaks down a man in a link position is as helpless as any other machine component in the system. We have tended to design out his ability to take over as a manual backup to the system. At the same time the jobs performed by the machine have become more and more important and the necessity for a manual backup consequently greater. How to design a complex automated system to facilitate its being backed up manually is a neglected area. One thing seems certain. It will most probably call for "degradation" in design, that is, systematically introducing features which would not have been necessary were no manual backup needed. This is an important area for future human factors engineering research.

Another area of complementarity which is gaining in significance as the systems are getting more and more complex is that of responsibility. Assuming we lick the problems of reliability, we can depend upon the machines to do those activities assigned to them consistently well, but we never can assign them any responsibility for getting the task done; responsibility can be assigned to men only. For every task, or for every activity entailed by the task, there must be a man who has assigned responsiblity to see that the job be done as efficiently as warranted. This necessitates two things: the specification of clear-cut responsibilities for *every* man in the system and supplying the men with means which will enable them to exercise effective control over those system tasks and activities for which they are responsible. You may think that this is obvious—yes it is. But it is surprising how rare, and then how ineffective, our planning and design in this area are. Experience to date with automated systems shows that the responsibilities of the individuals involved are generally nebulous so that when something unexpected occurs people often do not know who is to do what. Even to the extent that these responsibilities are clarified with time and experience, the system hardware often makes it difficult for men to assume these responsibilities, the means for man to exercise control over the areas of his responsibility being inadequate or lacking.

The complementarity of men and machines is probably much more profound and subtle than these aspects which I have just highlighted. Many other aspects will undoubtedly be identified, elaborated and ordered to the extent that we start thinking about how one complements the other. In other words, to the extent that we start *humanizing* human factors engineering. It is not surprising that the ten years of lack of progress pointed to by Swain and Wohl (1961) were accompanied by the conceptual definition of treating man as a machine component. Man is not a machine, at least not a machine like the machines men make. And this brings me to the last point I would like to make in this paper.

When we plan to use a machine we always take the physical environment of the machine into account; that is, its power supply, its maintenance requirements, the physical setting in which it has to operate, etc. We have also taken the physical environment of man into account, to a greater or lesser extent; that is, illumination and ventilation of the working area, noise level, physical difficulties, hours of labor, coffee breaks, etc. But a fundamental difference between men and machines is that men also have a psychological environment for which an adequate physical environment is a necessary condition but is ultimately secondary in importance. This is the truth embedded in the adage: man does not live by bread alone. The psychological environment is subsumed under one word: motivation. The problems of human motivation are at present eschewed by human factors engineering.

You can lead a horse to water but cannot make him drink. In this respect a man is very similar to a horse. Unless the human operator is motivated, he will not function as a complement to machines, and the motivation to function as a complement must be embedded *within the task itself*. Unless a task represents a challenge to the human operator, he will *not* use his flexibility or his judgement, he will *not* learn nor will he assume responsibility, nor will he serve efficiently as a manual backup. By designing man–machine systems for man to do *least*, we also eliminate all challenge from the job. We must clarify to ourselves what it is that makes a job a challenge to man and build in those challenges in every task, activity and responsibility we assign to the human operator. Otherwise man will not complement the machines but will begin to function like a machine.

And here too men differ significantly from machines. When a man is forced to function like a machine he realizes that he is being used inefficiently and he experiences it as being used stupidly. Men cannot tolerate such stupidity. Overtly or covertly men resist and rebel against it. Nothing could be more inefficient and self-defeating in the long run than the construction of man–machine systems which cause the human component in the system to rebel against the system.

Herein lies the main future challenge to human factors engineering.

REFERENCES

Birmingham, H. P., and Taylor, F. V. (1954) "A Design Philosophy for Man–machine Control Systems," *Proc. IRE,* vol. 42, 1748-58.

Craik, K. J. W. (1947a) "Theory of the Human Operator in Control Systems: 1. The Operator as an Engineering System." *British Journal of Psychology,* vol. 38, pp. 56-61.

Craik, K. J. W. (1947b) "Theory of Human Operator in Control Systems: 2. Man as an Element in a Control System." *British Journal of Psychology,* vol. 38, pp. 142-8.

Einstein, A., and Infeld, L. (1942) *The Evolution of Physics.* Simon and Schuster.

Fitts, P. M. ed. (1951) *Human Engineering for an Effective Air Navigation and Traffic Control System.* National Research Council.

Swain, A. D., and Wohl, J. G. (1961) *Factors Affecting Degree of Automation in Test and Checkout Equipment.* Dunlap & Associates.

3
Operating Units*
Robert Boguslaw

Utopia is a place that seems to belong either to the past or to the future, and we tend to think of utopians as being either starry-eyed philosophers or wild-eyed reformers. But there is a new breed of utopians afoot, threatening to rush down all the exciting pathways and blind alleys frequented by utopians since the days of Plato. These are the people who are known by such titles as system engineer, computer manufacturer, operations researcher, computer programmer, data processing specialist, or, more simply, system designer.

This book deals with some of the problems confronting these new utopians—the social engineers of our times. But, perhaps much more to the point, it deals with some of the problems they are in the process of preparing for the rest of us.[. . .]

Different system designers characteristically begin their work not only with queries about system functions but with different answers to questions such as the following: What is the problem you are trying to solve? Why are you trying to solve it? What *kind* of solution would you accept as satisfactory? How much time and effort are you prepared to devote to the enterprise? How enduring must your solution be?

Differences in the approach to system design involve implicit if not explicit differences in these answers. They also imply gross differences in methodology and technique. We may distinguish four approaches to system design used by both the classical and the new utopians. They are the Formalist Approach, the Heuristic Approach, the Operating Unit Approach, and the Ad Hoc Approach.[. . .]

In explicating the operating unit approach to system design, it seems only fair to warn readers that this seems to be the chosen approach for many technically illiterate, would-be roboteers—and for many technically qualified misanthropes as well.[. . .]

The operating unit approach begins neither with models of the system nor with selected principles. It begins with people or machines carefully selected or tooled to possess certain performance characteristics. The system or organization or utopia that ultimately unfolds will incorporate solutions that these units provide.

It is obvious that the various systems that get developed through the use of this

---

*The assumptions and implicit value premises underlying the design of the work organizations are revealed in the issues, raised by Boguslaw, for development of computer (automated) systems [Eds.].

Excerpts from Robert Boguslaw. *The New Utopians: A Study of System Design and Social Change,* © Reprinted by permission of Prentice–Hall, Inc., Englewood Cliffs, New Jersey.

approach are, to a considerable extent, based upon the range of flexibility possessed by the operating units. It is becoming increasingly apparent that flexibility in this sense is much more than a simple distinction between man and machine. Man may be inflexible, machines may be flexible—or vice versa. Under some conditions, it may be highly desirable to limit the range of operating unit flexibility to insure reliability and predictability of system performance. Under other conditions, the reverse may be true.

Thus, in B. F. Skinner's (1948) fictional utopia, called *Walden Two,* it is clear that the flexibility of the human operating units is drastically limited to suit the requirements of the system as seen by its designer, an experimental psychologist named Frazier. The behavior of these units (people) is highly reliable, although no one has attempted to specify the situations in which they are to perform. One might almost postulate an infinity of possible system designs that might in fact emerge, and conceivably an infinity of principles or heuristics to which these systems could be required to adhere. Reliability in performance is achieved through conditioning the components to behave in a 'reasonable' fashion.

Walden Two has been called an "ignoble utopia," because it urges men to be something less than human (Heilbroner, 1953). "Human" in this context apparently refers to the properties of free choice or the wide range of possible responses that hopefully characterizes the unconditioned human being. It is perhaps a significant commentary on contemporary psychological and social science that its efforts often appear directed toward making men less than human through the perfecting of behavioral control techniques, while contemporary physical science seems to be moving in the direction of increasing the number of possible machine responses to environmental stimuli.

There exists a striking similarity between the use of human operating units in the *Walden Two* system and the use of physical equipment employed in contemporary system engineering.[. . .]

But what, specifically, is it that operating units are called upon to do? Briefly, they must sense, measure, compare, process, and regulate or handle (Folley and Van Cott, 1960).

Sensing refers to the job of detecting signals or information in the environment of the system. These signals may include radar returns, dial readings, and so on. The components involved may include such things as a photoelectric cell, a sound-pressure meter, and the human eye, ear, nose, skin or tongue. If the signals are enlarged or magnified by the system, we are in the presence of an *amplification* function. If some of the signals are suppressed or screened, we have a *filtering* function.

Measuring refers to the job of comparing information that has been sensed with a precalibrated standard or scale. It is possible to *store* measurements in a memory for use at some future time. Components used for this purpose include magnetized tape or disks, punched or marked cards, charged meshes of wire, mechanical relays, or the human brain.

Comparing consists of determining the difference between one measurement and another. Differences are called error signals or simply errors.

Processing consists of combining the available information with a number of different actions to produce some desired decision consequence.

Regulation or *handling* means acting upon a decision to produce some desired condition or result. Examples of this include: milling a cast to a specified tolerance, controlling the rate of flow of a liquid, and generating a message to another system or to men. The regulation function may be found associated with an actuating function and a power supply that starts and stops handling. It may also be found associated with a *monitoring* function that inspects the quality or quantity of an output.

When a system is conceptualized in these terms, an indispensable portion of its description consists of identifying the *program* it must execute. This is a set of commands given to the system for performing certain operations. When a commander or executive is available he may issue these commands as required. This, in effect, is "real-time" programming. It is also possible, of course, to use some sort of memory to store and issue instructions to the system as they become necessary (Folley and Van Cott, 1960, p. 5).

But the concept of "program" as used in this context can be quite deceptive. It seems to imply that when "programmed," the system does only what it is told to do in the program, that is, that the actions it will take are listed in the program. But of course this is scarcely the case. The operating units of the system do what it is possible for them to do. What it is possible for them to do is dependent upon their own structural characteristics, the characteristics of their environment (including other units within the system), and the characteristics of their own internal states at the moment of action. One way of "telling" a radar system to ignore random blips is to issue an instruction to the radar operator. You then have a "programmed" operator. Another way of doing essentially the same thing is to substitute for the human operator a piece of equipment that will "see" only nonrandom blips. The instruction to the piece of equipment does not exist in any usual sense of the term, yet the decision to use the equipment has the same kind of system effect as does the instruction. In one case, the command is contained within a "program"; in the other it is not.[. . .]

In *Walden Two,* the problem of controlling the component operating units was accomplished through the behavioral engineering technique of psychological conditioning. As Frazier explains it, a code of conduct had been worked out that would presumably keep things running smoothly if everyone concerned behaved according to plan. It was recognized that to anticipate all future situations would be an impossible task. The planners, therefore, relied upon "self-control" that permitted each individual to act essentially as a servomechanism obeying commands generated within the code of conduct.

The problem that contemporary system engineers have solved no better than the designers of *Walden Two* is that of how to build a mechanism for generating an ever appropriate code of conduct. Such a mechanism must be able to size up its environment, decide upon some universally acceptable values, and accomplish all this without doing violence to the structure of its operating units. Engineers understand very well what it means to overload an electrical circuit or to place an excessive strain upon a mechanical assembly. Where these operating units are human, the evidence of strain, load, or deterioration may not be quite so apparent.

Gardner Murphy (1958), whose primary concern is human beings reminds us that most of our traditional utopias forget that men do not stay put. "A utopia which would fit the men of today," he tells us, "would be insipid or become a straitjacket to the men of tomorrow" (p. 309). For one thing, the sheer specifications of these human equipments change. People produce people who produce people ad infinitum. But the people thus produced are by no means carbon copies of their predecessors. They vary in size, weight, memory, capacity, access time to memory, ability to manipulate the contents of memory, and in many other similar ways. Furthermore, they may be affected in unpredicted ways by new experiences or fresh sensations. As a human operating unit wears out, one searches in vain through the parts catalogue for an exact replacement.

The operating unit approach, it is clear, can indeed provide some solutions to the problem of system design for emergent situations. But a fundamental contradiction remains—the historical dilemma between freedom and control. To the extent that we increase predictability and performance reliability by selecting predictable and reliable components, to that extent we reduce the system's freedom and its capacity to deal with emergent situations effectively. In this sense, reliable components reduce overall system effectiveness. As we proceed in the other direction—that is, in the direction of building a system with self-sufficient operating units—we reduce the effectiveness of our control mechanism. This design problem poses the basic dilemma of freedom versus control. We shall keep exploring this dilemma throughout the remainder of our discussion.[. . .]

If one wishes to adhere to this engineering frame of reference, it is possible to think of human beings as materials with more or less specifiable performance characteristics. Assuming that you have an order to give, and that part of your circuit includes people, it becomes necessary to understand the amount of work that can be accomplished by these people components, the time necessary to accomplish the work, the reliability of performance, the maintenance schedule required, and so on.

The customary consequence of adhering to this frame of reference is to conclude that human components are exasperatingly unreliable, limited and inefficient. Furthermore, they are very difficult to control. The most obvious analogy to the physical control system involves the use of formal authority and its delegation as the energy or power source necessary to insure that the desired signals pass through the entire system. This of course, is the basis for the insistence upon unquestioning obedience to orders traditionally found not only in military organizations but in all bureaucracies of both private industry and government organizations. Human groups unfortunately (or fortunately) have devised many mechanisms for disrupting systems that exercise control exclusively or even primarily through the use of authority.

What happens when authority control systems run amuck is an endless source of case history material for management development seminars. The case of the employees who do *everything* they are ordered to do by their supervisor—neither more nor less—is a classic. They ignore obvious emergent situations and engage in assigned repetitive tasks beyond reasonable termination points. The supervisor is gradually forced into behavior indistinguishable from that of a computer programmer giving instructions to a stupid but completely obedient machine. The case of the industrial work group ordered to use a new, unwanted piece of equipment is perennially effective slapstick comedy material; the ingenious steps taken by members of the group to prove the existence of unsuspected faults in the new equipment provide universally understandable material for comedy writers. The list of examples could be continued indefinitely. The point to be made is simply this: the idea of control results in highly unreliable performance when applied to human components of a system.[. . .]

THE USE OF HUMAN OPERATING UNITS—A DIGRESSION

Our immediate concern, let us remember, is the explication of the operating unit approach to system design, no matter *what* materials are used. We must take care to prevent this discussion from degenerating into a single-sided analysis of the complex characteristics of one type of system material: namely, human beings.

What we need is an inventory of the ways in which human behavior can be controlled, and a description of some instruments that will help us achieve control. If this provides us sufficient "handles" on human materials so that we can think of them as one thinks of metal parts, electric power or chemical reactions, then we have succeeded in placing human materials on the same footing as any other materials and can proceed with our problems of system design. Once we have equated all possible materials, one simply checks the catalogue for the price, operating characteristics, and reliability of this material and plugs it in where indicated. For an engineer or industrial designer, these are precisely the terms upon which human beings must be considered. This is not, of course, to imply that engineers are cruel, heartless or inhuman. They are, as they would put it, "simply trying to do a job." It is, they would assert, 'inhuman' to insist that human beings perform duties that can be passed on to nonhuman materials. This frees human beings for golf, philosophy, music and business deals.[. . .]

There are, however, many disadvantages in the use of human operating units. They are somewhat fragile; they are subject to fatigue, obsolescence, disease and death; they are frequently stupid, unreliable, and limited in memory capacity. But beyond all this, they sometimes seek to design their own system circuitry. This, in a material, is unforgivable. Any system utilizing them must devise appropriate safeguards.[. . .]

A "good" or "effective" operating unit is one that has "adjusted" to its environment. It accepts the environmental conditions postulated by its system designer as a "given," and it does what its structure permits it to do. The central difficulty that arises lies in the definition of "environment." A "bad" thermo-nuclear weapon would be one that exploded before some "responsible" human being "pressed the button," or because it simply "felt" like exploding. Human beings generally don't want "intelligent" thermonuclear weapons. But the man who presses the button is part of the environment of the weapon. The factors that lead to the button's being pressed are equally part of this environment. The social, economic, emotional, political or other issues that help determine whether the button will be pressed are all part of the bomb's environment. Do you design a bomb to be detonated with one finger, two fingers, or two hundred million fingers? This is all part of the system design problem when you design systems with the operating unit approach.

The safest procedure is to build a system with operating units resembling Mr. Zero of Elmer L. Rice's (1922) *The Adding Machine*. Whether serving as a Roman galley slave, a serf or an American bookkeeper about to be displaced by an adding machine, Mr. Zero is completely reliable, noninnovative and safe. The designer of his universe is undoubtedly a shrewd, cost-conscious engineer. He collects used souls in a sort of heavenly dry-dock, cleans and repairs them, and ships them out to occupy new bodies. For purposes of minimizing costs and maximizing efficiency within a predictable cosmos, this is obviously a highly intelligent solution. There is, of course, no requirement for Mr. Zero to be intelligent; he remains eternally a Zero.

This is not to imply that Mr. Zero is incapable of independent action. He can learn to speak, read, write, hold a job, raise a family, quarrel with his wife, and discuss politics. It is not necessary to program his daily activities; they will fall well within specified tolerances. His purpose in the scheme of things is simply to be himself. One might, of course, find it interesting to speculate about the long-range objectives of his designer, which are not specified—but that, as our new utopians might say, is another problem.

In any event, his designer seems to be faced with a constantly changing universe. He deals with this dynamic universe by using dependable operating units like Mr. Zero. In doing so, he is confronted with the same issue that other operating unit system designers must resolve: How much self-determination should these operating units be allowed to possess?[. . .]

If a robot is allowed too much independent action, it may begin to assert the pre-eminence of its own goals over those of its designer. It is then a "rebel" and its behavior is appropriately referred to as a "revolt."

But how "intelligent" must an operating unit be before it is able to revolt? Or conversely, how "stupid" must the designer insist that his operating unit be to insure reliable system performance? And, from the perspective of the operating unit, what are the necessary and sufficient conditions for effective rebellion?[. . .]

Decisions made by operating units acting either independently or as direct agents of a designer affect human populations directly through their impact upon the conditions of human existence. It is not only the human beings serving as operating units who are affected, but those outside the system as well. The critical point is not the location of people with respect to the system, but the nature of the decisions made and the actions taken which affect their destinies.

In this context, discussions about whether man should be adjusted to physical equipment or vice versa become gigantic *non sequiturs*. When the operating units are not simply tools but machines in varying states of operating independence, it is men who must adjust. Hannah Arendt (1958) has observed, "Even the most primitive tool remains a servant unable to guide or replace the hand. Even the most primitive machine guides the body's labor and eventually replaces it altogether" (p. 129).

But this, of course, is a profound understatement. The replacement is much more than a simple substitution of machine for human labor. It is becoming increasingly more obvious that a surrender of decision-making prerogatives is involved. The values of human populations increasingly become excluded from the dialogue between operating units and their environments. Operating units requirements become both the short-run and long-range goals of human populations. The information necessary to understand operating unit characteristics becomes the content of educational programs; operating unit characteristics shape society's demand for natural resources, economic arrangements, philosophical orientations, and family life. This is the strength and the tragedy of human beings in search of systems within which they can assume their roles as operating units.[. . .]

SOME SIMPLE IMPLICATIONS OF THE UTOPIAN RENAISSANCE

To the bona fida utopian, empiricism is not enough. He is not content with simply designing systems, organizations or societies that operate efficiently and effectively—he feels that they must act in ways he would assess as being "good" rather than "bad." He has a more or less well-defined set of values at stake and is, to a considerable extent, a moralist as well as an engineer. Of course, it is quite possible to value efficiency or effectiveness above all other things, and this can, under some circumstances, lead to bizarre or even macabre consequences. For example, the characteristic American impatience with obvious inefficiency in other societies is a well-known phenomenon. Visions of cattle roaming the streets of Indian cities while human populations starve is a favorite illustration used by efficiency worshippers to demonstrate the tragic consequences of nonefficiency ideologies.[. . .]

The problem, of course, is not simply one of introducing greater degrees of specificity into the definition of various principles. We have seen how such specificity can result in procedure rigidity and lost games. If, however, we leave the path of specificity and follow one leading from low-level generality to high-level generality to still-higher-level generality, we ultimately arrive at the place called "values."

Now this is a region where many, if not most, scientists feel uncomfortable. It sounds and looks like something outside the science ballpark. If you insist upon going there, you are probably interested in things other than the science game.

What is the science game?

The obvious reply is to insist that science is a game whose objective is "truth." If you find truth, you win; if you fail to find truth, you lose. And for many people in our society—scientists and non-scientists alike—science is the game we should all be playing. We are told by serious thinkers that science is not merely a value prescribing the conduct of the scientist as he works alone, but that it is the overriding value for our entire Western society (see Bronowski, 1959). If this is the case, a whole series of instrumental heuristics is indicated. They follow naturally and logically from the requirements to do those things which will help uncover truth. They include "independence," "dissent," and even "freedom." A truth-seeker must be independent—and society must protect his independence. He must be original—and society must protect his originality. He may wish to dissent—and society must provide him the opportunity to do so.

It would therefore seem that establishing the value of truth provides a means for achieving the historic American dream. It seems to invite the use of freedom of thought, speech and individual dignity. But this, unfortunately, is not the case. Indeed, it is possible to invoke the negative of each of the indicated instrumental heuristics and to show how necessary this negative is for achieving truth in some situations.[. . .]

Truth as a means to an end became a necessary antidote to esoteric representations of reality insisted upon by medicine men, soothsayers, pundits and politicians. The history of empiricism and scientific research is a history of debunked old-wives' tales. These tales served as instrumental heuristics for the ignorant, the superstitious, and representatives of special interests. But when truth alone becomes the end of human existence, one must not be surprised if humanity ultimately emerges as the loser.

The spawn of truth is efficiency. Efficiency as an instrumental heuristic leads to more rapid transportation, more automobiles, shoes, solid-state computers—and thermonuclear weapons.

Truth and efficiency are highly effective as instrumental heuristics. But as value heuristics they ignore the prejudices some of us have about the distinctive importance of human beings. There is nothing scientific or efficient about this prejudice; it simply exists. It says that the molecules that make up a human being are somehow more important than the molecules of a tree or a steel cabinet or a factory. This prejudice is something like the prejudice of ethnocentrism. We condemn ethnocentrism because it asserts the importance of one group of human beings over another group of human beings. Humanism simply asserts that humanity is more important than nonhumanity—and this is inconsistent with an orientation that values only truth and efficiency. Within a rigidly defined framework of these values, it is simply not true that the molecules of humanity have priority over other molecules.

Within the framework of systems, organizations and engineered societies, human beings become operating units. And now we must ask: what are these things called human beings in an operational sense? How do we deal with them in the context of our design specifications?[. . .]

The workaday new utopians seem to have implicitly turned Max Weber's Ethic on its head to read, "Hard work is simply a temporarily unautomated task. It is a necessary evil until we get a piece of gear, or a computer large enough, or a program checked out well enough to do the job economically. Until then, you working stiffs can hang around—but, for the long run, we really don't either want you or need you."

Depending upon one's religious orientation, this reversal may be viewed as either a good or bad thing in itself. Its potential implications for persons who continue to live in an economic situation whose traditional values are being overturned are, in any event, enormous.[. . .]

Here one may speculate regarding the successor to the Protestant Ethic. Will the unspoken creed, which once could be verbalized as "I may not be a brain but I can always make a living with these hands; I am fundamentally the producer," be replaced by another, which when verbalized might say, "All these hands (or all this mind) can do is what some machine hasn't yet gotten around to doing. The real producers in our society are the scientists, the engineers and maybe even the boss. I am not *really* a producer—I feel alienated from the productive process. I am the one who's asking the others for a free ride. I am the one who, in effect, is doing the exploiting—why not do it deliberately and systematically?"

Many segments of society can be characterized by what has been called the "powerless" form of alienation—"the expectancy or probability held by the individual that his own behavior cannot determine the occurrence of the outcomes, or reinforcements, he seeks" (Seeman, 1959, p. 784). The notion that those strange men who write equations on blackboards are the real arbiters of all our destinies is one that must be obliterated in any society that wishes to continue functioning in even an approximately democratic fashion.

Other segments are subject to the kind of alienation called "isolation." This results from assigning low reward value to goals or beliefs that are typically high-valued in a given society (Seeman, 1959, p. 789). Included among the groups affected are unquestionably some social scientists, some philosophers, and possibly some former bomber pilots. Funds for research on missile fuels are demonstrably more available than, say, funds for research in basic social theory, or philosophical theory, or manned bomber tactics. For some bomber pilots this may result in irrational and intemperate attacks upon the effectiveness of missiles. The rebellion of social scientists and philosophers against this imbalance in value structures can, and frequently does, take the form of avoiding professional involvement with some of the most centrally significant social issues in the contemporary world.

One implication of all this seems clear. In terms of sheer self-survival, it is necessary to expand the educational base of leaders and rank-and-file members of union and management organizations, military men, philosophers, social scientists and others through broad educational programs. Such programs should be addressed not only to the problem of making people more at ease with the concept of computers and computer programming, but also more fundamentally toward helping them become perceptive about the implications that contemporary large-scale system design has for each one of us. This should permit union leaders, social scientists, academicians, management, and government officials, as well as an informed public, to participate along with more hardware-oriented engineers in the design of large-scale systems at an early stage of formulation of these projects. This must be done to insure that the human implications of proposed automated systems are fully explored as fundamental design variables.

In turn, physical scientists and engineers must become increasingly more sensitive to the human purposes that improvements in automated technology will serve. They must broaden the educational base of their training so that they do indeed consider *all* significant variables in designing systems—rather than merely those that lend themselves to hardware implementation or formal modeling.[. . .]

REFERENCES

Arendt, H. (1958) *The Human Condition*. Doubleday.

Bronowski, J. (1959) "The Values of Science." In Maslow, A. H., ed. *New Knowledge in Human Values*. Harper & Row, pp. 54–60.

Folley, J. D., and Van Cott, H. P. (1960) *Human Factors Methods for Systems Design*. American Institute for Research under Office of Naval Research. Contract no. Nonr-2700[00], pp. 4–5.

Heilbroner, R. L. (1953) *The Worldly Philosophers*. Simon & Schuster.

Murphy, G. (1958) *Human Potentialities*. Basic Books.

Rice, E. L. (1922) *The Adding Machine*. Samuel French.

Seeman, M. (1959) "On the Meaning of Alienation." *American Sociological Review*, vol. 24.

Skinner, B. F. (1948) *Walden Two*. Macmillan Co.

4
History of
Work Concepts
Peter Warr and Toby Wall

The acquisition and application of knowledge are in part determined by society's contemporary value systems. There are wide areas of understanding and action in which accepted truth varies from generation to generation, and doctrines about industry and its employees have both reflected and influenced more general ideologies. The changes which have occurred in industrial society's orientation to work are in this way reflected in the main themes of industrial psychology through this century. Not surprisingly these themes have progressed from the simple to the complex, but they have also shifted from a rather single-minded concern for productive efficiency and the rights of the employer to a more wide-ranging perspective which incorporates employee well-being as well as efficiency and profitability.

Four research themes . . . have influenced both thinking and practice in the organization of work. The principal spokesman for these themes are Frederick Taylor (1856–1915), Elton Mayo (1880–1949), Abraham Maslow (1908–70) and Frederick Herzberg (born 1923).

Excerpts from P. Warr and T. Wall. *Work and Well Being*. Maryland: Penguin Books, 1975, Chapter 2, "Theories of Work Attitudes," pp. 24–38.

SCIENTIFIC MANAGEMENT

The first of these theorists systematically to consider what motivated people at work was Taylor, an engineer working in American industry at the turn of the century. Taylor's main concern was to increase efficiency, and his approach, described for example in *The Principles of Scientific Management* (1911, reprinted in 1947) is of interest both because of its influence upon subsequent job attitude research and for its more general relationship to the field of industrial psychology.

The basic aim of scientific management was the development of a "science" to replace the "rules of thumb" typically used by managers of the day. Taylor pointed to the fact that whereas managers had reliable and useful information concerning the capacity and efficiency of their machines, they had no such information about their employees. With this in mind he focused his attention upon two problems, how to make work methods more efficient, and how to encourage men to work harder.

Taylor advocated the following procedure for improving efficiency in manual work. A number of individuals who were exceptionally skillful at the work in question were to be found, the physical movements they used were to be closely scrutinized, and each movement or unit of activity carefully timed. From all the different elementary movements demonstrated by the skillful group the most rapid, and the slowest and redundant, were to be identified. Finally, a new method of working which capitalized on the rapid movements and avoided the slow and unnecessary ones was to be developed. A similar procedure was to be followed for establishing the best equipment to use during each stage of the work, and for the layout of the physical environment. Having decided the "best method" in this manner, it was to be put into practice by training individuals in its use. The training should be so exact that every employee would carry out the same movements in the same order, hour after hour, day after day. With a number of routine manual jobs this was put into practice with spectacular effects in terms of increased output, and this aspect of Taylor's work provided the impetus for later developments in the field of work study.

Taylor appreciated, however, that the success of a method devised in this manner depended not only upon the elimination of the least efficient physical movements, but also upon the cooperation of those trained in its use. He proposed two "laws" of human motivation which would encourage employee cooperation and which, he claimed, were derived from "carefully planned and executed experiments extending through a term of years." (The exact nature of these experiments, however, remains obscure.) The first of his "laws" concerned the effect of the "task idea" upon the individual. Taylor expressed this concept in the following way:

> ... The average workman will work with the greatest satisfaction, both to himself and his employer, when he is given each day a definite task which he is to perform in a given time, and which constitutes a proper day's work for a good workman. This furnishes the workman

with a clear-cut standard, by which he can throughout the day measure
his own progress, and the accomplishment of which affords him the
greatest satisfaction [1947, pp. 120–21].

This notion was put into practice by giving specific production goals to each
individual and by ensuring close supervision throughout the work. In today's
language the 'task idea' is similar to "feedback," "knowledge of results" or "role
clarity." The second "law" concerned the economic returns the individual obtained from work. Taylor argued that employees would only work at their best
speed if they were assured of a "large and permanent increase in their pay." Such
an increase should be made contingent upon the attainment of prescribed levels of
performance. Thus the desire for money which all men were assumed to possess
could be directly harnessed to work activity so as to increase performance and
efficiency. Employees were assumed to be rational people who made their own
sensible decisions about financial gain and loss.

It is through the explicit formulation and use of this second "law" that Taylor
has been particularly influential. The assumption that man works primarily for
money and will rationally choose to do that which provides the greatest personal
economic gain is the lesson conventionally culled from scientific management.
Certainly, the relationship between payment by results and work performance has
been sufficiently well illustrated to ensure the use of financial incentive schemes
throughout the industrial world. It is only to be regretted that other aspects of
Taylor's thinking did not exert an equal influence over the development of
industrial psychology. His writing reveals, if only in embryonic form, a concern
for issues including those that today have become known as performance appraisal, job analysis, job evaluation, job design, ergonomics, selection and training.
His research is also important for its deliberate use of the methodological techniques of control and criterion groups.

Rarely, however, is he credited with these contributions. It is his strong
emphasis on man's desire for money, and his contention that management should
manipulate pay in order to obtain greater effort from employees, that have
survived over the years. Understandably, then, it has become customary to
denigrate Taylor's work for its exploitative implications. While his methods did
improve the individual's pay they regularly resulted in a proportionately greater
benefit for the employer. Moreover, his belief that workmen were basically lazy
and should not, for their own good, be allowed to earn too much, has not endeared
him to those with less élitist tendencies.

In spite of these features one should not lose sight of the influence exerted by
Taylor over our views of human nature. We believe it to be unfortunate, and to a
large extent the fault of those who followed and reacted against Taylor, that
important aspects of his approach have been virtually ignored. The concept of the
"task idea," for example, took many years to re-emerge, and his concern for
scientifically acceptable methodology influenced even those who disagreed with
his conclusions. It should also be noted that economics and technological characteristics have altered since his time. He was working within an expanding econ-

omy with a low rate of change. Jobs were differentiated, less interdependent than today, and technological factors closely determined the nature of work. The jobs he studied were relatively unsophisticated, quite unlike many present-day tasks involving monitored decision-making based upon detailed knowledge. This is not to say that Taylor should receive especial praise; but it would be wrong to bury him.[. . .]

THE HAWTHORNE STUDIES

[. . .]The Hawthorne Works were part of the Western Electric Company.* This was a progressive company for its day, employing around 29,000 people, and paying relatively high wages in addition to providing pension schemes, sickness benefits and recreational facilities. Between 1924 and 1926 a series of studies, later known as the Illumination Experiments, were launched at the Hawthorne Works. These studies reflected the assumptions of their time—efficiency was the overriding concern and the rational individual the object of study. The initial aims were in keeping with prevalent scientific management ideals, in that the researchers intended to measure and control physical features of work in order to increase individual output and efficiency. In three departments, where women employers wound coils, assembled relays and inspected small parts, a number of engineers investigated the relationship between light intensity and work performance.

In the first study the illumination in the workrooms was steadily increased and the effect on production observed. The expectancy was that output would vary systematically with light intensity, but no such simple pattern occurred. In one department production fluctuated randomly relative to illumination. Production in the other two departments did increase, but this increase showed a tenuous and erratic relationship with light intensity. The experimenters next carried out investigations in which two comparable groups of employees were selected for study. The intensity of illumination was kept constant for one group acting as a control for the other. In the latter, lighting levels were gradually increased over time. As predicted, the output of this experimental group increased. But so too did the performance of the control group. With commendable persistence the investigators devised a third series of experiments. Again, the control group illumination was kept constant, but the experimental group received an ever-*decreasing* level of illumination. Once again, however, output rose in both groups, until the experimental group protested that they could no longer see what they were doing. By now the investigators had no option but to abandon their simple hypothesis that on its own light intensity directly affected productivity. Quite clearly other factors were more responsible for the variations in performance. [. . .]

What, then, accounted for the increased productivity? The change from the large-group to the small-group payment scheme was judged to be of some importance, but the full explanation came to focus upon social factors within the group.

*Editor's Note: See Roethlisberger and Dickson (1939).

Supervision was free and easy, the operatives were able to set their own work pace, and they developed their own norms, practices and values. The removal of the girls from their usual work environment set them apart and intensified the interaction among them. An interest was shown in each individual, and the production record of the group became a source of pride. A sense of cooperation between supervisor and operative was also developed. As a result of these changes in the social milieu, the attitudes of the employees in the experiment became more and more favourable. In other words, an increased involvement in the job was reflected in a steady improvement in production.

The importance of social relationships was further illustrated in two other investigations conducted at the Hawthorne Works. The first of these was a mass interview programme, involving over 21,000 employees, which aimed to discover the nature of attitudes towards work. People were found to have strong views about the physical conditions of their work and about pay, but in practice it was the content and style of their personal relationships which really mattered to them. How their foreman treated them, and how they got along with their colleagues were matters which arose repeatedly throughout the interview programme.

The importance of such issues was further highlighted in the final part of the investigation. This took place in the Bank Wiring Observation Room and was designed to shed more light on what happens within working groups. (Note how far this aim has shifted from the initial objectives of the Illumination Experiments.) Fourteen men were closely studied over a period of six months in 1931 and 1932. Their behaviour and work output were continuously recorded, but no experimental changes in working conditions were introduced. Of the fourteen operatives, nine were employed to wire banks of terminals, three soldered these banks and two worked as inspectors. A fairly complex group payment scheme was employed, and it soon became apparent that the employees did not understand the detailed operation of this scheme although they had a clear enough idea about what they would earn for specified levels of output.

In practice, however, the incentive scheme was not operating as management intended, since the employees did not attempt to maximize their earnings by working harder. Instead the group established its own norms of output. Individuals encouraged each other to keep closely to the agreed production level. If they exceeded this they were expected to record their output as lower than it really was, and the excess would then be recorded in periods of under-production. The social norms of the work-group were clearly having a marked influence on what people did at their work. Taylor's view of rational-economic man seemed to the investigators to be quite inappropriate in this case.[. . .]

In retrospect it seems obvious that social factors matter to people in their jobs, but the significance of the studies should be assessed within their historical context. They changed the focus of attention from the physical aspects of the work environment and the incentive value of pay to a consideration of interpersonal relations and communications, group norms and values, participation, supervision, morale and satisfaction. Man was no longer seen as a simple animal driven by a desire for money and at the mercy of his environment. A more complex view had emerged [Mayo 1946, Homans 1950].[. . .]

MASLOW'S THEORY OF HUMAN NATURE

A third influence upon job attitude research is to be found in the work of Maslow (1943, 1968, 1970, 1973). This differs in two main ways from the approaches already described in this chapter. Firstly, his theory of human nature was not developed specifically as an attempt to understand people at work. Maslow was more a clinical, humanistic psychologist than one concerned with industrial and other organizations. As such his work is broader in scope, being concerned with motivation in life more generally; we have already mentioned some of his views on psychological growth (page 17). Secondly, his theory is not only an attempt to identify people's wants; it goes beyond identification to specify the relationships between them in terms of their hierarchical organization.

Maslow postulated that man has five classes of "basic needs." The first is a physiological need, a desire for food, water and other prerequisites of life. The second, a safety need, involves a wish for security and the avoidance of physical danger. The third class—social needs—involves a desire for affection and friendship. The fourth is a need for esteem, a desire for a high evaluation of oneself, for self-respect. The final need is for "self-actualization." This is the most original aspect of his theory and at the same time the concept most difficult to define.

Maslow distinguishes between "becoming" and "being." We are all the time in the process of moving towards our full potential, towards the actualization of what we might be. This process of movement is one of "becoming," and we are closer on some occasions than others to "being" our true selves. Maslow writes of self-actualization as both a process and as a momentary experience of being.[. . .]

In Maslow's theory, then, the need to self-actualize is a particularly important one. He argues that the five kinds of basic needs form a hierarchy, from self-actualization at the top, through esteem, social and safety needs to physiological needs. The lower-order needs are seen as prepotent: they are personally most significant until they are satisfied to some acceptable degree, and only then do the higher needs gradually come into play. The higher needs are extremely important, but not until the others are satisfied. Conversely the lower needs can monopolize consciousness and behaviour when they have not been met. Man does not live by bread alone, but when he has no bread his active wants are exclusively to do with food.

These thoughts have been incorporated into the mainstream of occupational and organizational psychology by the recognition that employment in most industrialized societies caters quite well for lower-level needs. The wants which the theory predicts to be important to people are the higher-level ones to do with esteem and actualization. So what has work to offer here? For manual workers in most jobs it offers very little indeed. Can we then design jobs so that people's work engages their higher-level needs? This clearly presents difficult technological and financial problems.

Maslow's theory can be discussed on several levels. The conclusion of the last paragraph suggests that managers and employers might reject it on practical grounds, and certainly many so do. Yet we believe that a large number of people in professional and managerial jobs know for themselves what Maslow is driving at. His writings are florid and idealistic, but his notions of self-actualization strike home to many.[. . .]

A second level of criticism of Maslow's theory is, however, possible. This concerns his identification of separate needs which are ordered hierarchically. Several research programmes have employed separate measures (e.g. Porter 1961, 1962, 1963; Porter and Lawler, 1968) but there is ample evidence of overlap between the supposedly discrete want-systems (e.g. Payne 1970; Schneider and Alderfer, 1973).[. . .]

HERZBERG'S TWO-FACTOR THEORY

A related theory which from its inception has been aimed specifically at the organization of work is that of Herzberg et al. (1959). During the late 1960s this theory generated more research investigations than any other in the field of job attitudes. Outside academic circles it was also very influential, partly because of Herzberg's persuasive skill as a consultant and conference participant.

The central proposition of the two-factor theory is that the determinants of job satisfaction are qualitatively different from the determinants of job dissatisfaction.[. . .]

Engineers and accountants, who were asked to describe the causes of their satisfactions and dissatisfactions at work, gave support for the theory; and subsequent studies of the same type yielded broadly consistent results. Five factors stood out as determinants of job satisfaction: achievement, advancement, recognition, responsibility and the work itself. These Herzberg labelled "motivators" and he argued that they were factors intrinsic to the performance of work itself. In contrast, the factors of company policy and administration, supervision, interpersonal relations and work conditions were strongly related to job dissatisfaction, but apparently unimportant as determinants of satisfaction. This latter set of factors Herzberg called "hygiene factors," on the medical analogy that without them we are unhealthy, yet increasing them beyond an acceptable level does not make us positively more healthy. Herzberg argued that hygiene factors are extrinsic to the performance of work, being aspects of the work environment rather than of the work itself. Thus a dichotomy is proposed where factors of one kind (intrinsic to the job) promote a job satisfaction and factors of a different nature (extrinsic to the job) determine job dissatisfaction. This view is in conflict with the traditional idea that any job factor may cause satisfaction or dissatisfaction depending upon the degree to which it is present or absent.

Herzberg went on to interpret these findings as suggesting that man has two separate and distinct sets of needs—those concerned with the avoidance of pain which are serviced by hygiene factors, and those towards self-actualization reflected in motivators: " . . . the human animal has two categories of needs. One stems from his animal disposition . . . it is centred on the avoidance of loss of life, hunger, pain, sexual deprivation and other primary drives . . . The other segment of man's nature is [a] ... compelling urge to realize his own potentiality by continuous psychological growth" (Herzberg, 1966, p. 56). The parallel between the hygiene-motivator dichotomy and Maslow's distinction between low-level "deficit" motives (physiological and safety needs) and higher-level "growth" motives (self-actualization and esteem) is marked.[...]

CONCLUSIONS

We have briefly described some of the more important theoretical influences upon both job attitude research and management practices. In doing this we have taken the view that each of the approaches considered was an element in an ever-broadening view of human nature as it relates to the work environment. We should emphasize, however, that each theory did not evolve in a vacuum; rather it was a development from the inadequacy of its predecessors. Thus the influence of the Hawthorne studies may be attributed to the fact that they provided a plausible alternative to the clearly restricted views of Taylor as well as to their emphasis on social factors. Maslow's theory has been influential because the notion that man wanted only money or social contact was obviously too simple. Finally, the influence of Herzberg's work is a result of its applicability for research and management practice, an applicability lacking in Maslow's more general formulation.[...]

REFERENCES

Herzberg, F. (1966) *Work and the Nature of Man.* World Publishing Company.
Herzberg, F., Mausner, B., and Snyderman, B. (1959) *The Motivation to Work.* Wiley.
Homans, G. C. (1950) *The Human Group.* Harcourt Brace.
Maslow, A. H. (1943) "A Theory of Human Motivation." *Psychological Review,* Vol. 50, pp. 370–96.
Maslow, A. H. (1968) *Toward a Psychology of Being,* second edition. Van Nostrand.
Maslow, A. H. (1970) *Motivation and Personality,* revised edition. Harper & Row.
Maslow, A. H. (1973) *The Farther Reaches of Human Nature.* Penguin.
May, R. (1967) *Psychology and the Human Dilemma.* Van Nostrand.
Mayo, E. (1946) *The Human Problems of an Industrial Civilization.* Harvard University Graduate School of Business Administration.
Payne, R. L. (1970) "Factor Analysis of a Maslow-type Need-satisfaction Questionnaire." *Personnel Psychology,* Vol. 23, pp. 251–68.
Porter, L. W. (1962) "Job Attitudes in Management: (I) Perceived Differences in Need Fulfillment as a Function of Job Level." *Journal of Applied Psychology,* Vol. 46, pp. 375–84.
Porter, L. W. (1963) "Job Attitudes in Management: (II) Perceived Importance in Needs as a Function of Job Level." *Journal of Applied Psychology,* Vol. 47, pp. 141–8.
Porter, L. W., and Lawler, E. E. (1965) "Properties of Organization Structure in Relation to Job Attitudes and Job Behavior." *Psychological Bulletin,* Vol. 64, pp. 23–51.
Porter, L. W., and Lawler, E. E. (1968) *Managerial Attitudes and Performance.* Irwin.

Roethlisberger, F. J., and Dickson, W. J. (1939) *Management and the Worker—An Account of a Research Program Conducted by the Western Electric Company, Hawthorne Works, Chicago*. Harvard University Press.

Schneider, B., and Alderfer, C. P. (1973) "Three Studies of Need Satisfaction in Organizations." *Administrative Science Quarterly*, Vol. 18, pp. 489–505.

Taylor, F. W. (1911) *The Principles of Scientific Management*. Harper. Reprinted as:

Taylor, F. W. (1947) *Scientific Management*. Harper.

5
Job Design:
Historical Overview

Louis E. Davis

Twenty-five years ago, the author and colleagues began to research, develop and apply a related set of concepts concerned with the design of jobs. At that time, the term job design first was introduced into the literature. The purpose of this paper is to review the developing trends in and point to the future direction of job design.

HISTORY OF ORIGINS

When Davis and Canter (1955) introduced the concept of job design, they said that "It is our purpose to point out that little attention has been devoted to the question, what constitutes an effectively designed job? Is it possible to improve the organization of work and the dividing up of the work into jobs so that the individual performing in the job can improve his productive contribution?" In that statement of purpose, they introduce the need to examine the process of rationalization; that is, fractionated tasks, rigid methods and boundaries, separation of planning and doing and strict hierarchy. They go on to develop this process by indicating "the assumption is very widely held that once established the job and its contents are unalterable and inviolate, that the alternatives available in specifying the design of a job are severely limited." Davis and Canter indicated that there are a variety of alternatives as to how jobs can be constituted and that the approaches used in rationalization may, in fact, be antithetical to the desired outcomes of effective performance of work. The notion of jobs as instruments for satisfying personal

Excerpts from Louis E. Davis. "Job Design: Overview and Future Direction." *Journal of Contemporary Business*, Vol. 6, 1977, No. 2, pp. 85–102.

needs of the job holders was not yet indicated very strongly. Davis and Canter raised two propositions that now have become quite widely accepted. One is the need for the amelioration of rationalization and the second is the need for understanding that jobs and organizations are social inventions put together to suit specific needs and reflect the culture, the ideology and the governing concepts or the ethos of the time.

Job design originally was defined as "the organization (or structuring) of a job to satisfy the technical-organizational requirements of the work to be accomplished and the human requirements of the person performing the work." Jobs were seen "as being composed of assigned tasks" and "the process of job design is accomplished by carrying out the following three activities: (1) specifying the content of individual tasks, (2) specifying the method of performing each task, including the machinery and tools used and any special techniques, (3) combining individual tasks into specific jobs." The first and third activities were viewed as determining the content of the job and the concern of job design, while the second was perceived as indicating how the job was to be performed and dealt with in the design of work methods.

Davis and Canter also introduced a reconceptualization of the organization of work in systematic terms, referring to work systems requiring a fit among the organization, the technology and the requirements of individuals. This reconceptualization still is not totally accepted among many social scientists and industrial engineers. Additionally, in their discussion of the conventional methods of designing jobs, they point to the rigidity of rationalization, a notion that was not to be recognized for a number of years. Davis and Canter warn of the danger of designing jobs to suit technological requirements as follows:

> One major difficulty is found in the initial lack of flexibility of the design of the jobs. Any changes in design quite often result in resistance to change, voluntary restrictions in output, etc., on the part of the workers, i.e., the jobs have been so shaped by the technical process requirements that any extensive process change causes almost every job to be altered radically with resulting worker insecurity reactions. There is a further and possibly even more crucial difficulty. After the job content has been specified, the worker is usually selected to fit the "job" and the trend is to give him a minimum choice, if any, of the methods he will use or the standards of performance he must meet, and of the situation in which he must work.

Here the long-standing issue of industrial psychology is being confronted by examining the proposition of fitting square pegs in round holes when the shape of the hole itself can be changed.

To buttress the argument for the need to look at jobs in the way suggested, the authors begin to point out the false premises of rationalization or scientific management, pointing to the waste of human resources and to inadequate criteria for measuring effectiveness. Under scientific management, the choices in job design are made without considering the hidden costs in time, money, flexibility, cooperation and psychological stress. Thus the costs of items such as labor turnover, absenteeism, amount of learning time, lack of flexibility in work skills and product quality deficiencies are not considered in designing jobs conventionally. Interestingly, 25 years later there still is no systematic means of examining costs/benefits of alternative job configurations. The philosophy of designing jobs was built upon the concept that still persists of minimizing *immediate** financial costs with little operational consideration given to the concept of minimizing *total** costs. When undergirded by the concept of minimal dependence of the organization on the individual, this leads to the plug-in-man concept in organization design which is accomplished by having the work content highly repetitious, lowering skill requirements and requiring very short training cycles.[. . .]

EARLY RESEARCH

The first field experiment on job design in an industrial plant was conducted by A. R. Marks. The study was directed toward restructuring the content of jobs to examine their effects on economic productivity; the results were reported by Davis and Canter in 1956.

A number of hypotheses were tested, including increasing the number of tasks in a job; grouping together in jobs those tasks that were related sequentially in the technical process; including in the job those tasks that contained the final activities in the process or the subprocess; putting tasks in the job that would increase worker responsibility, for example, ones that enlarge the area of decision making in regard to work rate, work methods or set-up and increase autonomy in regard to quality decisions, material supply, etc.; and putting together tasks that would increase the opportunity for the worker to see the part his or her contribution made to the work process.

This experiment was conducted in an assembly department of a unionized pharmaceutical plant, and the nature of the assembly line in that department made it impossible to examine separately the effects of attempting to use these hypotheses. Very briefly, the experiment introduced a series of changes that altered the straight assembly line operation with serial individual work stations, to group assembly and, finally, ending with each individual assembling the total product off the line. The original assembly line had nine different kinds of work stations and required twenty-nine people who rotated positions and performed carefully specified, minutely subdivided tasks. Inspectors examined the product at the end of the line. Six people were required to supply the line and perform the inspection, and the conveyor paced the work of all people working in the assembly line. The individual total product assembly performed at individual work stations yielded no gain in productivity and a remarkably high gain in the quality of this product, which already was at a very high quality level. As measured in defects per inspected lot, the average quality improved from a defect level of 0.72 percent per

---

* Editors' note: Italics added.

lot to 0.11 percent per lot. Workers developed a more favorable attitude towards individual responsibility, individual work rate, effort expenditure, distribution of work load and product preparation as compared with the lack of personal responsibility for the product on the conveyor line. After experience with the total product, assembly line workers disliked, by comparison, the lack of personal responsibility characteristic of assembly line work.

In 1957 the variables and requirements for building a theory of job design were postulated. Viewing job design as the creation and specification of job content must be seen as a design problem which raises the needs to: a) identify boundaries and evaluate boundary conditions, b) identify factors operating and determine the effect of each, c) determine methods of estimating and controlling the factors operating, d) develop systematic design methods and means of predicting consequences, and e) develop criteria for evaluation and methods of feedback (Davis 1957).

Twenty-three hypotheses were proposed which related to more effective performance and to higher satisfaction of needs on the part of those performing jobs. Some of the hypotheses on this list concern putting together tasks that constitute "meaningful" units of activity for workers; providing a sequence of tasks or operations (or organization of work) that provides a "meaningful" relationship between jobs; putting together tasks that would include in a job each of the four types of work activity inherent in productive work [namely production (processing), auxiliary (supply, tooling), preparatory (set-up) and control (inspection)]. Additional similar hypotheses included dividing the product into units (parts, components, documents) which were "meaningful" entities to the worker; arranging facilities and communications so that feedback on all aspects of performance and production needs took place automatically and constantly; providing "meaningful" measures of performance to individuals and providing "meaningful" incentives or rewards. The development of the various hypotheses and conduct of the first experiment in this early period of 1953–57 provided background which, when taken with other developments that followed in the 1960s, provided the basis for job design today.

DEVELOPMENTS OF THE 1960s

A number of critical developments occurred in the 1960s which shifted concern with specific job design per se to a concern with organization and technology in the form of sociotechnical systems in which job design becomes a dependent outcome. The developments that gave rise to the change of focus in job design ultimately led to the view that jobs as organizational units are not conceptually appropriate bases for analysis, design or redesign of work systems. Also, jobs are not a practically appropriate unit for making changes in organizations to enhance organizational effectiveness and improve the quality of working life. The dominant view of the United States in the 1960s, which still may be the case, was that jobs are the organization, for they are the visible link between men and women and how the work of society and its organizations is accomplished. Of course jobs are the most visible aspect of the organization; they are named in union contracts, in job titles and are the focus of considerable conflict. Jobs are what men and women prepare themselves to do, are alienated from, and become obsolete in their abilities to perform. Behind the popular focus is the not-so-invisible reality that in technologically advanced societies, organizations and jobs are man-made inventions designed to suit a number of technical and social system needs and are changing constantly. Thus perceived, jobs are inventions coming out of the design of larger organizational and technical system. Therefore good strategy suggests the need for examination of the larger systems to make available significant opportunities for change and for fundamental research into the processes of design.

TECHNOLOGY

More pernicious and enduring than fractionation of work in organization and job structures is the effect of technological determinism which enters through the design of technical systems and their accompanying artifacts—machines, tools, computers, programs, etc. The dominant view of the 1960s which still is prevalent today, of the relationship of technology, organization and job structure, carefully nurtured for the past 150 years, is the dangerously simplistic perspective of technological determinism. This holds that technology evolves according to its own inherent logic and needs, regardless of social environment and culture. Further, it holds that to use technology effectively, and thus to gain its benefits for society, technological development and application must be uninhibited by any considerations other than those thought relevant by its developers—that is, engineers or technologists.

Technological determinism generally has been invoked to support the organizational and institutional status quo of the now fading industrial era. For example, the claim is made that organization structure and behavior are predetermined by technology and are unalterably locked into its needs. While it has been shown that there are some correlations between technology and organizational structure and processes, choices are possible, based on social system values and assumptions. Additionally, it is both misleading and defeatist to accept the determination of technological form and its unalterable application. It is well known that *many* technological alternatives are considered by technical system planners who then propose only one alternative as a final suggestion. In job design development, therefore, it became a requirement to look at the design process of production technology itself to see which social system planning and psychosocial assumptions were considered in the design of various technical system alternatives. Further there is the need to make explicit the economic and social, as well as technical, factors included implicitly in the design process of choosing a technological form. The design and development of *technology* consists of *the application of science to invent a technique and its supportive artifacts (machines)* *to accomplish transformation of objects (materials, information, people) in support of certain objectives.* * The invention of a technique may be engineering, to an overwhelming extent, but also in part, it is social system design. In the design of a work system there are two sets of antecedent determinants that constrain the choices available for design of tasks and job structure. First there are the social choices already contained within the technological design; second, there are the social choices contained within the organization design undertaken to use the technology. Rarely is technological determinism found in the pure sense of technological or scientific variables exclusively determining the design or configuration of a technical system. On the contrary, technical system designs most frequently incorporate social system choices made intentionally or included accidentally either casually or as a result of an omission in planning. In this sense, engineers or technologists can be called social system engineers, and they are crucial to evolving new organizational forms and new job structures. In part, this recognition of technology as social engineering led to the search for concepts to examine the interaction between technology and individual and organizational needs, ultimately leading to joining job design concepts with those of sociotechnical systems.[. . .]

From Jobs to Roles

The consequences of conducting research and design in a systems context are engagements with larger organizational entities, with greater complexity, with roles rather than jobs of members in the functioning of the organization and viewing existing (and classic) job designs as comprising only some of the "tasks" or activities carried out by an organizational member. Thus from the late 1960s the concept of role design began to enter into consideration as distinct from the concept of job design. This shift permitted the introduction of the concepts of discretionary tasks versus prescribed tasks which previously had constituted the realm of classic job design. In this respect it was similar to the job enrichment activities of Herzberg (1968) who stressed vertical enrichment rather than horizontal enlargement.[. . .]

Sociotechnical systems theory conceives of the working world as consisting of independent technological systems and social systems operating under joint causation. This leads to the central concept of joint optimization, which states that when achievement of an objective depends on independent correlated systems, such as a technological and a social system, it is impossible to optimize for overall performance without seeking to optimize these correlative systems jointly. Among a number of concepts that derive from these propositions, the concept of boundary control is of great importance for the design of jobs and of organizational units. Questions are raised regarding tasks and relationships to be included within the boundary of the "job" or "organizational unit" for self-regulation and control of functioning and the functions to be performed by higher levels that will maintain the boundary of a stable organizational unit.

---

* Editors' note: Italics added.

A number of other developments occurred in the 1960s which influenced job design. The first of these, complementarity, is an unusual concept and one not recognized properly. It was formulated by Jordan,* who in 1963 stated a systems concept for task allocation in joint man-machine systems. This contributed to the need to deal with technical and social system interactions. A second development was that of job enrichment which strongly emphasized the work itself and recognized the relationship of motivation and satisfaction to the intrinsic substantive contents of jobs. This work began to emphasize the characteristics of jobs leading to better performance and higher satisfactions. Research on the characteristics of motivating jobs was continued by Hackman and Lawler (1971). The preceding two developments continued to treat jobs and organizations in the conventional fashion, overlooking the effects of technology and considering the organization to be independent of its environments.

REFERENCES

Davis, L. E. and Canter, R. R. (1955) "Job Design." *Journal of Industrial Engineering,* Volume 6, p. 3.

Davis, L. E. and Canter, R. R. (1956) "Job Design Research." *Journal of Industrial Engineering,* Volume 7, p. 6.

Davis, L. E. (1957) "Toward a Theory of Job Design." *Journal of Industrial Engineering,* Volume 8, p. 19.

Hackman, J. R. and Lawler, E. E. (1971) "Employee Reactions to Job Characteristics." *Journal of Applied Psychology,* Volume 55, p. 265.

Herzberg, F. (1968) "One More Time: How Do You Motivate Employees?" *Harvard Business Review,* Volume 46, p. 53.

Jordan, N. (1963) "Allocation of Functions Between Man and Machines in Automated Systems." *Journal of Applied Psychology,* Volume 47, p. 161.

---

* Editors' note: See reading 2 in this volume.

Part 2

THE
CURRENT CONDITION

Introduction

INTRODUCTION

What was seen not very long ago as an avant garde—some would say elitist—concern for the quality of life at the workplace has evolved into a central concern in advanced Western industrial countries. The issue is deep and reflects extensive changes in the values of these societies. At present industrial-era job designs are still predominant, even as the post-industrial world is emerging. The conflicts generated between what is provided in such job designs and the changing expectations and needs of all who work are not likely to be easily or soon overcome. This is evidenced in reading 7 by Hedberg and Mumford and in reading 8 by Taylor.

Hazlehurst, Bradbury, and Corlett (reading 6) remind us that technology only partially influences the form of organizations and jobs. How technology is perceived and how managers view their workers strongly influence the design of organizations and jobs. As this paper shows, very different applications come from the same technology. Additionally, the authors indicate that numerically controlled machines are similar to continuous process technology machines in reducing the need for some conventional skills while increasing the need for perceptual and conceptual skills.

Hedberg and Mumford's paper (reading 7) does little to reassure us that less simplistic and more realistic criteria are used in the sophisticated world's computer systems design and electronic data processing. Their study of systems analysts' organizational model and individual model of man shows wide divergence between the way systems analysts design systems and what their personal, more democratic values are. In this newer and growing sector of employment we see the dogma and practices of scientific management, circa 1911, imposed in the latter 1970s, through tightly structured and limited job content and tight work control. Systems designers still see necessity in such restrictions. These designs exacerbate one of the central problems of the last twenty-five years of the twentieth century: namely, the design of new systems based on old shopworn concepts that no longer match values, expectations, and needs of present society. The problem arises in what follows—the costly dislocating efforts to change these very systems because of the disaffection and conflict they generate.

Taylor (reading 8) reexamines job design criteria twenty years after the first—and until now the only—available survey (by Davis, Canter, and Hoffman) of American industrial practice in the design of jobs. Now, as then, the most important consideration determining the assignment of work to people is the minimization of the direct time required to perform an activity.

Last, Mire (reading 9) shows us how central "the humanization of work" and "democracy at the workplace" have become to European unions. Growing numbers of trade union leaders are convinced that unions' responsibilities and obligations must extend to the worker's need for human dignity and respect as well as to his material needs. Depending upon local situations, different unions are responding differently.

6
Numerically Controlled Machine Tools and Machinists' Skills
—R. J. Hazlehurst, R. J. Bradbury, and E. N. Corlett

This paper describes an investigation into the nature and extent of changes in job skills brought about by the introduction of numerically controlled (NC) machine tools.

A numerically controlled machine tool is directed in its operation by numerical input information, either to be read by the operator, or in machine readable form such as punched paper tape. Like any other machine tool, an NC machine is equipped with a work holding device and a cutting tool, and means for causing related movements between the workpiece and the cutting tool so as to form new surfaces. The novel character of numerical control lies in the substitution of automatic for manual control of these related movements. It is claimed that data can be transferred directly from a drawing or planning layout into a form which is accepted by the machine and transplanted into servo-controlled machine movements without the need for intervention by a machine operator.

In its simplest form NC controls only the machine table movements. In the more sophisticated systems, speed and feed changes, table indexing and tool changing movements are also tape controlled.

Four job skills were identified in machine tool operation: motor, perceptual, conceptual and discretionary.[. . .]

Sixteen jobs,* eight NC and the eight jobs replaced by NC machines, were studied by direct observation and interview in four companies. Detailed job skills analyses were prepared which described important features and emphasised their distinguishing characteristics. Each job had tasks which imposed different demands. For example, a machine setter operator might require a high level of conceptual skill in setting up a new piece of work, but once the machine was running, the work, from the conceptual viewpoint, might become largely routine for long periods. Another operator might be required to maintain a high level of perceptual vigilance throughout a lengthy operation the setting up of which was

Excerpts from R. J. Hazlehurst, R. J. Bradbury, and E. N. Corlett. "A Comparison of the Skills of Machinists on Numerically Controlled and Conventional Machines." *Occupational Psychology*, vol. 43, nos. 3 and 4, 1969, pp. 169–182.

* Editor's Note: The authors' use of "jobs" here is in the job-shop sense, i.e., a piece of work to be done or part of a product to be made. Elsewhere they use the conventional definition of jobs, i.e., the duties or assignment of an individual.

perceptually simple. Accordingly each job was seen as divided into three principal tasks.

1. *Setting up*—which included both the initial set up and the loading of the workpiece into the fixture.
2. *Operating*—controlling and adjusting the machine and tools while cutting metal.
3. *Checking*—which included the operator's checking of other people's work as well as any gauging or inspection of his own.

For every job, each of these three tasks was separately analysed and described to indicate its important features.

Each task thus described was allocated to one of the five degrees for each of the four skills, so that each job was awarded twelve scores. From these data skill profiles were drawn, and skill levels in pairs of jobs—each NC job and the job it replaced—were compared.[. . .]

MOTOR SKILLS

[. . .] Within the context of machine tool operation, motor skills include: small delicate movements, especially fine finger work as in using a micrometer or limit gauge, or in the precise setting of the vernier table-setting dial to give a desired depth of cut or degree of offset; rapid highly dextrous movements requiring the co-ordination of different limbs in space and time, for example using both hands, simultaneously or in succession, on different machine controls (e.g. handwheels or buttons) to achieve smooth regular table slide and machine head movements; or the steady controlled arm movement in hand feeding a drill press or tapping machine. Lesser degrees of motor skill are observable in tasks requiring more gross, less precise movements, or less frequent, regular or rapid movements, or having less varied demands on the operator.

PERCEPTUAL SKILLS

[. . .] Such perceptual loads and skills may be recognisable in machine tool operation. The skills depend on those receptors which make possible the judgement of sensory qualities and the recognition of sensory cues. The monitoring of sounds, vibrations and other signals which indicate how a process is running fall into this category, and also the visual and tactile discrimination required in judging surface finish, depth of cut, metal flaws, sharpness of cutting tools and so on. Activities such as reading micrometers, control indicators and aligning graticules involve perceptual skill. The number of machine controls and information sources and the complexity and frequency of their use create different perceptual loads. Varying degrees of perceptual skill are also associated with different demands on the operator's alertness, vigilance and powers of concentration. Thus a task which requires rapid hand movements to cause frequent changes of cutter direction, where it is difficult for the operator to observe the cutting action, and where the machine controls are insensitive, puts high demands upon perceptual skill.

CONCEPTUAL SKILLS

[...]Within the context of machine tool operation, the extent to which operators are required to understand and translate abstract, symbolic information in the form of drawings, layouts, planning sheets, programmes, punched tapes, display codes, inspection sheets and so on may be regarded as one measure of the conceptual skill employed. The degree of directness or indirectness of machine controls involves differing amounts of conceptual skill. Thus the direct relationship between a pillar drill hand feed lever and the movements of the spindle imposes no load; the inter-related push buttons on a remote console which cause complex table, head and spindle feed movements, do. Conceptual skill is also involved in making calculations to establish co-ordinate and datum dimensions from complex drawings. Essentially the five degrees of conceptual skill used in this study represent a scale of increasing difficulty for the operator in relating and synthesising information involving varying degrees of symbolism from a varying number of sources. The sources are the machine controls, functions and displays, which are of varying degrees of complexity, compatibility and remoteness and interact with each other to a degree varying with the task in hand.

DISCRETIONARY SKILLS

In the performance of the tasks which form their job, operators find it necessary to make decisions, to use independent action and to exercise resourcefulness to a greater or lesser extent according to the complexity of the work. In so doing they exercise discretion or discretionary skills. The extent to which they do so may be related to changes in the method of controlling their machine tools, such as the introduction of numerical control.

Bartlett, discussing a paper by Mackworth (1956), suggested that the difference between skilled and routine performance is that in skilled performance decisions have to be made at key points. In machine tool operation the output variables of dimensional accuracy, surface finish and rate of metal removal are all influenced by operator discretion. The way in which an operator ensures efficient location, and the decisions he makes about tools, speeds and feeds, sequence of operations, or how to improvise a set up, all represent varying degrees of discretion.

RESULTS

The study provides evidence to support the following broad general statements about the effects of introducing NC machines.

1. The extent to which physical effort is diminished largely depends on the extent to which the machine is "automated." Where the tape control is limited to table co-ordinate positioning, overall activity is probably increased because of the speeding up of positioning movements.
2. NC involves some reduction in the demand for motor skills and the associated perceptual load related to precision and accuracy of movement.
3. NC involves an appreciable increase in the demand for perceptual skills associated with vigilance, machine monitoring and controls.
4. NC involves an appreciable increase in the demand for conceptual skill associated with the interpretation of symbolic information in the form of drawings, planning instructions and calculations.
5. NC involves an appreciable reduction in the number of decisions an operator is required to make.
6. Only in one job was an NC operator found to be working more than one machine, but so was his counterpart on the conventional machine.

The variety of the skill profiles [obtained] suggests that, in addition to the technical differences between NC and conventional machines, other factors account for the lack of overall pattern in skill changes; and that some NC jobs have more in common with the jobs they replace than with other NC machines. The following paragraphs discuss some such factors. *

The Effects of Company Policies on Job Skills

Some companies regard NC machines as highly specialised, to be treated in ways related to their particular characteristics, while others regard NC as normal machine tools and subject them to the same work programming, planning and loading systems as conventional machines. Policy decisions about the number of hours per day the machines are to be worked, supervisory training, number of men per machine, whether to use setter/operators or operators, and so on, depend upon the depth of understanding by managers of the machines' fundamental characteristics, and how managers decide to use NC to deal with their own products and circumstances. All these decisions affect the job skills demanded of operators.

Precision

The precision required for the workpiece in relation to the machine's inherent accuracy affects the perceptual and conceptual demands on operators and the extent to which they monitor performance and make adjustments.

Batch Sizes

These, depending on company manufacturing policy, significantly affect job skills. Long runs allow operators to build up experience of components which

---

* Editors' Note: Italics added.

enables them to recognize deviations from standard. Short runs mean that setter/ operators have to make repeated set-ups, and often have to use manual control of the machine rather than tape input.

Inspection System

Varying degrees of prescription are in force, in different companies, leaving varying amounts of discretion to operators. In one company, the decision to work 24 hours per day in three shifts meant that two operators per machine were required to deal with meal breaks. In order to keep them fully occupied they were required to perform complete inspection checks on 75 percent of production.

Programmes

The technical ability and quality of programmers affect operator job skills. Where programmes are produced by experienced men, fully conversant with the machines and their problems, the operators learn to rely on the tape, the programme and the tooling laid down. Where this is not the case operators may be expected to check the programmes, to advise the programmers, and to request modifications if necessary. Skill in performing these functions becomes an expected part of the setter/operator job.

The Operator's Concept of His Job

The operator's view of the important features of his job affect job skills. Where NC operators were aware of the high cost-centre rates, they developed skills to deal rapidly with programme stop checks, axis offsetting and so on. In companies where conformity with inspection standards was felt to be of prime importance, these skills were not developed, but great attention was paid to getting the job right, regardless of machine utilisation.

Ergonomic Aspects

Ergonomic aspects of the machine design also affect the skills required. Some machines provide displays with unequivocal, easy to read information which facilitates rapid decision making. Others provide a confusing coded display which inhibits prompt action, but which stimulates the development of conceptual skills, while adding to the operator's uncertainty about the outcome of his activities.

It appears that the great majority of job skills needed for NC will already be possessed by conventional operators. Where skill profiles indicate extra perceptual and conceptual demands, operators, selected for their adaptability, might benefit from specific training programmes dealing for example with tape language, display codes and programme sheets. The development of training devices to simulate such aspects of machine operation as controlling machine functions from insensitive remote controls, or by keying or dialling information, might be worthwhile if the rapid transfer of large numbers of operators to NC machines becomes necessary.

REFERENCES

Mackworth, N. H. (1956) "Work Design and Training for Future Industrial Skills" (The 1955 Sir Alfred Herbert Paper). *Institution of Production Engineers' Journal*, 35, (4), 214–240.

7
Design of
Computer Systems
Bo Hedberg and Enid Mumford

COMPUTER SYSTEMS AND WORK DESIGN: PROBLEMS OF PHILOSOPHY AND VISION

At this moment in time two sets of *values* present in society are in conflict with each other. On the one hand we have a powerful technical value system which tells us to make maximum possible use of technology so that we may become more wealthy and comfortable. On the other hand we have a humanistic value system which tells us to beware of technology for it is a mirage which will lead us to disaster rather than success. Somewhere in between these two value systems is another which says technology is essentially neutral; whether it produces gains or losses depends entirely on the decisions that are taken on how it shall be used. Supporters of this middle position are a group of researchers from seven European countries who are working together in an attempt to influence one form of technology—computers—to move in a direction which produces human as well as technical gains. This paper is a report on one aspect of our research. We argue that computers and *information technology* represent a powerful resource for improvement at all levels of society, but for this improvement to come about, alternative ways of using the technology must be identified and choices made in terms of human psychological needs.[. . .]

Excerpts from B. Hedberg and E. Mumford. "The Design of Computer Systems." In E. Mumford and H. Sackman, eds. *Human Choice and Computers*. New York: North Holland Publishing Company, 1975, pp. 31–59.

One of our principal research hypotheses is that computer systems associated with the solution of particular business problems allow for different forms of *work organization* and different job structures. In other words, that systems involving computers such as stock control, order processing or production control are not technologically deterministic but permit the designing of these systems in a manner which successfully meets the needs of people. This will include factors related to the performance of work such as fast, accurate, clear information and factors related to needs for job satisfaction such as work interest and challenge.

A second hypothesis, and the one on which this paper focusses, is that we are not at present getting computer systems which are consciously designed to increase job satisfaction, because the reward system and the values which influence systems designers are not of a kind which motivate them to do this. These values may be the systems designer's own individual or professional values or they may be top management or user values to which systems designers have to respond. *In this paper we shall discuss only the values of the systems designers.* We recognise that top management values and reward systems or, in some situations, the values of user management and staff, together with time constraints, technical constraints, financial constraints, etc., imposed by management or by the existing hardware or software support may have considerable impact on the way computer systems are designed, but we believe that the values of the systems designers exercise a strong enough influence over the design process for these to warrant separate examination. It is therefore this aspect of our research which we shall examine here. Using the data collected so far we shall examine the *models of men* which the systems designers in our survey have told us they use.

Systems design means technical and social change. The design group alters important variables in the multivariate system which we call organization. Not only the technology, but also the work roles of individuals, the nature and performance of their task, and the structure which is designed to keep the organizational components together can be subject to change. The complexity of the design task is considerable and the consequences of various design alternatives are often hard to evaluate. It is reasonable to assume that values play an important part in guiding the designers' choice between different design alternatives.

We shall argue that systems are designed in terms of a vision of man and man's needs and abilities which is greatly influenced by the systems designers' own values, training and experience. In a situation where the potential users of the system may lack time, EDP knowledge, and perhaps the motivation to become involved in the design process, the systems designer is left to create his own organizational reality and this may not coincide with the reality of people in user departments where new computer systems are introduced. We hypothesize that systems designers, in an attempt to regulate and reduce the variety of the systems design process, build simple conceptual models of the design universe and the people located in it. These models do not typically include human factors such as a desire for job satisfaction.

Such models assist the systems designer to bring order to the design process and when translated into objectives and procedures they determine the manner in which he approaches his work and the criteria which he uses for evaluating the success of his work. But they are likely to be derived from his own value system and, if there are no other active participants to the systems design process, will incorporate concepts of human and organizational needs which are related principally to the organizational reality perceived by the systems designer and not to the view of reality held by workers and managers in the situation where computer systems are introduced.

The thesis of this paper is that if the computer man is left to create his own organizational world and the rules by which it is to operate, then he will not design computer systems which fit the organizational worlds of the workers and managers who use his systems.

THE ORGANIZATIONAL MODEL OF MAN HELD
BY THE MAJORITY OF SYSTEMS DESIGNERS

Systems designers were given two sets of statements, representing the extremes of an opinion scale (graded 1–7) and asked to indicate where they stood on the scale. The results are set out below. . . . Diagram A sets out the average view of the respondents. The statistical means of each distribution are connected by the graphs.[. . .]

Statements on the left of the scale represent, using the terminology of McGregor (1960), a Theory X view of the firm. A tightly structured organization, with precise job definitions and clear lines of hierarchical authority. Statements on the right represent a Theory Y position. A flexible organization, which has a great deal of control located with employees instead of supervision. It can be seen that the British systems designers are not consistent. At the task, or operational level—the work which the employee does, they favour well defined, structured and stable jobs; they want job methods to be carefully defined by O & M, Management Services or supervision; they want targets to be set and monitored by supervision, and they want close supervision, tight controls and well maintained discipline. Yet at the same time they favour the downward delegation of authority and the provision of nonfinancial motivators such as work challenge.

The areas where they want structure and definition are those over which they have a great deal of influence when they design systems, namely job content and work controls. Yet it can be argued that by imposing a tight structure and tight controls they eliminate opportunities for challenging work and for group decision taking. This could suggest a perhaps unrecognised conflict between the way they design systems and their personal, more democratic values.

The Swedish systems designers are somewhat more consistent in their Theory Y-oriented view of the firm. However, the profiles of the two graphs are rather similar. All observations from the Swedish sample fall on the Y side of the British data and on the Y half of the scales. The majority opinions of the two groups are close to one another on statements F and G where the variance in both studies is relatively low. The opinions are quite far apart for statements A, B, D and E, where the values in both studies is relatively high.

DIAGRAM A: Organizational Model of Man

Use the following scale to indicate what you believe to be the best form of department structure for non-specialist, non-management staff (put an X on the scale for each pair of properties).

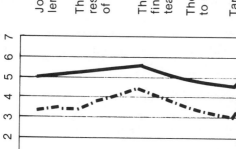
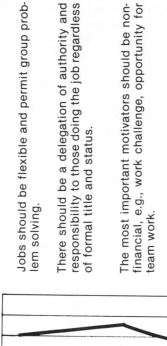

A. Jobs should be clearly defined, structured and stable.

Jobs should be flexible and permit group problem solving.

B. There should be a clear hierarchy of authority with the person at the top carrying ultimate responsibility for all aspects of work.

There should be a delegation of authority and responsibility to those doing the job regardless of formal title and status.

C. The most important motivators should be financial, e.g., high earnings and cash bonuses.

The most important motivators should be non-financial, e.g., work challenge, opportunity for team work.

D. Job methods should be carefully defined by systems and procedures specialists, management services, or supervision.

The development of job methods should be left to the group and individual doing the job.

E. Targets should be set by supervision and monitored by supervision.

Targets should be left to the employee groups to set and monitor.

F. Groups and individuals should be given the specific information they need to do the job but no more.

Everyone should have access to all information which they regard as relevant to their work.

G. Decisions on what is to be done and how it is to be done should be left entirely to management.

Decisions should be arrived at through group discussions involving all employees.

H. There should be close supervision, tight controls and well maintained discipline.

There should be loose supervision, few controls and a reliance on employee self discipline.

——— *Swedish Study [N = 20]*
–·–·– *British Study [N = 41]*

Although the majority of the Swedish systems designers feel that jobs should be flexible and permit group problem solving (statement A), that authority and responsibility should be delegated (statement B) and that job methods and targets should be decided upon by the group or by the individual himself (statements D and E), the spread of opinions on those items is noticeable. Likewise while the majority of the British respondents favour delegation of authority and responsibility (statement B) several members of their group question that position.

The data seems to indicate that Swedish systems designers are consistently more Y-oriented in their perceptions of the ideal organization than their British colleagues. The latter are less willing to let the employees of an organization take responsibility for job definitions, job methods and work targets. At the present point in time the limitations of our data prevent us making too definite conclusions about differences. However, the welfare gap between the two countries seems to have some correspondence in an opinion gap between the two professional groups concerning worker demands and quality of working life. If there is a bias in the British material, it seems reasonable to assume that the group which answered would be more Y-oriented and aware of human needs than the average British computer specialist.

[...]We were therefore interested in finding out the organizational design principles that were used by our system designers. We asked two open ended questions.

(1) Describe briefly some of the properties which you consider important to a well functioning organization.
(2) When you design a system in what ways do you think you are contributing to the well being of the organization?

[...] In answer to the second question, the comments fell into the following categories.

SYSTEMS DESIGN CONTRIBUTIONS TO ORGANIZATIONAL WELL BEING

	N	Greater efficiency	Better information for management	More job satisfaction	Financial savings	Staff savings
British	62	31%	27%	18%	15%	10%
Swedish	23	45%	35%	15%	0%	4%

Job satisfaction was seen as increasing as a result of the systems designer's ability to reduce the amount of routine work.

These comments suggest that at the organizational level systems designers perceive themselves as having a rather limited role. Their contribution is to assist the organization to become more efficient through speeding up work procedures and providing information that is useful to management.

It seems as if the British systems designers have no conception of themselves as organizational designers using computer systems to produce new organizational forms. They possess no intellectual constructs which would enable them to assume this kind of role. But here again we find the same interesting contradiction which we noted in Diagram A. They place most emphasis on the human relations climate and personnel policies of the company as assisting its effective operation and they believe they can assist this to some extent through removing boring work and thus increasing job satisfaction. Yet, they see their principal work activities as increasing efficiency through stream-lining procedures and providing better information. They do not appear to appreciate the potential of computer technology for improving the overall quality of working life. They do not design their systems to facilitate good human relationships.

Although the assessment of contributions to the organization is similar in the two groups, the Swedish systems designers mention more often their role as change agents in an organizational context. Several of the respondents use terms like organizational change, change processes and organizational development. A few give as an important contribution that they try to provide their clients with a better understanding of the totality of their organization. The zero value given to "financial savings" in the Swedish data should be interpreted in the light of the designers' recent experiences with a large, advanced but expensive real-time system which was designed to improve services rather than to cut costs.

THE INDIVIDUAL MODEL OF MAN HELD BY
THE MAJORITY OF SYSTEMS DESIGNERS

In order to find out how systems designers perceived the individual users for whom they were designing systems, they were asked to complete another opinion scale. The statistical means of each distribution are connected in the graphs of Diagram B.

The right side of the scale (items A–I) represents McGregor's Theory Y man—a responsible, self achieving individual who can take full control of his work environment. The left hand side of the scale is McGregor's Theory X man—a different kind of individual who likes order, wishes to work within tightly specified boundaries and does not want to have a great deal of personal control over his activities.

As in the "Organizational Model of Man" case the British systems designers are closer to a Theory X view of the people for whom they are designing systems than are their Swedish colleagues. The latter are still on the Y half of the scale in all cases but two. However, the variance is sometimes considerable both in the Swedish and British answer distributions.

Although basically Y-oriented, the Swedish systems designers are not sure that their clients would function well within less structured, or well defined jobs. They also feel that to a certain extent their clients need to be told what to do and how to

DIAGRAM B: Individual Model of Man

Use the following scale to describe the average human being (non-specialist and non-management) for whom you design computerized systems (put an X on the scale for each pair of properties).

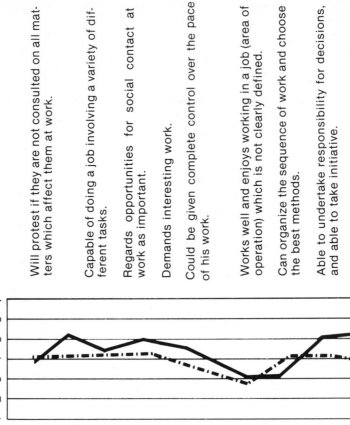

A.	Leaves other people to make most of the decisions on things which affect them at work.		Will protest if they are not consulted on all matters which affect them at work.
B.	Capable of handling only a limited range of tasks in their job.		Capable of doing a job involving a variety of different tasks.
C.	Not concerned about having social contact at work.		Regards opportunities for social contact at work as important.
D.	Can tolerate boring work.		Demands interesting work.
E.	Work best if the pace of the work is outside control.		Could be given complete control over the pace of his work.
F.	Needs or wants to have a well defined job (area of operation) which he/she sticks to most of the time.		Works well and enjoys working in a job (area of operation) which is not clearly defined.
G.	Needs to be told what to do next and how to do it.		Can organize the sequence of work and choose the best methods.
H.	Unable to undertake responsibility for decisions, and unable to take initiative.		Able to undertake responsibility for decisions, and able to take initiative.
I.	Has a low level of skill and/or knowledge (expertise).		Has a high level of skill and/or knowledge (expertise).

Swedish Study [N = 25]

United Kingdom Study [N = 41]

do it. The resulting model of man, as provided by the Swedish sample, is clearly not entirely consistent with the same group's model of the organization. Although they state that employees in an ideal organization should be free to determine their job methods, set their own performance targets etc., their model of the average employee does not really assume that the capacity for doing so is at hand.

It should be noted that the "Organizational Model of Man" questions (Diagram A) were concerned with future visions of a better organization. The "Individual Model of Man" (Diagram B) is concerned with the present state (the average human beings for whom you design computerized systems). The gap between the British and Swedish average is less noticeable in the description of the present characteristics of the users than in the descriptions of future organizational visions. This might imply that the Swedish computer specialists find themselves in a more pronounced conflict situation between societal values which favour Y-oriented organizations, and their own perception of the actual humans they have to work with than is the case with the British respondents.

In order to obtain more detailed information on their models of man, the systems designers were asked a number of open ended questions. These were,

(1) Give a short description of the basic characteristics of the human beings (non-management, non-specialist) for whom you typically design computer systems. What strengths and shortcomings do they have? How do these strengths and shortcomings affect your design approach?
(2) Describe briefly some of the factors which you consider contribute to employee job satisfaction?
(3) When you design a system in what ways do you think you are contributing to an increase in employee job satisfaction?

There was considerable unanimity concerning the basic characteristics of the user populations. 81% of the British comments referred to shortcomings like institutionalization (13%), resistance to change (29%) and limitation of outlook (39%). 41% of the Swedish comments were primarily concerned with the same factors: institutionalization (8%), resistance to change (14%) and limitation of outlook (19%). 22% of the Swedish systems designers mentioned a lack of EDP knowledge or knowledge about new methods as the primary weakness of their clients.

The strength of these individuals was seen as their considerable knowledge of their own job. A job which many had done for a number of years. (Mentioned by 32% of the Swedish respondents.) Their principal weakness was described as a dislike of change together with a reluctance to divulge information to the systems designers unless this was specifically asked for. Inability to make existing demands explicit and to think in "systems concepts" were other weaknesses mentioned. These strengths and weaknesses affected the system design by influencing the systems designers to make the systems as simple and error proof as possible with input forms easy to complete and output easy to understand. A number spoke of introducing computer systems gradually in order to get them accepted, others of trying to make their systems flexible and related to user work needs.

Yet the question on which factors contribute to job satisfaction produced answers totally at variance with the narrow, conservative kind of individual the systems designer saw himself as designing systems for. We shall analyse the answers in terms of a model job satisfaction developed by Mumford (72). This measures of job satisfaction on five variables. (1) the knowledge fit—the extent to which an individual's skills and knowledge are used and developed. (2) the psychological fit—opportunities for achievement, recognition, responsibility, advancement and status (Herzberg, 1968). (3) the efficienty/reward fit—the extent to which the individual receives the kind of resources, controls and financial rewards that he thinks is appropriate. (4) the ethical fit—opportunities for involvement and participation. (5) the task fit—is the job designed so as to provide meaningful, interesting and challenging work in the performance of which it is possible to take decisions and use discretion? We received the following pattern of responses from the systems designers.

FACTORS WHICH YOU CONSIDER CONTRIBUTE TO JOB SATISFACTION (NUMBER OF COMMENTS)

	N	Knowledge factors	Psychological factors	Efficiency/ reward factors	Ethical factors	Task factors	Other
British study	112	2%	21%	13%	7%	32%	24%
Swedish study	46	4%	17%	26%	15%	24%	13%

Task factors were mentioned most frequently in the British study as contributing to job satisfaction, particularly the need to have a meaningful, challenging job, and work interest. Psychological factors came next with emphasis on recognition, achievement and opportunities for advancement. In the "other" category working conditions and "good" management were mentioned frequently. Task factors played an important role also in the Swedish study. Efficiency/reward factors such as proper resources for action were, however, considered to be even more important. Ethical factors like opportunities for self determination and participation were mentioned more frequently by the Swedish than by the British respondents.

In answer to the question "when you design a system in what way do you think you are contributing to an increase in employee satisfaction," the British majority response was "by making the job less routine." The computer was seen as taking over the very simple work, leaving the user with more interesting activities, such as dealing with exceptions. However, a number of the systems designers in both the British and Swedish samples said that they did not think that they were contributing to job satisfaction. 25% of the respondents in the Swedish group felt that they could contribute to employee job satisfaction by removing repetitive and simple jobs, by matching the needs and demands of the clients (35%), by allowing the potential users of the system to participate in the design process (10%), by designing a technically perfect and well-functioning ("simple" and "reliable") system (20%), and by decentralization and delegation of authority through the system (10%).

These answers are extremely interesting for they suggest that at both the organizational and the individual level the systems designers in our sample operate with two models of man—one operational, one theoretical. One which they use when actually designing systems for users, the other which they produce when asked to consider the subject of human needs such as job satisfaction at an intellectual level. The first, operational model of man is close to McGregor's Theory X concept. In terms of organizational design it implies tightly structured jobs which are defined by the systems designers or their O & M colleagues. It also implies targets and controls set and imposed by supervision, and not by the employees themselves. At a theoretical level we get a totally different organizational model, one which has rather few structural concepts embedded in it but which sees the successful organization in terms of good human relations.

The most important thing seems to be to establish real communication between experts and clients in design groups and to change the content of the joint discussion. Rather than discussing the tools, the users should help establish the goals. The *value system* rather than the actual computerized system should be the focus of interest. Perhaps the strongest influence that will change the practical model of man held by the systems designer will be when the users get up and shout "we are not as you think we are." They may need both trade union and top management support to enable them to do this.

REFERENCES

Herzberg, F. (1968) *Work and the Nature of Man*. London: Staples Press.
McGregor, D. (1960) *The Human Side of Enterprise*. New York: McGraw-Hill.

8
Job Design Criteria
Twenty Years Later
James C. Taylor

INTRODUCTION

In 1955, the *Journal of Industrial Engineering* carried the results of a study by Davis, Canter, and Hoffman which examined the criteria used by production planners and designers in manufacturing. The authors had based their analysis on the response to a questionnaire sent to a representative sample of large American industrial firms, and on the results of interviews with a number of other large manufacturing companies. Davis et al. took the position that there were underlying principles for designing production processes that would carry over to the design of jobs. They proposed to bring these principles to light in order to better understand the manner in which the content of jobs was designed in American industry. Their results indicated that the most important consideration in job design was the minimization of the time required to perform the operation. They reported that the principles of job design they found reflected the mass-production precepts of specialized jobs and repetitive work, which minimized the individual employee's contribution to the production process. They cited, for example, designer preference for emphasizing highly specified, low-skill operations, to the detriment of increased job satisfaction. Davis et al. concluded that to counter this, comprehensive criteria of effective job design must include not only the immediate and direct cost of production time, but also the more indirect economic and social costs to companies and workers.

Although the study has been widely cited over the years, its impact on both designer practices and on further research concerning them appears limited. This results in part from the fact that the problems associated with suboptimization of short-term technical costs have only gradually become apparent in manufacturing engineering (cf., Kildrige & Wester, 1963; Ingall, 1965; Davis, 1966; Basu, 1973). Today, with productivity and quality of working life viewed as complementary and integrated issues at the national level—and attracting increased attention and concern internationally—the time has come for the reexamination of the issues raised in that early study.

No direct replications of the study by Davis et al. are known. Developments in computer application and information system design have revealed the potential for a similar design constraint in the larger universe of white collar administrative and service organizations (cf., Boguslaw, 1965). This possibility was further

This paper is being published for the first time in this volume.

explored in a study of British and Swedish information system analysts* (Hedberg and Mumford, 1975). Like Davis and his colleagues, Hedberg and Mumford tapped some of the values and models underlying the design of work systems and the content of jobs in those systems. They set out to examine the values of systems analysts toward the psychological aspects of the computerized systems jobs they design.[. . .]

Although Hedberg and Mumford do not confirm the findings of Davis, Canter, and Hoffman, their finding that jobs are designed to be carefully defined and monitored is suggestive of the 1955 study. In addition, Mumford and Hedberg contribute the additional finding that technical designers may be working in a system which requires them to design jobs whose content conflicts with their personal values. The question of whether this possible dilemma results from the policies of their employing organizations or from the design conventions they acquire during their professional training remains unanswered.

The evidence from the Davis et al. study and the Hedberg and Mumford research suggests that technical systems designers in general meet the criteria of cost performance by detailed specification and definition of job content. That this is viewed as a short-term solution and that it may be inconsistent with the designers' personal models of man is also possible. Despite these tentative findings, little is actually known about the status of job design criteria among engineers and systems analysts today. We also know little about the dilemmas and role conflicts that organizations create for their technical designers.

THE STUDY

The present study examines these issues among American work system designers. It assesses current criteria for job design, examines the constraints technical designers might experience, and presents their models of man. In measuring these aspects of designers' perceptions, it takes into account the similarities and differences between those who design industrial production systems (production engineers) and those who design computer information and decision-making systems (information systems analysts). The two samples were drawn to ensure representation from both manufacturing and information systems.

Following the approach taken by Davis et al. and Hedberg and Mumford, a questionnaire survey was developed which asked engineers and systems analysts about various aspects of their design experience and some of their attitudes and feelings. The questions themselves form five general sets or classes. The results reported below are presented in the order of those five sets of items.

The first four classes of questions are intended to parallel those asked in the Davis et al. study. Their original survey had posed questions referring to twenty-four different specific manufacturing operations. This methodology was appropriate for their original sample of manufacturing organizations. For the joint sample of manufacturing designers and informations systems designers in the present study, however, a general questionnaire format was considered more useful.

---

*Editors' Note: Reprinted as reading 7 in this volume.

Although this study is therefore not a literal replication of the 1955 Davis et al. study, the essential content of their examination is carefully paralleled in the present questionnaire instrument.

The content of the first set of questions deals with seven major considerations (criteria) for breaking work system designs into separate tasks. The second set of questions assesses five practices followed in combining separate tasks into jobs for people. The third set of questions identifies the parties responsible both for choosing tasks to be assigned to people, and for combining these tasks into jobs. Set Four assesses the impact of five constraints in the organizational environment, while the fifth set of questions replicates those in the Hedberg and Mumford study. In this fifth set, one group of eight pairs of statements deals with the favored form of job design and work organization; and the other set of nine pairs with the characteristics of the average job holder in the respondents' companies.

Sample

During 1976, the questionnaire was mailed to a total of 240 technical designers employed in California. One-half (120) of this number was randomly drawn from the production engineers and engineering managers identified in the subscription list of a widely circulated manufacturing journal (*Factory*). The other half (120) of the sample was similarly drawn from the systems analysts and EDP managers appearing in the subscription list of a popular computer and information systems magazine (*Datamation*). Ninety-five completed questionnaires were returned (a usable response rate of 40%). In all, 53 systems analysts and 42 engineers responded.

Results

In Table 1, seven considerations for breaking technical processes into human tasks that result in greatest product quality at lowest cost are ranked in order of their perceived importance to those questioned. They were drawn primarily from the set developed in the 1955 study. The first two criteria in Table 1, "throughput per unit time" and "use of machine resources," are ranked highest by both groups. These criteria are well known in engineering practice and values. In 1955, Davis and his colleagues reported that these two criteria also ranked at the top of their list. In the present case, systems analysts ranked management information systems third— not surprisingly, since a valued product of computer systems is the creation of additional or better information. Thus, a major factor in breaking EDP systems down into tasks for people should be management control information of the arrangement.

Both systems analysts and engineers give a relatively high rank importance to "making jobs simple to perform" (rank "4" for the former; "3" for the latter), and a low rank to "improving job satisfaction" ("6" in both samples). This finding is in substantial agreement with that of Davis et al. for job designers in the earlier study. Davis and his colleagues interpreted that finding as an attempt by designers to minimize total costs of production: to minimize immediate costs by minimizing skills, and deemphasizing job satisfaction in design. Making work

TABLE 1
IMPORTANCE OF SEVEN CONSIDERATIONS IN
BREAKING WORK FLOW INTO TASKS FOR PEOPLE
TO PROVIDE GREATEST PRODUCT QUALITY
AT LOWEST COST

	Rank Order	
	Engineers	Systems Analysts
Maximizing throughput per unit of time	1	1
Efficient use of machine resources	2	2
Making jobs as simple to perform as possible	3	4
Reducing manpower	4	5
Providing Management with better information	5	3
Providing more job satisfaction	6	6
Minimizing floor space requirements	7	7

simple and jobs satisfying are usually considered contradictory goals, illustrating the thesis that simplified work primarily reduces short-term costs, while satisfaction does not. It follows that the choices made in the present study suggest that designers are more preoccupied with immediate benefits than with total costs, an attitude which confirms the central finding of Davis, Canter, and Hoffman.

Table 2 presents various ways in which tasks are assigned to workers. The question asked the engineers and systems analysts to rate each of the five proce-

TABLE 2
COMBINING TASKS INTO JOBS FOR PEOPLE

Methods for Combining Tasks into Jobs	Average Extent to Which the Methods are Used (Higher Score = Greater Extent)	
	Engineers	Systems Analysts
Assign each employee a *specific group of tasks* as a full time job.	3.8	3.8
Assign each employee *one particular task* as a full time job.	3.1	2.7
Assign each employee *one particular task* and *rotate* employees at intervals	2.5	1.9
Assign each employee a *whole production process* as a full time job.	2.1	2.5
Assign *groups of employees* to *specific groups of tasks* allowing them to assign the individual tasks informally among themselves.	1.9	2.1

dures (listed in Table 2) on a five point scale, ranging from "used to a very little extent" (1) to "used to a very great extent" (5). The results in Table 2 are remarkably like those obtained by Davis, Canter, and Hoffman in response to a similar question on combining tasks into jobs in assembly operations. Both the earlier study and the present one reveal that the two methods most frequently employed to combine tasks into specific jobs are (a) assigning an employee a specific group of tasks, (but not a whole production process) as a full-time job, and (b) assigning an employee one particular task as a full-time job. These results can be taken as additional evidence that companies continue to limit the content of individual jobs to a great extent, which further explains the high ranking given to fragmentation of work, in Table 1 above.

Table 3 presents the results of an item dealing with responsibility for performing job design functions. Davis et al. had found that first line supervisors, as well as the various engineering departments, were reportedly involved in specifying the

TABLE 3
RESPONSIBILITY FOR JOB DESIGN
Percent of Instances
(Reported by Engineers—Engr.
and reported by Systems Analyists—Sys. An.)

	Task Content (Chooses or Orders Tasks in the Production Process)					
	Always		Sometimes		Rarely or Never	
Responsibility of:	Eng.	Sys. An.	Engr.	Sys. An.	Engr.	Sys. An.
Supervisors or Foremen	51%	36%	36%	52%	13%	12%
Production Engineers	33%	39%	47%	50%	19%	11%
Systems Analyists	32%	49%	29%	40%	39%	11%
Industrial Engineers	12%	11%	50%	74%	39%	16%
Personnel Analysts	6%	8%	0%	20%	94%	73%

*Percentages equal 100% for each sample for each row.

task content and job content. In fact, the present findings in Table 3 resemble the earlier results very much. Fifty-one percent of the engineers and 36% of the systems analysts report the foreman or supervisor as "always involved" in specifying the content of tasks. Both engineering and system analyst samples agree that production (manufacturing) engineers are heavily involved in specifying task content (33% and 39% report them to be "always involved"). They disagree about the job design responsibility of the systems analyst which may well reflect real differences between that designer's role in computer-based technologies and his role in more conventional technologies. The findings in Table 3 suggest the definition of designers (engineers and systems analysts) in the present study may be an unnecessarily narrow one, given the prominent role played by first line supervision. This replication of earlier findings by Davis et al.

confirms the thesis that job design is the outcome of a complex system of interrelated disciplines, duties, and techniques, for which no one is solely resonsible. This further suggests that the generally observed design criteria of minimizing immediate costs by making jobs as simple as possible to perform (Tables 1 and 2) may not be held as personal values by those involved in the process of job design. The following data will shed additional light on the issue.

Both the Davis et al. and Hedberg and Mumford studies recognized the potential effect of influences other than the designer on ultimate job content. While the latter study acknowledged the probable impact of top management values, time constraints, technical and financial constraints, the former study actually examined a variety of restrictions. Davis and his colleagues reported that respondents found training requirements most restricted job design—with union agreements also exerting considerable influence.

Table 4 shows present respondents' reports of the actual effects of five posited constraints on their ability to design jobs. The question required the respondent to rate each constraint according to actual effect on a five-point scale, from "restricts

TABLE 4
REPORTED EFFECTS OF FIVE POTENTIAL
RESTRICTIONS ON ABILITY TO DESIGN JOBS

Potential Constraints Of:	Average Extent of Restrictions (Higher Score = Greater Restriction)	
	Reported By:	
	Engineers	Systems Analysts
Union Management Agreements	3.1	1.4
Physical Requirements, Training Requirements, Working Conditions	3.0	2.5
Federal or State Legislation	2.8	1.9
Top Management Policies	2.4	2.7
Centralized Personnel Policies	2.1	1.6

to a very little extent" (1) to "restricts to a very great extent" (5). This question is intended to explore the extent to which these technical systems designers are free to specify the content of jobs. The earlier study by Davis et al. had reported that training requirements greatly influenced specification of job content. Where they existed, union agreements also imposed restrictions. As Table 4 indicates, the engineering sample reports that union contracts, federal or state legislation, and training requirements exert the greatest restrictions on assigning tasks to jobs. The engineering sample results appear similar to the 1955 study results, while the systems analysts tend to see the strongest constraint being from top management policy.

TABLE 5. The Preferred Structure of Jobs and Work

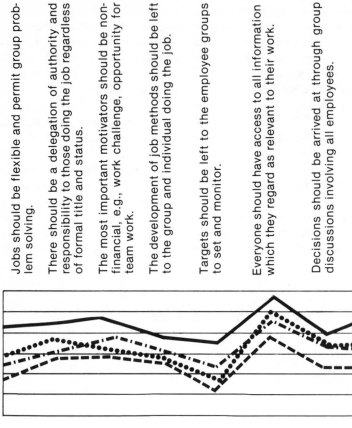

		Jobs should be flexible and permit group problem solving.
A.	Jobs should be clearly defined, structured and stable.	
B.	There should be a clear hierarchy of authority with the person at the top carrying ultimate responsibility for all aspects of work.	There should be a delegation of authority and responsibility to those doing the job regardless of formal title and status.
C.	The most important motivators should be financial, e.g., high earnings and cash bonuses.	The most important motivators should be non-financial, e.g., work challenge, opportunity for team work.
D.	Job methods should be carefully defined by systems and procedures specialists, management services, or supervision.	The development of job methods should be left to the group and individual doing the job.
E.	Targets should be set by supervision and monitored by supervision.	Targets should be left to the employee groups to set and monitor.
F.	Groups and individuals should be given the specific information they need to do the job but no more.	Everyone should have access to all information which they regard as relevant to their work.
G.	Decisions on what is to be done and how it is to be done should be left entirely to management.	Decisions should be arrived at through group discussions involving all employees.
H.	There should be close supervision, tight controls and well maintained discipline.	There should be loose supervision, few controls and a reliance on employee self discipline.

US Engineers
UK Systems Analysts
US Systems Analysts
Swedish Systems Analysts

The final items reported here reveal some attitudes regarding the favored form of job design (the organizational model of man) and opinions about job holders (the individual model of man). Tables 5 and 6 present these "models of man" profiles for the two samples in the present study, together with the profiles for the Swedish and British samples of computer-based systems designers reported in the Hedberg and Mumford study.

The shape of the profiles in Table 5—preferred structure of work—are remarkably similar for the four samples. In fact, they are statistically indistinguishable in terms of profile shape, although there are significant differences in absolute levels between the highest and lowest scores on some of the items A through H. This shared profile shape reveals that all of these technical systems designers prefer that the jobs they design be well defined (item A), and that these jobs be monitored (item E), while at the same time, they favor some delegation of authority to lower levels (item B), the creation of challenging jobs (item C), and general access to relevant information (item F). That both the present study and the study by Mumford and Hedberg report this internal inconsistency supports the observation made earlier: What designers say they do and what they want to do are not altogether the same. Likely sources of this inconsistency are the complexity and multiple responsibility found in job design (Table 3), and the variety of constraints on job design (Table 4).

Table 6 presents technical designers' views and opinions of the people who fill the jobs they design. Once again, the sample profiles are quite similar in shape. The location of the profiles in the middle range of the scale strongly suggests an individual model of man which is at variance with the short-term perspective implied by the use of mass-production precepts of specialized jobs, repetitive work, and assignment of simple, low-skilled jobs to workers. In general, these designers agree that the people in their organizations who fill the jobs they design are capable of doing a variety of tasks (item B), have considerable skill (item I), and demand interesting work (item D). However, the designers also report that these same workers leave decisions to others (item A), and want well-defined work (item F). Achieving tight control and highly structured jobs as shown in Table 5 may well undermine efforts to encourage application of greater skill, interesting challenging work, as suggested in Table 6.

In conclusion, it seems clear that twenty years of technological progress and innovation have had little corresponding effect on the professional values of design practitioners. The data presented in this paper suggest that both production engineers and systems analysts select job design criteria remarkably similar to those chosen by their predecessors in the 1950s. They still prefer to minimize the immediate costs of production rather than to emphasize a longer-term approach to job design which recognizes the economic costs of worker frustration and acknowledges employee satisfaction and motivation. The data also suggest that current criteria run counter to their professed view of the worker—"the individual model of man." In short, systems analysts and engineers appear to be caught between what they believe to be employees' needs and potential, and what they, as designers, are obliged to deliver.

TABLE 6. Characteristics of the Average *Non-Specialist, Non-Supervisory* Employee in Company for Whom the Jobs and Work Described Above are Designed

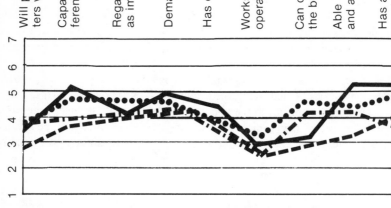

	Left characteristic	Right characteristic
A.	Leaves other people to make most of the decisions on things which affect them at work	Will protest if they are not consulted on all matters which affect them at work.
B.	Capable of handling only a limited range of tasks in their job.	Capable of doing a job involving a variety of different tasks.
C.	Not concerned about having social contact at work.	Regards opportunities for social contact at work as important
D.	Can tolerate boring work.	Demands interesting work.
E.	Work best if the pace of the work is outside control.	Has complete control over the pace of work.
F.	Needs or wants to have a well defined job (area of operation) which he/she sticks to most of the time.	Works well and enjoys working in a job (area of operation) which is not clearly defined.
G.	Needs to be told what to do next and how to do it.	Can organize the sequence of work and choose the best methods.
H.	Unable to undertake responsibility for decisions, and unable to take initiative.	Able to undertake responsibility for decisions, and able to take initiative.
I.	Has a low level of skill and/or knowledge (expertise).	Has a high level of skill and/or knowledge (expertise)

Legend:
— — US Engineers
— ·— UK Systems Analysts
•••• US Systems Analysts

REFERENCES

Basu, R. N. "The Practical Problems of Assembly Line Balancing." *The Production Engineer,* October, 1973, 369–370.

Boguslaw, R. (1965) *The New Utopians.* Englewood Cliffs, N.J.: Prentice Hall.

Davis, L. E. "Pacing Effects on Manned Assembly Lines." *The Journal of Industrial Engineering,* 1965, Vol. 16, 4.

Davis, L. E., Canter, R. R., and Hoffman, J. "Current Job Design Criteria." *The Journal of Industrial Engineering,* 1955, Vol. 16, 1–7.

Hedberg, B. and Mumford, E. "The Design of Computer Systems: Man's Vision of Man As an Integral Part of the System Design Process." In Mumford, E. and Sackman, H., eds. (1975) *Human Choices and Computers.* New York: North Holland Publishing Co.

Ingall, E. J. "A Review of Assembly Line Balancing." *The Journal of Industrial Engineering,* 1965, Vol. 16, 4.

Kildridge, M. D. and Wester, L. "The Assembly Line Model Mix Sequencing Problem." *Proceedings of the 3rd Industrial Conference on Operations Research,* Oslo, 1963.

9
Trade Unions
and Quality of Life
at the Workplace
Joseph Mire

Unions argue—not without justification—that all their activities, most notably collective bargaining at the shop and industry-wide level and/or their legislative efforts in the political arena have a significant impact on job satisfaction. They have been skeptical and suspicious of management efforts to increase job satisfaction, and they object to the manipulative character of so much of what has passed under the heading of "human relations." Even more importantly, they pointed to the failure of management to assure workers a share in resulting increases of

Excerpts from Joseph Mire. "Trade Unions and Union Participation in Management." In Louis E. Davis and Albert B. Cherns, eds. *The Quality of Working Life: Vol. 1, Problems, Prospects, and State of the Art.* New York: Free Press, 1975, chapter 28, pp. 410–438.

productivity. And, finally, trade unions have a very realistic fear that improved productivity and job satisfaction, no matter how it is brought about, may result in a reduction of the number of available jobs.

In recent years, however, there has been growing recognition that the improvement of the worker's economic, social, and political status has left largely unchanged their jobs at the workplace. Yet it is precisely the situation at the workplace which most fundamentally affects their well-being, both physical and mental. Workers continue to do monotonous and uninteresting work. They have little or no control over their jobs and few, if any, opportunities for initiative, independent thinking, personal growth, and maintaining their human dignity. The growth of industry has meant segmentation and depersonalization.

Worker participation in management in the past has meant primarily indirect participation through elected or appointed union representatives or shop stewards, involving relatively few people. Spokesmen for *direct* worker participation even claim that the institutionalized forms of indirect worker participation have, in fact, become barriers to direct participation, blocking efforts for the transfer of decision-making power to rank-and-file workers.

Trade unions in Western Europe have been baffled by workers' unrest in the face of rising standards of living and material well-being. There has been a notable increase in number of wildcat strikes and rejections of collective agreements negotiated by union leadership, and an additional factor has entered the picture: with rising levels of education, it becomes increasingly difficult to find enough "dumb people to do the dumb jobs." In many countries, critical shortages of labor can presently be met only by drawing on imported labor.

Thus the search is on for ways and means to improve communications, humanize work, democratize the workplace, and seek a wider distribution of decision making in order to enhance dignity and assure a better quality of life.

This survey was conducted to learn what trade unions in some Western European countries—and in Yugoslavia—are doing to improve job satisfaction through worker participation in management, emphasizing the transfer of some decision-making power directly to workers rather than to elected or appointed representatives such as shop stewards or unions.

AUSTRIA

The Austrian Federation of Trade Unions, for several years now, has been engaged in an intensive discussion of worker participation in management.[. . .] In his final address, the president of the federation noted: *"We are no longer merely interested in who gets what but also in who decides what. The division of decision making in the plant must concern us as much as the division of the fruits of production. And, next to achieving material benefits for the workers, we must also search for ways to improve the quality of life."*

To attack the problem of physical hardships, the federation has developed a *workplace simulator,* designed to measure the impact of heavy work, assembly-line work, and monotonous work, as well as of noise, heat, light, and draft on the heart and blood circulation. The simulator also demonstrates "model chairs" and other equipment for sedentary and nonsedentary occupations.

The Chamber of Labor has a more skeptical view of the possibilities of direct worker participation in management. There is fear that the transfer of decision making to the workers may threaten the position of shop stewards or that employers, under the pretext of increasing job satisfaction, would in fact drive a wedge between workers and the union and that job satisfaction could be manipulated to the point where workers would find their unions dispensable.

In short, the Chamber of Labor views worker participation in management essentially as a responsibility of shop stewards or union representatives, but not as one of workers at the shop level, a view shared by the majority of the Austrian union leadership.[. . .]

A very large sector of Austria's industry (some 70 percent) is nationalized. Contrary to expectations, these enterprises are not in the forefront of experimentation to improve worker participation in management. They seem to be permanently up against the twin problems of underinvestment and overstaffing. Political difficulties are another factor: to stay alive and survive, the nationalized industries have to lean constantly and heavily on the political power of the shop stewards and trade unions. Therefore, "any experimentation to promote direct worker participation at the risk of antagonizing the shop stewards is out of the question."

The Austrian Department of Labor has thus far paid little attention to the problem of job satisfaction and ways of dealing with it. Neither monotony nor assembly-line work is considered as yet to be of serious proportions since the number of workers involved is probably still very small. Nor does it have records of information on any work done in this field by private companies. It is believed, however, that in many places the workers may have a lot more to say about how to do their jobs than is generally assumed, the exact extent depending more often on the individual worker than on management.[. . .]

BELGIUM

Belgium is an example of successful multiunionism in labor relations inasmuch as strong federations of Christian, socialist and liberal-conservative persuasions exist side by side, cooperating fairly harmoniously in daily operations. Yet they do have different views on worker participation in management.

The Christian Trade Union Federation is strongly occupied with the problem of humanizing the workplace. Several committees at the local and national level have prepared detailed reports and recommendations containing the following proposals:

> define the rights of workers at the workplace;
> establish objective rules for hiring and firing of workers;

experiment with the establishment of semiautonomous work groups along the Scandinavian model;

equalize blue- and white-collar workers in respect to all social legislation and insurance;

improve the law on shop stewards to give them more information and decision-making power.

The federation is also studying Scandinavian and Yugoslav models, but so far is not participating in actual experiments.

The Socialist Trade Union Federation is interested only in indirect workers' participation, opposing co-determination as practiced in the German coal and steel industry where representatives of workers have equal representation with full rights and responsibilities at the board of directors. The socialist federation believes union representatives cannot sit on both sides of the bargaining table. It is also against more decision-making power for rank-and-file workers because it fears the development of plant egoism and that workers would have to spend too much time in meetings, and only "legitimate" unions can represent the workers' interests effectively. However, the federation is in favor of "workers' control," exercised through shop stewards or union representatives, the final goal being the self-management of workers.[. . .]

DENMARK

In 1967 the Danish Federation of Labor adopted a resolution calling for a study of the problems of democracy at the workplace. The study produced two major recommendations: (1) promote in industry the establishment of joint committees of cooperation, and (2) seek legislation to provide workers with a fair share of the economic growth through establishment of a "profit and investment fund for wage-earners."

The first recommendation was realized in 1970, when the Trade Union Federation and the Employers Federation signed an agreement setting up in all enterprises with at least fifty employees "committees of cooperation." Their dual purpose was to promote efficiency and increase job satisfaction. The committees are composed of an equal number of representatives from management and labor. The forms of cooperation vary from plant to plant, but in the summer of 1971 metal worker unions were participating in at least seven experimental programs in the iron and metal industry. The companies had been selected in an effort to provide a variety of experiences, that is, different-sized firms and different types of production, composition of work force, and geographic location. Also, in view of the risks involved, only companies with an established base for cooperation were included.[. . .]

WEST GERMANY

Democracy at the workplace has been a matter of furious debate for a number of years now and a rich literature is available covering every feasible aspect of the problem. Thus far the discussion has produced few positive and practical attempts to come to grips with the issue.

Supporters of direct worker participation come from a variety of positions and directions. For example, social psychologists and industrial engineers are interested in better efficiency and productivity; religious and social reformers are concerned about a more ethical and just society; trade union and political leaders fear that "Germany might slip again into a totalitarian society unless the worker is integrated, into both society and the economy," critics of indirect worker participation seek more direct participation as a counterweight to the presumed conservatism of union bureaucracy. There are some "weak" enterprises which turn to worker participation as a way to save their plants from bankruptcy; there is the league of young employers which has developed a model constitution for plant democracy; and, finally, there are forces on the extreme left who view worker participation at the grassroots as a means to undermine capitalism.

The very strong support given to the demands for democracy at the workplace by the "New Left" may well explain the slowness and hesitancy which has marked the attitude of German trade unions toward the implementation of such demands. Initially, there was much sympathy for the idea both within the German Federation of Trade Unions (DGB) as well as among some of its affiliates, notably the Metal Workers Union, the Postal Workers, and the Public Employees Union. Today, however, this support has largely evaporated.

The DGB continues to pay lip service to the demands for direct representation at the workplace, but only as part of its broader demand for worker participation at the top; that is, representation on the boards of directors of companies, as practiced in the steel and coal industries. Most efforts of the trade unions are directed at this aspect of their legislative program rather than at bringing about worker participation at the plant level.

An important exception is the very serious interest in this subject taken by a top official of the Wirtschaft and Sozialwissenschaftliches Institut in Düsseldorf (an independent research arm of the federation), who sees the problem largely as one of engineering; creating new instrumentalities for worker participation is less important than changing the organization of work. And since there is a shortage of literature on such questions as work requirements, work methods, modes of production, and so on, "progress can be achieved only piecemeal and empirically." Every job should demand some ability, *decision making, opportunity to advance,* and *social contacts.* Job design and job enlargements as well as job rotation are some tools available to accomplish these objectives.

The German Metal Workers Union, a few years ago, was the most outspoken proponent of the demand to give workers more decision-making powers at the shop level. Staff members critical of the institutionalization of the shop steward system drafted an amendment to the German Works Council Law, which would provide for the election of "group spokesmen": to give smaller units in the plant an opportunity to participate in the decision-making process along with the elected shop stewards. The initial reaction of the union leadership to this proposal was quite favorable, but it has since changed to absolute hostility, so much so that the matter can no longer even be discussed at union meetings or in union publications. They fear a weakening of the steward system or of the union, intergroup rivalries in the plant, and that management might use the system of "group spokesmen" to weaken union efforts to secure co-determination at the top.[. . .]

NORWAY

Norway is *the* country where worker participation at the grassroots is being tried in earnest, led by social scientists with the full support of management and the trade unions. Constructive employee-employer relations have been a mark of that country's industrial relations system for some time. Now an attempt is being made to go beyond consultation and negotiation between organizations of employers and workers to find ways and means for the transfer of some decision-making power to the workers themselves. Polls taken among workers convinced the union leadership, first, that the workers could handle more responsibility on their jobs and, second, that a large majority does want to assume such responsibility.

Since the matter of direct worker participation is new territory, it was agreed to embark on a slow step-by-step approach. A Joint Committee for Research and Development for Industrial Democracy was established which reviewed traditional approaches to worker participation in management. This was followed by an examination of additional areas to be covered by collective bargaining, such as providing more information on job problems to stewards and unions. Then the committee turned its attention to a number of enterprises, especially those with problems such as monotony, assembly-line work, and high turnover rates. If the companies were willing to participate in the experimental program, the committee commissioned a detailed examination of production processes and pay procedures. Action committees, composed equally of company and worker representatives, assisted in the examination. Next, the committee developed several strategies to promote direct worker participation in job design, job enlargement and enrichment, job rotation, and semiautonomous work groups. Finally, the committee arranged for sensitivity training of foremen as well as for permanent self-perpetuating programs of upgrading workers, overcoming in the process occasional serious opposition from skilled workers.

The committee set itself the following goals for a "satisfactory organization of the workplace": each worker should have a minimum of diversity on his job assignment; an *opportunity to learn* and continue to learn; a minimum of decision-making power; a *minimum of recognition;* and an *opportunity to relate* to what he does or produces.

Although the trade unions are fully committed to this program, they are not directly involved because the experiments are confined essentially to production problems and do not yet affect an appreciable number of workers. Union interest in the program, however, is genuine, especially among such unions as metal workers, chemical workers, and paper workers. Some resistance has come from the ranks of skilled workers, expressing concern about the threatened breakdown of demarcation lines between skilled, semiskilled, and unskilled occupations. Similarly, there has been opposition to the shift in the mode of wage payments, that is, away from piece rates for work performed to a system of rewarding knowledge and experience regardless of actual work rendered. As elsewhere, there has also been some resistance from the foremen, since the semiautonomous work groups have assumed much of the responsibility which was formerly theirs.

Norway seems to present the most conspicuous effort to enhance direct worker participation in management. It is an *article of faith that the more the worker is enabled to control his work, the more will he be willing to accept a positive commitment.* The results so far bear out this expectation. Progress in productivity has been substantial and so has been the growth in income of workers.

As in other countries, the nationalized industries and communal enterprises have done no better than enterprises in the private sector in decentralizing decision making. Because of this, the Department of Labor has recently established a special committee to look into the now ongoing experimental programs in the private sector, with a view of adopting some of the experiences for the public sector.

SWEDEN

Interest in promoting worker participation in management arose almost simultaneously in government, labor, and management circles. In a speech of December 1970, the Swedish prime minister noted that while standards of living for workers had been much improved with respect to housing, nutrition, and education, the plant where the worker spends some 2,000 hours annually has changed little, and work may be as dissatisfying as ever. "The task of the 70s," he said, "must be to give workers a better surrounding and more say over his work at the workplace."

The Swedish Federation of Labor then suggested an action program to "democratize enterprises," in response to which the government established three commissions dealing with job security, work environment, and the right to allocate work, respectively.

Management, plagued by serious labor shortages, high absentee rates (10 to 11 percent in the metal industry), job dissatisfaction, and, consequently, rising personnel costs, was more than receptive. To come to grips with these problems, one company, LKAB, experimented with job rotation, job enlargement, allocation and wider distribution of decision making, election of spokesmen for smaller units of workers, and, finally, a promise to put workers willing to work for better productivity on monthly salary.

As in Norway, labor-management relations in Sweden at the top level have been excellent for many years, but there has been little concern for the human problems of the workers at the workplace. This is now being changed: the Swedish Federation of Trade Unions is actively participating in a number of models designed to improve job satisfaction. A joint labor-management development council on cooperation has been established to provide a framework for the initiation of programs and dissemination of information. In 1969 the government set up a similar committee to sponsor experiments in the public sector. In May 1972 labor and management signed an "Agreement on Rationalization" which concerns productivity, job satisfaction, work environment, and job security.*[...]

SWITZERLAND

Early in 1971 the Socialist Swiss Trade Union Federation adopted a program for worker participation in management, which was subsequently endorsed by the Christian as well as the Protestant Trade Union Federation. Apparently, this was the first time that all three federations agreed on a joint political initiative. They are seeking a nationwide referendum to the effect that the parliament legislate participation of workers and/or their representatives in management. The president of the socialist federation defined the purpose of their initiative as an effort "to secure workers participation at the workplace, in the plant, and at the board of directors of large enterprises." He denied any ideological motivation, stating that their concern was solely for a more balanced power position of labor and management at all levels. The spokesman for the Christian Trade Union Federation emphasized concern for the maintenance of harmony in industry which, he thought, was threatened because of the *"changing character of control."* [...]

YUGOSLAVIA

The Yugoslav system of self-management has four functional components:

1. The workers' collective, the plant meeting of all employees.
2. The workers' council, elected by the workers' collectives for 2 years, which approves all decisions involving planning research, production, hiring and firing, investments, worker welfare, allocation of profits, and budget matters.
3. The management board, composed of technicians and also elected by the workers' collective for 2-year terms, decides on day-by-day plant operations.
4. The plant director, elected by the workers' council for a 4-year period, manages the plant and develops plans for production, sales, and invest-

---

*Editors' Note: Since 1975 new Swedish labor relations laws have been introduced, opening all aspects of work design to collective bargaining.

ment. Formerly, he was responsible to the government, but now he is responsible to the three instrumentalities discussed above. He is elected on the basis of proposals submitted by a commission in which management and workers are equally represented.

One important fact should be noted. The system of self-management evolved primarily in order to get the government and the Communist party out of the economy, so as to eliminate political interference and bureaucratic excesses. By general consent, the major concern of the reform was not so much the expansion of workers' democracy as the promotion of economic and organizational efficiency.

This four-tier model of self-management is seen by some observers as proof that direct worker participation in management has its severe limits. By any measure, it is the members of the workers' council rather than the workers themselves who share, with the management board and the plant director, in the decision making. Tests conducted in various plants bear this out inasmuch as job satisfaction is substantially greater among members of the workers' council than among rank-and-file workers. The required rotation of membership on the council and management board helps in providing more workers with opportunities to participate in the decision-making process. It also guards against institutionalization and bureaucratization of the system except, of course, for the position of the plant director, who does not have to rotate and is thus in an advantageous position.

It would seem fair to say that the system of self-management is superior to the former economy directed by a centralized bureaucracy. There have been over the past few years significant improvements in efficiency and productivity; the growth rate has been high and constant. Much less clear, however, is the impact of the reform on the decision-making power of rank-and-file workers, that is, on democracy at the workplace. At least one trade union official felt that the alienation of workers is worse now than before, because social values are changing and expectations are higher than they were under the former system.

Direct worker participation seems to fall short of expectations. For example, the plant director, although dependent on the workers' council for appointment and reappointment as well as for approval of all matters of significance, has considerable power. As a rule, he has superior knowledge and skills which members of the workers' council cannot hope to match since educational levels are still low in comparison with Western Europe, and more than 50 percent of the work force is said to have less than eight years of schooling. Nevertheless, the opportunity for workers to share in the decision making is there, though it is sometimes not used or used to a very modest degree. Confronted by a choise of more say on how to do the job or more efficiency and subsequently more income, most workers presumably choose the latter, wherever they are—East or West.

Workers' councils vary greatly in effectiveness. They may be rubber stamps in some plants, and in others they do not exist at all. Nor, for that matter, are the government or the Communist party now effectively deprived of all influence on the economy.

The government can intervene at any time if it finds that decisions of the workers' councils are contrary to the interest of the total economy; for example, if a plant charges what are considered inflationary prices or fails to set aside sufficient funds for investment or resorts to excessive borrowing for investment purposes. These are instances in which the government has intervened. Likewise, the government may choose not to intervene and have the enterprise suffer the consequence of irrational decisions such as, for instance, underinvestment. Moreover, the government, through its power of taxation and credit policies, can decisively affect the amount of income available for distribution to all employees of a plant. And finally it could, of course, also change the system of self-management or abandon it altogether.

The role of the trade unions under the system of self-management is apparently undergoing some changes. Formerly their responsibility was merely to support the concept of self-management and provide educational training opportunities for workers as well as members of the workers' council and of the management board. Unions were assigned a supportive role, but not direct voice in the management of the plant. The practice is somewhat different now. The workers' councils call on them not infrequently for assistance in evaluating proposals submitted to them by the plant director, especially those concerned with the distribution of income. Unions have also been called upon to mediate conflicts within the labor force; for instance, in disputes involving shares going to employees.[. . .]

CONCLUSION

"Democracy at the workplace" and "humanization of work" have become regular and popular items on the agenda of trade union meetings throughout Western Europe, though there is no agreement on their precise meaning or specific strategies to accomplish these goals. Some favor them as a means of "destroying" the system, others as a bridge to "save" the system. In between, a growing number of trade union leaders are less concerned about either ideology, but convinced that unions' responsibilities and obligations must extend to the worker's need for human dignity and respect as well as to his material needs.

From the discussions this author had with unions and management, and from reading their literature, the following conclusions emerge as a *tentative* consensus on the conditions for the successful transfer of decision-making power to workers:

1. It must not adversely affect efficiency—and therefore, workers' income—or both management *and* workers will oppose it.
2. It must not threaten or impinge upon established rights of stewards and/or union—or there will be strenuous opposition from these sources.
3. Enterprises with an established history of constructive employer-employee relations offer the best prospects for pilot projects.
4. A broad program of education and skill training for all workers has to be an integral part of all programs for humanizing work.
5. The context of a full-employment economy may be a necessary condition to ease fears that improved efficiency will result in unemployment.
6. More research is required on alternative modes of production, alternative methods of working and work requirements.

14. Job Enlargement: Effects of Culture on Worker Responses (1973) —Gerald I. Susman

15. Job Satisfaction and Quality of Working Life: A Reassessment (1976) —James C. Taylor

INTRODUCTION

The papers in Part 3 unequivocally support a central position regarding job design taken in this book. This position, expected to grow in acceptance among organizational policy makers and designers of jobs and organizations, is that jobs and, of course, organizations are social inventions reflecting the values of the era and the culture of the region in which they exist. It follows from this that the design of jobs is social system design affected by technology—in short, sociotechnical system design.

Hackman and Lawler (reading 10) focus on intrinsic factors related to motivation, emphasizing job content, the individual workers and their relationship to their product. The job characteristics they develop reinforce the position that job content is a matter of social system choice.

Emery (reading 11) insightfully shows us that the designs of the assembly line and assembly jobs are crucially linked to concepts of organization and to values regarding people who are to fill these jobs. He indicates that the application of assembly technology can lead to different assembly technical systems. When the technical system is viewed explicitly as a sociotechnical system rather than exclusively as a collection of machines, different designs result. The Volvo Kalmar automobile assembly plant illustrates that even the choice of the mechanical belt itself, taken by many to be the assembly line, is a social system choice. Again this analysis reinforces the position of this book, that design of technical systems unavoidably includes social system choices.

Davis (reading 12) indicates the changes in the post-industrial era wrought by the application of sophisticated process technologies. Here people are required to respond to "stochastic" events rather than execute the routines of conventional "deterministic" production technologies. High levels of investment in complex technical systems result in the automation of all programmable tasks but increase the dependence on organization members for those responses necessary to maintain continuous operations. It is this new relationship between people and production processes that calls for new forms of organization and jobs.

Davis and Taylor (reading 13) indicate that technological determinism, a piece of conventional wisdom, limits the choices that society is able to make concerning many aspects of its development. They indicate to the contrary that technology is neither value-free nor develops according to its own rules, but that there are choices that must be made in the design of technical systems to suit the values and objectives of society.

Design of jobs and organizations have been plagued by the argument over differences in cultures, namely, that rural workers hold tightly to traditional values of autonomy and independence concerning work whereas urban workers have strong instrumental values regarding work. Susman (reading 14) indicates that the differences between urban and rural workers are inconclusive. It may be that Susman's more recent data reflect changes in individuals, whether urban or rural, that are congruent with the values of an urbanized industrial society.

Last, Taylor (reading 15) focuses on the increasingly recognized impotence of job satisfaction measurement as it has developed historically. He shows that job satisfaction measures are themselves part of a social systems design. Therefore, what is to be measured and how that measurement is to be undertaken must be congruent with the design of the social system and its objectives.

10
Job Characteristics
and Motivation:
A Conceptual Framework

J. Richard Hackman and Edward E. Lawler, III

Researchers and managers alike are increasingly attending to the way jobs are designed as an important factor in determining the motivation, satisfaction, and performance of employees at work. This is not to say that jobs previously have been seen as irrelevant to organizational administration. On the contrary, earlier in this century when scientific management was in its prime, considerable research effort was expended to find ways that jobs could be simplified, specialized, standardized, and routinized. At the same time, industrial psychologists were developing rather complex and sophisticated procedures for describing and analyzing jobs in terms of their simplest components, as a means of evaluating the skill levels required for different jobs. The results of job analyses have been used to establish fair rates of pay, for training purposes, and in personnel selection (see,

Excerpts from J. Richard Hackman and Edward E. Lawler, III. "Employee Reactions to Job Characteristics." *Journal of Applied Psychology*, vol. 55, 1971, pp. 259–265.

for example, Ghiselli and Brown, 1955; Lytle, 1946; Stigers and Reed, 1944). The general expectation of the scientific management approach was that by simplifying jobs, work could be carried out more efficiently; less-skilled employees would be required; the control of management over production would be increased; and, ultimately, organizational profits would be enhanced.

In recent years, numerous scholars have documented a number of unintended and unfortunate consequences of the trend toward work simplification (for example, Argyris, 1964; Blauner, 1964; Davis, 1957; Friedmann, 1961; Guest, 1955; Herzberg, Mausner and Snyderman, 1959; Walker, 1950; Walker and Guest, 1952). In brief, it has been shown that simple, routine nonchallenging jobs often lead to high employee dissatisfaction, to increased absenteeism and turnover, and to substantial difficulties in effectively managing employees who work on simplified jobs.[1] The expected increases in profitability from work simplification have not materialized as had been hoped, and the reasons apparently have very much to do with the human problems encountered when jobs are standardized and simplified.

Partially in response to the above findings, a number of researchers began experimentally enlarging various jobs to determine whether or not worker productivity and satisfaction would increase if jobs were designed so as to be more generally meaningful and challenging to employees. By and large, those job enlargement experiments which have been reported in the literature have been considered successful (see, for example, Biggane and Stewart, 1963; Conant and Kilbridge, 1965; Davis and Valfer, 1965; Ford, 1969; Kilbridge, 1960; Pelissier, 1965). With few exceptions, however, job enlargement experiments have been case studies and often have lacked appropriate experimental controls. Hulin and Blood (1968) review the research literature on job enlargement in some detail and are especially attentive to possible difficulties in procedure and methodology which may cast doubt on the generality or the validity of the findings reported.

Perhaps equally as disturbing as the uneven level of methodological rigor which has characterized job enlargement studies is the almost total absence of any systematic conceptual or theoretical basis for the studies which have been done. As a result, after dozens of experiments, little cumulative knowledge has been gained regarding the effects and effectiveness of job redesign. Job enlargement experiments, for example, have typically involved a number of simultaneous changes—such as in the amount of variety in the work, the amount of responsibility required, the degree to which working with others is an important part of the enlarged job, etc. Very little is known about which of these (or of other) aspects of the redesigned job are in fact responsible for observed behavioral and attitudinal changes. Further, the generality of job enlargement effects is largely unknown (e.g., whether they are effective only for certain types of workers or whether they are relevant only to certain kinds of jobs). More case studies are not likely to contribute very much to the development of answers to crucial questions such as

---

[1] These observations have not, however, gone unchallenged. See, for example, Kilbridge (1961) and MacKinney, Wernimont and Galitz (1962).

these. Instead, what appears to be needed are conceptual frameworks which generate testable propositions about how job characteristics affect employees under various circumstances, and empirical research which is designed explicitly to test these propositions. This article proposes one way of conceptualizing the impact of job characteristics on individual work behavior and attitudes.[. . .]

PREVIOUS THEORY AND RESEARCH

Some progress toward the development of theory relevant to job design has been made in recent years. The well-known two-factor theory of Herzberg (Herzberg, Mausner and Snyderman, 1959; Herzberg, 1966), for example, can be used to derive general propositions regarding conditions on the job which will be motivating and satisfying to employees. In particular, the theory suggests that a job should enhance employee motivation to the extent that it provides opportunities for (a) achievement, (b) recognition, (c) responsibility, (d) advancement, and (e) growth in competence. These principles have given rise to a series of generally successful job enlargement experiments in the American Telephone and Telegraph Company (summarized by Ford, 1969).

Unfortunately, a number of researchers have been unable to provide empirical support for some of the major tenets of the theory from which the principles used in the AT&T studies were derived (e.g., Dunnette, Campbell and Hakel, 1967; Hinton, 1968; King, 1970), and the general conceptual status of the theory must presently be considered uncertain. Further, the theory has not yet been elaborated to specify how characteristics of workers interact with the presence or absence of the five motivating conditions in determining worker performance and satisfaction. Finally, the theory in its present form does not specify how the presence or absence of the motivating conditions can be measured for existing jobs. This makes it very difficult to test the theory and to generate unambiguous predictions from it about the effects of specific changes which may be contemplated for existing jobs.

The problem of measuring job characteristics has been explicitly and carefully dealt with by Turner and Lawrence (1965). These authors developed operational measures of six 'requisite task attributes' which, on the basis of a review of existing literature and an a priori conceptual framework, were predicted to be positively related to worker satisfaction and attendance. The six attributes are: (a) variety, (b) autonomy, (c) required interaction, (d) optional interaction, (e) knowledge and skill required, and (f) responsibility.[. . .]

Examination of the relationships among the six requisite task attributes for forty-seven jobs revealed that the attributes were very closely related to one another. Therefore, Turner and Lawrence developed a summary measure called the Requisite Task Attribute Index (RTA Index) by formulating a linear combination of the six separately measured attributes. This summary index was then used in ascertaining the relationships between the attributes of the jobs and worker job satisfaction and attendance.

The authors' expectation that employees working on jobs which were high on the RTA Index would have higher job satisfaction and lower absenteeism was not fully supported. Instead, it appeared that the predicted relationship between the RTA Index and employee reactions held only for workers from factories located in small towns.[. . .]

Blood and Hulin (1967) and Hulin and Blood (1968) provide additional data on the importance of subcultural factors in determining worker responses to the makeup of their jobs. These authors hypothesize that an important moderating factor is alienation from the traditional work norms which characterize the middle class. When employees hold traditional values regarding the value of work and achievement in work settings (as would be expected of the employees in small town factories in the Turner and Lawrence study), more complex jobs should be responded to positively. When employees are alienated from these norms (as might be expected in urban workers), more complex jobs should be responded to negatively. Blood and Hulin (1967) provide data supporting this general proposition and propose a three-dimensional response surface (Hulin and Blood, 1968) which specifies the expected interrelationships among worker alienation, job level, and satisfaction with work.[. . .]

Both Turner and Lawrence (1965) and Hulin and Blood (1968) choose to deal with individual differences on a subcultural or sociological level (i.e. in terms of differences between town and city workers or in terms of the alienation of city workers from middle-class work norms).

An alternative strategy would be to attempt to conceptualize and measure the relevant individual differences directly at the individual level of analysis. The town–city conceptualization assumes a substantial homogeneity of worker characteristics and response tendencies for employees within the two cultural settings. To the extent that there are substantial individual differences among town workers and among city workers, an attempt to measure relevant individual differences directly at the individual level would seem to have considerable merit. The difficulty in implementing this alternative approach, of course, is that it requires prior specification on a conceptual level of what specific differences among people are responsible for the results reported by Turner and Lawrence (1965) and Blood and Hulin (1967), i.e. what it is about people that moderates the way they react to their jobs. In the following paragraphs, we will propose such a conceptualization, and derive from it a number of predictions about the effects of job characteristics on employee satisfaction and motivation.

JOBS AND INDIVIDUALS:
A CONCEPTUAL FRAMEWORK

The present conceptualization of the interaction between job characteristics and individual differences is based primarily on the expectancy theory of motivation, as formulated by Lewin (1938) and Tolman (1959), and as applied to work settings by Vroom (1964), Porter and Lawler (1968), and others. In particular, five propositions based on expectancy theory are suggested below, which address the specific problem of how employee motivation can be enhanced through the design of jobs.

1. To the extent that an individual believes that he can obtain an outcome he values by engaging in some particular behavior or class of behaviors, the likelihood that he will actually engage in that behavior is enhanced. Relevant valued outcomes can be both intrinsic (e.g., feelings of accomplishment or of personal worth) and extrinsic (e.g., material goods); the only requirement is that the outcomes be valued by the individual. When an individual anticipates obtaining some valued outcome as a result of a contemplated action or course of action, that outcome may be termed an incentive for engaging in the action.

2. Outcomes are valued by individuals to the extent that they satisfy the physiological or psychological needs of the individual, or to the extent that they lead to other outcomes which satisfy such needs or are expected by the individual to do so. Such need satisfaction need not, of course, be in the objective best interest of the individual. People frequently strive for satisfying states of affairs which are quite inconsistent with their long-term well-being (Locke, 1969). Nevertheless, if an outcome is not somehow linked to satisfaction, it will not continue to be valued and therefore cannot continue to serve as an incentive.

3. Thus, to the extent that conditions at work can be arranged so that employees can satisfy their own needs best by working effectively toward organizational goals, employees will in fact tend to work hard toward the achievement of these goals (McGregor, 1960).

4. Most lower level needs (e.g. physical well-being, security) can be, and often are, reasonably well satisfied for individuals in contemporary society on a continuing basis and, therefore, will not serve as motivational incentives except under unusual circumstances. This is not the case, however, for certain higher order needs (e.g. needs for personal growth and development or for feelings of worthwhile accomplishment). A person may experience higher order need satisfaction on a continuing basis without the strength of desire for additional satisfaction of these needs diminishing. Indeed, it may be that additional satisfaction of higher order needs actually increase their strength (Alderfer, 1969). This is an important possibility since it suggests that the opportunity for the development of continuing (and possibly even increasing) motivation is much more a reality when higher order needs are engaged than is the case for more easily satisfied lower order needs. There is, of course, a major cost associated with any motivational approach in which higher order needs are central: not all employees can or will respond to opportunities for the satisfaction of higher order needs, and thus motivational approaches based on these needs cannot be applied indiscriminantly. Maslow (1943, 1954) and Alderfer (1969, 1971) discuss in much more complete detail the nature of higher order needs and their motivational implications.

5. Individuals who are capable of higher order need satisfaction will in fact experience such satisfaction when they learn that they have, as a result of their own efforts, accomplished something that they personally believe is worthwhile or meaningful (see Argyris, 1964; Lewin, Dembo, Festinger and Sears, 1944).

Specifically, individuals who desire higher order need satisfactions should be most likely to obtain them when they work effectively on meaningful jobs which provide feedback on the adequacy of their personal work activities. To establish conditions for internal work motivation, then, it appears that a job must: (a) allow workers to feel personally responsible for an identifiable and meaningful portion of the work, (b) provide work outcomes which are intrinsically meaningful or otherwise experienced as worthwhile, and (c) provide feedback about performance effectiveness. The harder and better an individual works on such a job, the more opportunities he will have to experience higher order need satisfactions and the more incentive there can be for continued effective performance. Higher order need satisfactions, therefore, are seen as (a) a result of, rather than a determinant of, effective performance (Lawler and Porter, 1967), and (b) an incentive for continued efforts to perform effectively.[2]

The five propositions outlined above lead to the conclusion that it may be possible under specifiable conditions simultaneously to achieve high employee satisfaction and high employee effort toward organizational goals. Specifically, the long-term congruence of high satisfaction and high effort is seen as depending upon (a) the existence of employee desires for higher order need satisfaction and (b) conditions on the job such that working hard and effectively toward organizational goals will bring about satisfaction of these needs.

CHARACTERISTICS OF MOTIVATING JOBS

The three general job characteristics identified above as central in developing a congruence between individual need satisfaction and organizational goal achievement must be described in more measurable terms if the validity of the conceptualization proposed here is to be tested. In the following paragraphs, therefore, each of the three general characterisitcs are examined in somewhat more detail. In addition, it will be proposed that four of the requisite task attributes proposed by Turner and Lawrence (1965) are likely to be useful as measures of the three general job characteristics.

1. The job must allow.a worker to feel personally responsible for a meaningful portion of his work. What is accomplished must be through the individual's own efforts. He must realize that the work he does is his own. And he must believe that he personally is responsible for whatever successes and failures occur as a result of his work. Only if what is accomplished is seen as one's own can an individual experience a feeling of personal success and a gain in self-esteem. This does not mean, of course, that feelings of personal responsibility for work outcomes cannot occur in team projects; all that is required is for team members to feel that their own efforts are important in accomplishing the task at hand.

---

[2] It should be noted that only higher order satisfactions are predicted to be increased by effective work on a job with the characteristics outlined above; other satisfactions, e.g. pay satisfaction, satisfaction with supervision, may not be affected.

The autonomy dimension, as specified by Turner and Lawrence (1965), would seem to tap the degree to which workers feel personal responsibilty for their work. In jobs high on measured autonomy, workers will tend to feel that they own the outcomes of their work; in jobs low on autonomy, a worker may more often feel that successes and failures on the job are more often due to the good work, or to the incompetence, of other workers or of his supervisor.[3]

2. The job must provide outcomes which are intrinsically meaningful or otherwise experienced as worthwhile to the individual. If a worker feels that the results of his efforts are not very important, it is unlikely that he will feel especially good if he works effectively. Instead, he must achieve something that he personally feels is worthwhile and important if he is to be able to experience positive feelings about himself as a result of his efforts. It clearly is not possible to indicate for people in general what kinds of job characteristics will be likely to provide outcomes seen as meaningful and worthwhile; people differ too much in the kinds of things they value for any statement of such generality to be made. It is possible, however, to provide some such specifications for individuals who have high desires, for higher order need satisfaction and, of course, these are the individuals to whom the present conceptualization is intended to apply.

There are at least two ways that work can come to be experienced as meaningful for employees with relatively high desires for higher order need satisfaction. The first is for the job to be a sufficiently whole piece of work that the worker can perceive that he has produced or accomplished something of consequence. In terms of a Turner and Lawrence task attribute, this would be expected to be the case when a job is high on task identity. According to Turner and Lawrence (1965, p. 157), jobs high on task identity are characterized by (a) a very clear cycle of perceived closure—the job provides a distinct sense of the beginning and ending of a transformation process, (b) high visibility of the transformation to the worker, (c) high visibility of the transformation in the finished product, and (d) a transformation of considerable magnitude. For a worker who has high needs for developing and using his competence, a job with such characteristics generally would be expected to be experienced as highly meaningful and worthwhile.

In addition, the experienced meaningfulness of work may be enhanced when a job provides a worker with the opportunity to accomplish something by using skills and abilities which he personally values. For example, a strongly motivated duffer feels good when he hits a solid tee shot, even though the broader significance of this event is doubtful. His golfing skills are on the line when he steps to the tee; those skills are important to him; he performs well—and that, in itself, is enough.

---

[3]Having high autonomy on the job does not, of course, necessarily imply that one will have major control over the work outcomes achieved. There may be a number of factors in the work environment which affect the nature of work outcomes, over which the worker has little meaningful control. For example, a football quarterback has high autonomy in selection of plays but only a moderate level of personal control over the outcomes obtained from execution of the plays. Thus, work autonomy is probably best viewed as a necessary but not sufficient condition for feeling personal responsibility for work outcomes.

Jobs high on the Turner and Lawrence (1965) dimension of variety would be expected to provide opportunities for workers to experience this kind of meaningfulness on the job, since high variety jobs typically tap a number of different skills which may be important to the employee. Thus, working on high variety jobs may become personally meaningful to some employees through a process very analogous to that which makes golf meaningful to the duffer. It should be noted, however, that only variety which does in fact challenge the worker will be expected to be experienced as meaningful to workers with desires for higher order need satisfaction; screwing many different sizes of nuts on many different colors of bolts, if this could be considered variety, would not be expected to be experienced as meaningful.[4]

To summarize, it may be that jobs can come to be experienced as meaningful to employees to the extent that they involve doing a whole piece of work of some significance, i.e. have high task identity, and, at the same time, to the extent that they give employees the chance to use their valued skills and abilities, i.e. to be challenged, in doing the work. In many cases the latter condition may be met on jobs which have high variety.

3. The job must provide feedback about what is accomplished. Even if the two general conditions discussed above are met, an employee cannot experience higher order need satisfaction when he performs effectively unless he obtains some kind of feedback about how he is doing. Such feedback may come from doing the task itself, e.g. when a telephone operator successfully completes a long distance person-to-person call, but performance feedback also may come from some other person—an esteemed co-worker, a supervisor, etc. The crucial condition is that feedback be present in a form that is believable to the worker, so that a realistic basis exists for the satisfaction, or frustration, of higher needs.

It should be emphasized that, for all of the job characteristics discussed above, it is not their objective state which affects employee attitudes and behavior, but rather how they are experienced by the employees. Regardless of the amount of feedback (or variety, or autonomy, or task identity) a worker really has in his work, it is how much *he perceives that he has* which will affect his reactions to the job. Objective job characteristics are important because they do affect the perceptions and experiences of employees. But there are often substantial differences between objective job characteristics and how they are perceived by employees, and it is dangerous to assume that simply because the objective characteristics of a job have been measured, or changed, that the way that job is experienced by employees has been dealt with as well.

In summary, then, it has been argued that the characteristics of jobs can establish conditions which will enhance the intrinsic motivation of workers who

---

[4] It is also possible, of course, for a job to have too much variety. Activation theory (e.g. Scott, 1966) suggests that when variety is too high, employees may experience a general state of muscular and mental hypertension which can greatly handicap performance effectiveness. In addition, Hall and Lawler (1970) found that among research scientists, high job variety can be associated with low job satisfaction, apparently because jobs with high variety also tended to be low in task identity and feedback.

desire higher order need satisfaction. In particular, it has been suggested, in terms of a subset of the Turner and Lawrence (1965) dimensions, that such individuals will be able to obtain meaningful personal satisfaction when they perform well on jobs which they experience as high on variety, autonomy, task identity and feedback. Further, the harder and better an individual performs on a job which is perceived as high on these dimensions, the more satisfaction he is likely to feel.[. . .]

REFERENCES

Alderfer, C. P. (1969) "An Empirical Test of a New Theory of Human Needs." *Organizational Behavior and Human Performance,* vol. 4. pp. 142–75.

Alderfer, C. P. (1971) *Human Needs in Organizational Settings.* Free Press.

Argyris, C. (1964) *Integrating the Individual and the Organization.* Wiley.

Biggane, J. F., and Stewart, P. A. (1963) *Job Enlargement: A Case Study.* Research Series no. 25, State University of Iowa, Bureau of Labor and Management.

Blauner, R. (1964), *Alienation and Freedom.* University of Chicago Press.

Blood, M. R., and Hulin, C. L. (1967) "Alienation. Environmental Characteristics and Worker Responses." *Journal of Applied Psychology,* vol. 51, pp. 284–90.

Conant, E. H., and Kilbridge, M. D. (1965) "An Interdisciplinary Analysis of Job Enlargement: Technology, Costs and Behavioral Implications." *Industrial and Labor Relations Review,* vol. 3, pp. 377–95.

Davis, L. E. (1957) "Job Design and Productivity: A New Approach." *Personnel,* vol. 33, pp. 418–29.

Davis, L. E., and Valfer, E. S. (1965) "Intervening Responses to Changes in Supervisor Job Designs." *Occupational Psychology,* vol 39, pp. 171–89.

Dunnette, M. D., Campbell, J. P., and Hakel, M. D. (1967) "Factors Contributing to Job Satisfaction and Job Dissatisfaction in Six Occupational Groups." *Organizational Behavior and Human Performance,* vol. 2, pp. 143–74.

Ford, R. N. (1969) *Motivation Through the Work Itself.* American Management Association.

Friedmann, G. (1961) *The Anatomy of Work.* Free Press.

Ghiselli, E. E., and Brown, C. W. (1955) *Personal and Industrial Psychology.* McGraw-Hill.

Guest, R. H. (1955) "Men and Machines: An Assembly-line Worker Looks at His Job." *Personnel,* vol. 31. pp. 3–10.

Hall, D. T., and Lawler, E. E. (1970) "Job Design and Job Pressure as Facilitators of Professional—Organization Integration." *Administrative Science Quarterly,* vol. 15. pp. 271–81.

Herzberg, F. (1966) *Work and the Nature of Man.* Harcourt, Brace & World.

Herzberg, F., Mausner, B., and Snyderman, B. (1959) *The Motivation to Work.* Wiley.

Hinton, B. L. (1968) "An Empirical Investigation of the Herzberg Methodology and Two-factor Theory." *Organizational Behavior and Human Performance,* vol. 3, pp. 286–309.

Hulin, C. L., and Blood, M. R. (1968) "Job Enlargement, Individual Differences, and Worker Responses." *Psychological Bulletin,* vol. 69, pp. 41–55.

Kilbridge, M. D. (1960) "Reduced Costs Through Job Enlargement: A Case." *Journal of*

Business of the University of Chicago, vol. 33, pp. 357–62.

Kilbridge, M. D. (1961) "Turnover, Absence and Transfer Rates as Indicators of Employee Dissatisfaction with Repetitive Work." *Industrial and Labor Relations Review*, vol. 15, pp. 21–32.

King, N. A. (1970) "A Clarification and Evaluation of the Two-factor Theory of Job Satisfaction." *Psychological Bulletin*, vol. 74, pp. 18–31.

Lawler, E. E., and Porter, L. W. (1967) "Antecedent Attitudes of Effective Managerial Performance." *Organizational Behavior and Human Performance*, vol. 2, pp. 122–42.

Lewin, K. (1938) *The Conceptual Representation of the Measurement of Psychological Forces*. Duke University Press.

Lewin, K., Dembo, T., Festinger, L., and Sears, P. (1944) "Level of Aspiration." In J. McV. Hunt, ed. *Personality and the Behavior Disorders*. Ronald Press.

Locke, E. A. (1969) "What is Job Satisfaction?" *Organizational Behavior and Human Performance*, vol. 4, pp. 309–36.

Lytle, C. W. (1946) *Job Evaluation Methods*. Ronald Press.

MacKinney, A. C., Wernimont, P. F., and Galitz, W. O. (1962) "Has Specialization Reduced Job Satisfaction?" *Personnel*, vol. 39, pp. 8–17.

Maslow, A. H. (1943) "A Theory of Human Motivation." *Psychological Review*, vol. 50, pp. 370–96.

Maslow, A. H. (1954) *Motivation and Personality*. Harper.

McGregor, D. (1960) *The Human Side of Enterprise*. McGraw-Hill.

Pelissier, R. F. (1965) "Successful Experience with Job Design." *Personnel Administration*, vol. 28, pp. 12–16.

Porter, L. W., and Lawler, E. E. (1968) *Managerial Attitudes and Performance*. Irwin.

Scott, W. E. (1966) "Activation Theory and Task Design." *Organizational Behavior and Human Performance*, vol. 1, pp. 3–30.

Stigers, M. F., and Reed, E. G. (1944) *The Theory and Practice of Job Rating*. McGraw-Hill.

Tolman, E. C. (1959) "Principles of Purposive Behavior." In S. Koch ed. *Psychology: A Study of a Science*. McGraw-Hill, vol. 2.

Turner, A. N., and Lawrence, P. R. (1965) *Industrial Jobs and the Worker*. Harvard University Graduate School of Business Administration.

Vroom, V. H. (1964) *Work and Motivation*. Wiley.

Walker, C. R. (1950) "The Problem of the Repetitive Job." *Harvard Business Review*, vol. 28, pp. 54–8.

Walker, C. R., and Guest, R. H. (1952) *The Man on the Assembly Line*. Harvard University Press.

11
The Assembly Line—
Its Logic and Our Future
Fred E. Emery

Our problems of human management have emerged most clearly in the management of assembly lines, and most pungently in the conveyor belt assembly of automobiles.[. . .]

What I am suggesting is that the logic of the car assembly line is a keystone, probably *the* keystone, to prevailing 20th century concepts of human management. If you think, as I do, that the climate of opinion enables us to attempt to pull out this keystone then let us do so.

The logic of production by a continuous flow line was well understood in early phases of industrialisation. First Charles Babbage and then Karl Marx spelt out this logic. The logic was an "if X then Y" logic. If a complex production task was broken down into a set of constituent tasks then the level of craft skills required was lowered and hence the cost of labour was lowered. At the extreme a class of unskilled labour emerged to perform the very elementary tasks that practically always remained after a complex task had been broken down to its minimum skill requirements. Such unskilled labourers would have had no part to play in craft production.

There is another valuable side of this penny that was not obvious till a much later date. That is, if one lowers the level of craft skill needed for a product it becomes much easier to swing to production of major variations of that product, e.g., from swords to ploughshares. Massive re-skilling of craftsmen is not needed.

Once the partition of a task had been successful in reducing the necessary level of craft skills it was only natural that men should seek further partitions leading them into even broader and cheaper labour markets. World War II recently gave a further great stimulus to this approach. The military demanded large scale production of very complex machines when often the only available labour force was that conscripted from outside the traditional industrial work force, e.g., women, pensioners, and peasants. The lessons flowed over from the blue collar work to the organisation of offices—insurance and taxation offices, etc.—organised for mass flow production of documents.

However, to realise the economic advantages of task segmentation it was necessary to cope with several sources of cost *inherent* in the method—(a) transfer costs (b) standardisation (c) "balancing" (d) external co-ordination and "pacing."

Excerpts from Fred E. Emery. "The Assembly Line—Its Logic and Our Future." *National Labour Institute Bulletin* (New Delhi), vol. 1, no. 12, 1975, pp. 1–9.

(a) Transfer costs: Individual craft production requires a minimal movement of the object under production. Partitioning of production needs transport of the object between each of the work stations at which someone is performing a different sub-task. The costs are those of sheer physical movement and re-positioning so that the next operation can be proceeded with, and, also, the costs of "waiting time" when valuable semi-products are, as it were, simply in storage. Henry Ford's introduction of conveyor belts to car assembly seemed to be the natural outcome of the attempt to reduce these transport costs. Conveyor chains had already transformed the Chicago slaughterhouses. Palletisation and fork lift trucks continue to reduce these costs in assembly areas where continuous belts or chains are not justifiable.

(b) Standardisation: Partitioning of production process was simply not an economic proposition unless there was a fair probability that the separately produced parts could be re-constituted to yield a workable version of the final product (it would not have to be as good as the craft produced product if its costs was sufficiently lower). This was obvious enough with the 18th century flow line production of pulley blocks at the Woolwich Naval Arsenal and the early 19th century production of Whitney's muskets. Reduction of this inherent cost has a long history. From Maudsley's slide rest onwards there has been a continuous evolution in specialised tools, machines, jigs and fixtures to enable relatively unskilled labour to continuously replicate relatively skilled operations to a higher degree of standardisation.[. . .]

(c) "Balancing the line": This is a problem that does not arise with the individual craftsman. Whatever the problems with a given phase of production on a particular lot of raw materials he can proceed immediately to the next phase as soon as he is satisfied with what he has done. He does not have to wait to catch up with himself. When the task is partitioned, that is not possible. Each set of workers is skilled, or rather, semi-skilled, in only its sub-task. They are not skilled to help clear any bottleneck or make up any shortfall in other parts of the line; they can simply stand idle and wait. Theoretically, there is in a flow line an "iron law of *proportionality*" such as Marx writes of. Theoretically, it should be like the recipe of a cake; so many hours of this kind of labour, so many of that kind of labour etc. and hey presto, the final product. Unfortunately for the application of the theory, it is not as simple as making cakes.

Balancing the line, to reduce downtime, was an on-the-line art of observation until Taylor and Gilbreth came onto the scene, [followed by] M.T.M. At last the balancing of a line seemed to be a science. Controlled observation and measurements seemed to offer a way of balancing not just the major segments of a line but of scientifically planning the work load and skill level of each and every individual work station. Planning and measuring costs money, but there has seemed no other way to reduce the downtime losses inherent in the original fractionation of production.[. . .]

(d) External supervision and "pacing": So long as the individual craftsman produced the whole product, control and coordination of his work on the various sub-tasks was no problem. He managed that himself. With the fractionation of production a special class of work emerged, the work of supervision. Each person on the assembly line has to attend to his own piece of the work and hence someone else must coordinate what is happening at the different work stations, to re-allocate work when the line becomes unbalanced, to re-enforce work standards when individual performance drifts away from them.

A major headache has been the near universal tendency of workers on fractionated tasks to drift away from planned work times. The self-pacing that enables the craftsman-producer to vary his work pace and yet maintain good targets for over-all production times appears to be absent from small fractionated tasks that are repeated endlessly. Tighter supervision and incentive payment schemes seemed appropriate forms of the carrot and stick to replace this element of self-pacing. However, the moving line emerged as the major innovation. Once properly manned for a given speed it seemed that this speed has only to be maintained by the supervisors to ensure that planned work times would be maintained. Dawdling at any work station would quickly reveal itself in persons moving off station to try and finish their parts.[. . .]

The conveyor was not just a means of lowering transfer costs but also of reducing supervisory costs. At certain tempos the line even gave operators a satisfactory sense of work rhythm, a feeling of being drawn along by the work. Davis' 1966 study even suggests that the contribution to control may often be the main justification of the conveyor.

What I have spelt out is old hat to any production engineer. Nevertheless, it prepares the ground for the point of this paper.

We have heard a great deal lately about the demise of the automobile assembly line. The new Volvo plant at Kalmar does not even have conveyor belts. The EEC pronounced in 1973 that the assembly line would have to be abolished from the European car industry.

I suggest that the new Kalmar plant does not represent any departure from the basic principles of mass flow line production. In the first place, they are still seeking the maximum economic advantages to be gained from fractionation of the over-all task. In the second place, the plant and its organisation have been designed to reduce the same inherent costs of mass flow production, i.e., costs of transfer standardisation, balancing coordination and pacing. Kalmar is designed as a mass production flow line to produce an economically competitive product. There is no radical departure from the principles of flow line production, only from its practice.

Note, however, that I previously stressed that their aim was "maximum economic advantage from fractionation," *not* maximum fractionation.

What they have done is to recognise that the costs we have discussed are inherent in production based on fractionated tasks. The further one pushes fractionation the greater these costs become, particularly the costs other than transfer costs because they are more related to human responsiveness. *The objective of gaining maximum economic advantage from fractionation cannot be the objective of maximum fractionation.* There is some *optimal* level to be sought at a point before the gains are whittled away by rising costs.[. . .]

If we look at the traditional practices in designing a mass flow line we find a critical assumption has slipped in and been reinforced by the widespread reliance on M.T.M. as a planning tool and as a control tool. This assumption is that it must be possible for each individual worker to be held responsible by an external supervisor for his individual performance. On this assumption M.T.M. goes beyond being a planning tool to determine or re-determine the probable labour requirements of sections of the line. It becomes part of the detailed day-to-day supervisory control over production. Under this impetus fractionation heads down to the L.C.D. (Lowest Common Denominator) of the labour on the line.

The same assumption, that a line must be built up from the individually supervised one man-shift unit, has gone into the design of algorithms to determine line balance. Ingall (1965) has reviewed ten or so of the major algorithms. They all embody the same assumption. They go further along with M.T.M. to assert that this is a firm organisational building block by assuming that on the average, different operators work at the same pace; on the average, an individual operator works at the same pace throughout a shift; on the average, the cycle time of the operation is irrelevant; on the average, learning on the job can be ignored; on the average, variations in parts and equipment can be ignored.

An average is just that, an average. It represents the mean value of a set of different observed states of a system parameter. It does not even tell us whether the exact average state has ever occurred. One thing is pretty sure; at any one time on a line it is most improbable that all aspects are operating at their average value. Typically something is always non-average, wrong, and when one thing is wrong so are half a dozen other things.

The practical problem of balancing a line simply cannot be solved by abstracting this aspect from the total system of potential gains and inherent costs of flow production. As Ingall concludes in his review of assembly line balancing:

> Knowing whether these problems occur together is important because analysing them separately is not sufficient if they do. Using the "sum" of the results obtained by analysing each problem separately as the procedure for the combined problem can be a dangerous pastime (1965).[. . .]

Some people in the car industry during the fifties and the sixties became sensitive to the fact that pursuit of maximum fractionation was self-defeating; and they realised it was not at all like the engineering problem of pursuing maximum aircraft speed by reducing friction and drag. They realised it was not a problem to be solved by the grease of yet higher relative pay, by feather-bedding or by any of those things that Walter Reuther of the U.S. Automobile Workers' Union bitterly referred to as "gold-plating the sweat shop."

The response of these people to these critical insights was to look again at the building block, the one man-shift unit, to see what could be done about that. They did not question whether the individual was the appropriate block for building on.

One proposal to arise from this was to employ on the line only people who were at, or very close to, the lowest common denominator used by M.T.M. and the planners, i.e., donkeys for donkey work. This proposal does not look so good now that the international pool of cheap migrant labour dries up. In any case, there was little future in this proposal. Provided the line designers pursue the same twisted logic of maximum fractionation, they would inevitably design around an even lower cheaper common denominator and the other costs would rise again.

The other proposal was to discard the concept of an L.C.D. and accept the job enlargement or enrichment up to a point which would come closest to optimal fractionation for a majority of the people on the line. Imposing such enrichment on the minority whose optimal was below this level was an immediately obvious practical flaw. A more deep-seated flaw was that this job enrichment approach argued from consideration of only one aspect of the system—task fractionation. It did not simultaneously confront the other parameters of the system—balancing, pacing, etc.

As I have stressed these parameters constitute a *system* of production. If some people on the line are responsible for only one parameter and someone else has the problem of looking after the other parameters then you have designed in inefficiency and trouble (Ackoff and Emery, 1972, pp. 222–7). No designer in his right senses would design a purely technical system in that way, unless there was a very considerable time-lag between changes on that parameter and changes on the other system parameters. I think I am safe in saying that no such protective time-lag exists for the parameter of degree of task fractionation in a mass flow line. If something goes wrong with, for instance, the line balance or pace the operator can very quickly find himself frustrated by a stoppage and consequent break in his rhythm of work, or find himself temporarily slotted into some other strange station on the line.

An organisation like this is basically unstable and rendered even more so when the other party (or parties) looking after the other parameters live in the other more powerful world of management, i.e., when communications are subject to the constant distortion of messages going between "them" and "us." Inevitably the supervisors, M.T.M., work programmers, etc., respond to the predictable system problems by pushing for more fractionation and tighter controls.

The instability I am referring to is not that of the technical system of mass flow production. The instability is that of a superimposed organisation which has very different roots in history. This organisational instability has very serious practical consequences. Firstly, it makes it pretty well impossible to enrich individual jobs, whether this is done as a programme or slipped in by supervisors who have taken to heart their exposure to courses on human relations in industry. As the pressures build up the screws are back on again. Secondly, it is not just on the line that the pressures are experienced. As the instabilities cumulate to their recurrent crises on the line all levels of staff are sucked down to coping with deficiencies in performance of the levels below them. Even the plant manager can find himself living by the hour to hour performance of the line. Thirdly, the almost universal experience of these phenomena of instability has created a sustained history, almost an addiction to technical solutions that would design people out of the system, or at least create "fool-proof" technologies.

It is in looking at the mass flow production line as a *socio-technical system* that we come to what is really radical about the Kalmar design.

The designers approached their task with an awareness that the problems of flow line production could be theoretically approached in different organisational designs.[. . .]

The most striking outcome was the discovery that in an appropriately skilled and sized work group all of the key parameters of mass flow production could come together and be controlled vis-à-vis each other at that level. Picturesquely, this was labelled as "a lot of little factories within a factory." In terms of how we picture a factory, this the groups are not. Walk around Kalmar and you see nothing that even looks like a lot of little workshops producing their own cars. In system terms, however, it is a very apt description: a very valid design criterion.[. . .]

Formation of semi-autonomous groups on the Kalmar assembly line has given them a cycle time and buffers that would be negligible if split up for individual work stations. Split up into individual work stations, no one could take an untimed coffee break; grouped up, everyone can without increasing over-all downtime. On individual work stations everyone has to meet the standard work on that particular job minute by minute. In the group setting variations in individual levels of optimal performance can be met with hour by hour. Those that prefer repetitious simple tasks can get them; those that need to be told what to do will be told by others in the group. Within the range of their task the group can balance their work, without outside assistance. If quality control is amongst the group's responsibilities, and they are given time allowance for this, then it can be within their capabilities. Now we come to the fundamental matter—co-ordination, control and pacing.*

If a semi-autonomous work group is not willing to exercise control and co-ordination over its members then the design of flow lines must go back to the traditional model.

At this point I must rely on experience, not on theory. The experience over twenty odd years with a wide range of technologies and societies is simply this: *If reasonably sized groups have accepted a set of production targets and have the resources to pursue it at reasonable reward to themselves they will better achieve those targets than they would if each person was under external supervisory control.*[. . .]

I have suggested that the revolution at Kalmar has not been that of throwing out

---

* Volvo engineers came up with an ingenious technical solution to the transfer problems—the individual self propelled carriage. This allows the groups to vary the time put into each car whilst maintaining average flow onto the next groups.

the assembly line. The revolutionary change began with the eradication of an organisational principle of one man-one shift-one station, a principle that had no intrinsic relation to the design of assembly lines. Further, I have suggested that the pay off in the change began with selecting as the building block a socio-technical unit, an appropriately skilled and sized semi-autonomous group that had the potential of simultaneously controlling from their own immediate experience the basic set of parameters of gain and cost in the total system.

This was intended to be a technical paper for a body of professional production engineers. Hence, it might be excusable to expand a little on this last point. Just as in scientific fields one of the most critical strategic breakthroughs is the discovery of the appropriate "unit of analysis," so in production systems engineering it is the identification of the basic "unit of design." Identifying "unit operations" was such a classic breakthrough in the tremendously complex problems of chemical engineering. With this in mind the British Social Science Research Council funded an international, inter-disciplinary team "to devise a conceptual scheme for the analysis of men-machine-equipment relations with the more common unit operations" (Emery, 1966).

The conclusion of this study was that the *basic unit for design of socio-technical systems must itself be a socio-technical unit,* and, *have the characteristic of an open system.* "In design terms this represents the lowest level at which it is possible to jointly optimise the human and technical system with respect to environmental requirements (the over-all system inputs and outputs). Failure to recognise this may lead to design decisions being made solely on technical and economic cost criteria with consequent inefficiencies due to (a) excess operating costs (b) maintenance difficulties (c) lack of growth in system performance (d) high overheads for control and supervision, or (e) lack of adaptability to market shifts." (*ibid.* p. 4–5).

Now after nearly ten years of living with this conclusion I think I am prepared to argue even more strongly for a further conclusion unanimously arrived at by the study team: namely, that the best designs will be those that make the most use of the highest human potentials one could expect to find in any average group of 8 to 10 human beings. My argument is that: firstly there is a basic fact about systems that is simply ducked by the current plethora of so-called systems theoreticians, i.e., that "it is not simply the fact of linkages but rather the principle according to which all linkages fall together in *one controlling order* which makes an organization" (Feibleman and Friend, 1945 in Emery, 1969, p. 34); "Every system has one and only one construction principle . . . *unitas multiplex*" (Angyal, 1941 in Emery, 1969. p. 28).[. . .]

There is sufficient evidence that unions would agree to different designs that offer real advantages to their members. If what the unions are offered are aggregative designs from which the employers hope to maximise their economic gains from maximising fractionation then the unions must exploit this game to the maximum of their ability. Until recently the unions have not had the alternative possibility of sending the employers back to the drawing board. They have not had this possibility because they have not had the knowledge of alternatives that enabled Gyllenhamer of Volvo to send his designers back and back again to the drawing boards until they got a really new concept of the Kalmar plant.

The Kalmar design finished up as a genuine systems design. [Its] groups were enabled to confront and take responsibility for the basic parameters that determined whether they were an economically productive section. [Its] groups were enabled and encouraged to meet variance in their circumstances by re-arrangement of their own efforts. Adding further permanent members was very much a last resort, after making do with re-arrangement of themselves or working out arrangements for temporary borrowing of labour from neighbouring groups. As we had seen from the earliest coal mining studies, there was a marked reluctance of groups to accept any change of group membership until they had done their own best to cope with their work problem.

[Lastly] "the more the inherent properties of parts are utilised as co-determinants of positional values, the greater the organisation of the whole" (Angyal, *ibid.* p. 27). What this principal means is, quite simply, that the best design for any productive system will be that which not only allows that the goals of any sub-system, any part, embody in some manner the overall system goals, and allows that any such part is self-managing to the point that it will seek to cope with external variances by firstly re-arranging its own use of resources; the best design will be that which also recruits or develops its constituent parts so that they have the intrinsic properties suited to the demands on the position they occupy.

At the simplest level, this principle would indicate designing-in a degree of multi-skilling which could meet the probable re-arrangements of the section about its tasks. At a more sophisticated level of design, account would be taken of the human potentialities for reasoning, creativity and leadership that might be expected in any group of 8 to 10 human beings. This would mean designing the social system of the small group so that it becomes an instrument for its members— something they largely manage themselves, not vice versa. Then it would become *variety increasing* for them and they are enabled to pursue not only production goals but also proposals and even ideals that pertain to themselves (Ackoff and Emery, p. 216, Emery et al., 1974, pp. 60–70.[. . .]

Now, let me conclude with the observation that this is not quite how the Volvo design for Kalmar worked out. Volvo is a human organisation. Like ICI (U.K.) it made its name in management circles by introducing the principles of M.T.M. to Scandinavian manufacturers. They made quite a reputation out of the traditional forms of car assembly; and the economics were not bad. They eventually sensed an economic trap and in the design phase of Kalmar they eventually found a radical solution. In the run-in phase of Kalmar they found themselves with a belt-and-braces solution. The traditional departments were determined to show that they had something to offer.

One way or another they sold themselves into Kalmar. As Kalmar recently prepared itself to go into full on-line production the question was asked: "What are these supervisory and M.T.M. people doing here on the shop floor?" The question was critical. Most groups would not accept responsibility unless they were in fact allowed to be responsible. Supervisors were for their part, unwilling to draw their pay unless they exercised supervision, down to the individual.

The situation at Kalmar has been resolved in favour of the original radical design. My point in referring to this is that traditions, and that includes traditions about assembly line production, do not quietly go to rest as new ways emerge. They have got to be firmly buried.

REFERENCES

Ackoff, R. L. and Emery, F. E. (1972) *On Purposeful System*. London, Tavistock Press.

Amber, C. H. and Amber, P. S. (1962) *Anatomy of Automation*. N.Y., Prentice-Hall.

Basu, R. N. "The Practical Problems of Assembly Line Balancing." *The Production Engineer* (Oct. 1973) pp. 369–370.

Davis, L. E. "Pacing Effects on Manned Assembly Lines." *International Journal of Industrial Engineering* (1966) Vol, 4, p. 171.

Emery, F. E. "Report on a Theoretical Study of Unit Operations." (1966) *Tavistock Doc T900*, London, T.I.H.R.

Emery, F. E. ed. (1969) *Systems Thinking*. London, Penguin.

Emery, F. E. et al. (1974) *Futures We're In*. Canberra, CCE, ANU.

Ingall, E. J. "A Review of Assembly Line Balancing." *Journal of Industrial Engineering* (1965) Vol. 16, p. 4.

Kildridge, M. D. and Wester, L. "The Assembly Line Model-Mix Sequencing Problem." Proceedings of 3rd International Conference on O.R. Olso, (1963).

Mellor, D. P. (1958) *The Role of Science and Industry*. Canberra, Australian War Memorial.

Thorsrud, E. and Emery, F. E. (1969) *Form and Content in Industrial Democracy*. London, Tavistock.

Thorsrud, E. and Emery, F. E. (1969) *New Forms of Work Organisation*. In Norwegian. Olso, Tannum; Revised English edition, Emery, F. E. and Thorsrud, E. (1975) *Democracy at Work*. Canberra, Centre for Continuing Education, ANU.

Wild, R. "Group Working in Mass Production, Part 1: Flowline Work." *The Production Engineer* (Dec. 1973) pp. 457–461.

12
The Coming Crisis
for Production Management:
Technology and Organization
Louis E. Davis

INTRODUCTION

Events cast their shadows before them. Already, we can discern changes in our environment more than sufficient to show that Western industrial society is in transition from one historical era to another. It is the purpose of this paper to indicate that the environmental characteristics of the post-industrial era will lead to crisis and massive dislocation unless adaptation occurs. The anticipated consequences will be greatest, at first, for the production industries, because they stand at the confluence of changes involving technology, social values, the economic environment, organizational design, job design and the practices of managment.

Managers, as rational leaders, will seek to avoid these consequences by altering the forms of institutional regulation and control. It is a secondary purpose of this paper to describe some ways in which managers are already beginning this process. Specifically, examples will be given from the research results and organizational experiments of an international coalition of English, American and Norwegian researchers whose reports are referred to throughout this paper.[. . .]

THE POST-INDUSTRIAL CHALLENGE

Changes in Society

In recent years, changes in Western societal environments have been reflective of a rising level of expectations concerning material, social and personal needs. The seeming ease with which new (automated) technology satisfies material needs, coupled with the provision of subsistence-level support for its citizens by society, has stimulated a growing concern on the part of the individual over his relationship to work, its meaningfulness and its value—i.e. a concern for the quality of work life (see Davis, 1970s). In the US, questioning of the relationship between work and satisfaction of material needs is widespread through the ranks of university students, industrial workers and minority unemployed. The viability of the belief that individuals may be used to satisfy the economic goals of organiza-

Excerpts from Louis E. Davis. "The Coming Crisis for Production Management: Technology and Organization." *International Journal of Production Research,* vol. 9, 1971, pp. 65–82.

tions is being seriously questioned. It appears that people may no longer let themselves be used; they wish to see some relationship between their own work and the social life around them, and they wish some desirable future for themselves in their continuing relationship with organizations. No longer will workers patiently endure dehumanized work roles in order to achieve increased material rewards.

Among university students these expectations are leading to refusals to accept jobs with major corporations, in favour of more "socially oriented" institutions—an unfortunate loss of talented people. Even the unemployed are refusing to accept dead-end demeaning jobs (see Doeringer, 1969), appearing to be as selective about accepting jobs as are the employed about changing jobs. There appear to be means, partly provided by society, for subsisting in minority ghettos without entering the industrial world. For industrial workers there is a revival of concern with the once-buried question of alienation from work, job satisfaction, personal freedom and initiative, and the dignity of the individual in the work place. Although on the surface the expressed concern is over the effects of automation on job availability and greater sharing in wealth produced, restlessness in unions, their failure to grow in the non-industrial sectors and the frequent overthrow of union leaders are all indicators, in the US, of a changing field that stems from the increasingly tenuous relationship between work and satisfaction of material needs.

Another factor impelling social change is the continuously rising level of education that Western countries provide, which is changing the attitudes, the aspirations, and the expectations of major segments of society (see Bell, 1967). Future trends are already visible in California, where almost 50 percent of young people of college and university age are in school and where one-third of all the scientists and engineers in the US are employed.

Changes in Technology

One of the forces driving the transition into the post-industrial era is the growing application of automated, computer-aided production systems. This development is bringing about crucial changes in the relationship between technology and the social organization of production—changes of such magnitude that the displacement of men and skills by computers is reduced to the status of a relatively minor effect.

The most striking characteristic of sophisticated, automated technology is that it absorbs routine activities into the machines, creating a new relationship between the technology and its embedded social system; the humans in automated systems are interdependent components required to respond to *stochastic,* not deterministic, conditions—i.e. they operate in an environment whose "important events" are randomly occurring and unpredictable. Sophisticated skills must be maintained, though they may be called into use only very occasionally. This technological shift disturbs long-established boundaries between jobs and skills and between operations and maintenance. It has also contributed to a shift in the working population from providing goods to providing personal and societal services. As may be expected, there is a shift from blue-collar to white-collar work in clerical, technical and service jobs. At all levels of society, individuals find that they must change their careers or jobs over time.

Still further, the new technology requires a high degree of commitment and autonomy on the part of workers in the automated production processes (see Davis, 1970b). The required degree of autonomy is likely to be in serious conflict with the assumptions and values held within the bureaucratic techno-structure (see Galbraith, 1967).

Another feature is that there are in effect two intertwined technologies. The primary technology contains the transformations needed to produce the desired output. It is machine- and capital-intensive. The secondary technology contains the support and service activities, such as loading and unloading materials, tools, etc. It is labour-intensive and its variances are capable of stopping or reducing throughput, but enhancing the secondary technology will not enhance the primary technology and its throughputs.

Although it poses new problems, highly sophisticated technology possesses an unrecognized flexibility in relation to social systems. There exists an extensive array of configurations of the technology that can be designed to suit the social systems desired, within limits. This property disaffirms the notion of the "technological imperative" widely held by both engineers and social scientists. It places the burden on managers, hopefully aided by social scientists, to elucidate the characteristics of their particular social system suitable to the evolving post-industrial era.[. . .]

In production systems, stochastic events have two characteristics: unpredictability as to time and unpredictability as to nature. For economic reasons, they must be overcome as rapidly as possible, which imposes certain requirements on those who do the work. First, the workers must have a large repertoire of responses because the specific intervention that will be required is not known. Second, they cannot depend on supervision because they must respond immediately to events that occur irregularly and without warning. Third, they must be committed to undertaking the necessary tasks on their own initiative.

This makes a very different world, in which the organization is far more dependent on the individual (although there may be fewer individuals). From the point of view of the organization, the chain of causation is:

1. If the production process collapses, the economic goals of the organization will not be met.
2. If appropriate responses are not taken to stochastic events, the production process will collapse.
3. If the organization's members are not committed to their functions, the appropriate responses will not be made.
4. Commitment cannot be forced or bought; it can only arise out of the experiences of the individual with the quality of life in his working situation, i.e. with his job.

5. Therefore, automated industries seek to build into jobs the characteristics that will develop commitment on the part of the individual. The major characteristics are those of planning, self-control, self-regulation, i.e. of autonomy (see Davis, 1966).

A comparison between an industry that is highly automated and one that is not demonstrates these differences very clearly. In the oil-refining industry, the tasks that remain to be performed are almost entirely control and regulation, and the line between supervisor and worker is tenuous. The construction industry, on the other hand, still retains prominent roles for man as a source of energy and tool guidance, and supervision (often at several levels) mediates all system actions. Industrial relations officers in the oil industry are proud of their "advanced and enlightened" personnel practices. And indeed, these practices may be accurately described as enlightened. They were adopted because they are a necessary functional response to the demands of process technology.

Here is the point at which both the social and the technological forces can be seen working toward the same end, for "job characteristics that develop commitment" and thus promote the economic goals of the highly automated organization are exactly those that are beginning to emerge as demands for "meaningfulness" from the social environment—participation and control, personal freedom and initiative.

Nor is this linking of the two threads confined to industries that are as highly automated as oil and chemicals. Most industries are neither all automated nor all conventional; they utilize a mix of the two modes of production. If an industry has some employees whose jobs are designed to meet the requirements of automated technology, then the enhanced quality of their work life is visible to all the employees of the organization, creating demands by all employees for better, more meaningful jobs. It becomes very difficult to maintain a distinction in job design solely on the basis of a distinction in technological base.

Changes in Economic Organization

Developments in technology are interrelated with changes in economic organization. The scale of economic units is growing, stimulated by the developments of sophisticated production technology and organized knowledge leading to new products. In turn this is leading to new arrangements in the market, stimulating the development of higher-order interactions.

The organized use of knowledge brings about constant product innovation and for firms in electronics, aerospace, computers, information processing, etc., a new phenomenon in market relationship appears. Such firms are continually in the process of redefining their products and their futures—an exercise that reflects back on their internal organization structures and on the response flexibility of their members. Within these companies, there is an observable shift to high-talent personnel and to the development of strategies of distinctive competence, stores of experience, and built-in redundancy of response capabilities.

The Consequences of These Changes

A pervasive feature of the post-industrial environment is that it is taking on the quality of a turbulent field (see Emery and Trist, 1965). Turbulence arises from increased complexity and from the size of the total environment. It is compounded by increased interdependence of the environment's parts and the unpredictable connections arising between them as a result of accelerating but uneven change. The area of relevant uncertainty for individuals and organizations increases and tests the limits of human adaptability; earlier forms of adaptation, developed in response to a simpler environment, appear to suffice no longer. The turbulent environment requires that boundaries of organizations be extended into their technological, social and economic environments. The organization needs to identify the causal characteristics of the environments so that it can develop response strategies. The production organization, in particular, must provide a structure, a style of management and jobs so designed that adaptation can take place without massive dislocation.[. . .]

THE POST-INDUSTRIAL OPPORTUNITY

Although the presence of the features outlined in the previous section indicates that we are already well launched into the post-industrial era, Trist (1968) finds that we suffer from a cultural lag—the absence of a culture congruent with the identifiable needs of post-industrialism. Furthermore, in the turbulent environmental texture of the post-industrial era, the individual organization, city, state, or even nation—acting alone—may be unable to meet the demands of increasing levels of complexity. Resources will have to be pooled; there will be a need for more sharing, more trust and more cooperation.

Seldom does society have a second chance to redress deep-seated errors in social organization and members' roles; however, the opportunity may now be at hand to overcome alienation and provide humanly meaningful work in socio-technical institutions (see Fromm, 1968, and Emery, 1967). The development, over a period of nearly twenty years, of a body of theory (see Emery, 1969) concerned with the analysis and design of interacting technological and social systems has furthered the examination of questions of organization and job design in complex environments, too long considered to be exclusively an art form. The diffusion of knowledge about applications of these theories is itself changing the environment of other organizations. The concepts were first developed in Britain (see Emery and Trist, 1960) and followed by developments in the United States and recently in Norway, Canada and Sweden. They are far from having come into common practice. Their most comprehensive application is taking place in Norway, on a national scale, as a basis for developing organizational and job design strategies suitable to a democratic society.

Briefly, socio-technical systems theory rests on two essential premises. The first is that in any purposive organization in which men are required to perform the organization's activities, there is a joint system operating, a *socio-technical* system. When work is to be done, and when human beings are required actors in the performance of this work, then the desired output is achieved through the actions of a social system as well as a technological system. Further, these systems so interlock that the achievement of the output becomes a function of the appropriate joint operation of both systems. The operative word is "joint" for it is here that the socio-technical idea departs from more widely held views—those in which the social system is thought to be completely dependent on the technical system. The concept of joint optimization is proposed, which states that it is impossible to optimize for overall performance without seeking to optimize jointly the correlative independent social and technological systems.

The second premise is that every socio-technical system is embedded in an environment—an environment that is influenced by a culture and its values, an environment that is influenced by a set of generally acceptable practices, an environment that permits certain roles for the organisms in it. To understand a work system or an organization, one must understand the environmental forces that are operating on it. Without this understanding, it is impossible to develop an effective job or organization. This emphasis on environmental forces suggests, correctly, that the socio-technical systems idea falls within the larger body of "open system" theories. What does this mean? Simply, that there is a constant interchange between what goes on in a work system or an organization and what goes on in the environment; the boundaries between the environment and the system are highly permeable, and what goes on outside affects what goes on inside. When something occurs in the general society, it will inevitably affect what occurs in organizations. There may be a period of cultural lag, but sooner or later, the societal tremor will register on the organizational seismographs.

Significantly, socio-technical systems theory provides a basis for analysis and design overcoming the greatest inhibition to development of organization and job strategies in a growing turbulent environment. It breaks through the long-existing tight compartments between the worlds of those who plan, study and manage social systems and those who do so for technological systems. At once it makes nonsensical the existing positions of psychologists and sociologists that in purposive organizations the technology is unalterable and must be accepted as a given requirement. Most frequently, therefore, only variables and relationships not influenced by technology are examined and altered. Without inclusion of technology, which considerably determines what work is about and what demands exist for the individual and organization, not only are peripheral relations examined but they tend to become disproportionately magnified, making interpretation and use of findings difficult, if not impossible. Similarly, it makes nonsensical the "technological imperative" position of engineers, economists and managers who consider psychological and social requirements as constraints and at best as boundary conditions of technological systems. That a substantial part of technological system design includes social system design is neither understood nor appreciated. Frightful assumptions, supported by societal values, are made about men and groups and become built into machines and processes as requirements.

Socio-technical systems analysis provides a basis for determining appropriate boundaries of systems containing men, machines, materials and information. It considers the operation of such systems within the framework of an environment that is made an overt and specific object of the socio-technical study. It concerns itself with spontaneous reorganization or adaptation, with control of system variance, with growth, self-regulation, etc. These are aspects of system study that will become increasingly important as organizations in the post-industrial era are required to develop strategies that focus on adaptability and commitment. For these reasons, socio-technical systems analysis is felt to offer one of the best current approaches to meeting the post-industrial challenge.

The final section of this paper presents some selective aspects of socio-technical theory and application in greater detail. Wherever possible, actual field studies using the socio-technical approach are cited to support and illustrate the discussion.

RESULTS OF ORGANIZATIONAL AND JOB DESIGN RESEARCH

A number of developments, including on-site organizational experiments, lend strong support to the prospects of successfully developing suitable strategies of organization for the post-industrial era. In general, successful outcomes are measured by various objective criteria dependent on the finding of an accommodation between the demands of the organization and the technology on the one hand, and the needs and desires of people on the other, so that the needs of both were provided for. A summary report of US and English empirical studies appeared in Davis (1966).

The studies sought to find conditions in organization structure and job contents leading to cooperation, commitment, learning and growth, ability to change, and improved performance. The findings can be summarized under four categories of requirements: responsible autonomy, adaptability, variety and participation. When these factors were present, they led to learnings and behaviors that seemed to provide the sought-for organization and job response qualities. These studies lend support to the general model of responsible autonomous job and group behavior as a key facet in socio-technological relationships in production organizations.

By autonomy is meant that the content, structure and organization of jobs are such that individuals or groups performing those jobs can plan, regulate and control their own worlds.[. . .]

The results obtained indicated that when the attributes and characteristics of jobs were such that the individual or group became largely autonomous in the working situation, then meaningfulness, satisfaction and learning increased significantly, as did wide knowledge of process, identification with product, commitment to desired action and responsibility for outcomes. These supported the development of a job structure that permitted social interaction among job-holders and communication with peers and supervisors, particularly when the maintenance of continuity of operation was required. Simultaneously, high performance in quantity and quality of product or service outcomes was achieved. This has been demonstrated in such widely-different settings as the mining of coal (reported by Trist et al., 1963), the maintenance of a chemical refinery, and the manufacture of aircraft instruments (reported by Davis and Werling, 1960, and Davis and Valfer, 1966).

The second requirements category, which has mainly been the province of psychologists, is concerned with "adaptation." The contents of the job have to be such that the individual can learn from what is going on around him, can grow, can develop, can adjust. Slighted, but not overlooked, is the psychological concept of self-actualization or personal growth, which appears to be central to the development of motivation and commitment through satisfaction of higher order intrinsic needs of individuals. The most potent way of satisfying intrinsic needs may well be through job design (see Lawler, 1969). Too often jobs in conventional industrial organizations have simply required people to adapt to restricted, fractionated activities, overlooking their enormous capacity to learn and adapt to complexity.[. . .]

Where the socio-technical system was so designed that the necessary adaptive behavior was facilitated, positive results in economic performance and in satisfactions occurred at all levels in the organization, as demonstrated in studies in oil refineries, automated chemical plants, pulp and paper plants (see Thorsrud and Emery, 1969), and aircraft instrument plants (see Davis, 1966).

The third category is concerned with variety. Man, surely, has always known it, but only lately has it been demonstrated that part of what a living organism requires to function effectively is a variety of experiences. If people are to be alert and responsive to their working environments, they need variety in the work situation. Routine, repetitious tasks tend to extinguish the individual. He is there physically, but not in any other way; he has disappeared from the scene. Psychologists have also studied this phenomenon in various "deprived environments." Adult humans confined to "stimulus-free" environments begin to hallucinate. Workers may respond to the deprived work situation in much the same way—by disappearing (getting them back is another issue). Variety in industrial work has been the subject of study and controversy for fifty years. Recently, considerable attention has focused on the benefits to the individual and the organization of enlarging jobs to add variety (see Herzberg, 1966, and Davis, 1957).

There is another aspect of the need for variety that is less well-recognized in the industrial setting today, but that will become increasingly important in the emergent technological environment. The cyberneticist, Ashby (1960), has described this aspect of variety as a general criterion for intelligent behavior of any kind. To Ashby, adequate adaptation is only possible if an organism already has a stored set of responses of the requisite variety. This implies that in the work situation, where unexpected things will happen, the task content of a job and the training for that job should match this potential variability.

The last category concerns participation of the individual in the decisions affecting his work. Participation in development of job content and organizational relations, as well as in planning of changes, was fundamental to the outcomes achieved by the studies in Norway (see Thorsrud and Emery, 1969) and in the aircraft instrument industry (see Davis, 1962; 1966). Participation plays a role in learning and growth and permits those affected by changes in their roles and environments to develop assessments of the effects. An extensive literature on the process and dynamics of change (see Bennis, 1966) supports the findings of the field studies.

In a pioneering study, Lawrence and Lorsch (1967) examined the effects of uncertainty in technology and markets on the structure, relationship and performance of organizations. They found that where uncertainty is high, influence is high, i.e., if the situation becomes increasingly unpredictable, decision-making is forced down into the organization where the requisite expertise for daily decisions resides. Under environments of uncertainty, influence and authority are more evenly distributed; organizations become "polyarchic." Under environments of certainty or stability, organizations tend to be relatively less democratic, with influence, authority and responsibility centralized. These findings were derived from studies of firms in contrasting certain and uncertain environments.

Another category, which goes beyond the four and was implicit in them, concerns the total system of work. In the field studies, if tasks and activities within jobs fell into meaningful patterns, reflecting the interdependence between the individual job and the larger production system, then enhanced performance satisfaction and learning took place. In socio-technical terms, this interdependence is most closely associated with the points at which variance is introduced from one production process into another. When necessary skills, tasks and information were incorporated into the individual or group jobs, then adjustments could be made to handle error and exceptions within the affected subsystem; failing that, the variances were exported to other interconnecting systems. (In "deterministic" systems, the layer on layers of supervisors, buttressed by inspectors, utility men, and repairmen, etc., absorb the variances exported from the work-place.)

These organizational experiments indicate that individuals and organizations can change and adapt to turbulent environments. Nonetheless, in moving into the post-industrial era, considerable learning is still needed about building into the organizational milieu the capability for continuing change. A number of studies have indicated that, if spontaneous and innovative behaviors are to result, conditions will have to be developed to bring about internalization of organizational goals (see Katz and Kahn, 1966). Such internalization exists at the upper levels of organizations, but (except in the Norwegian experiments) is found in the lower levels only in voluntary organizations.

CONCLUSION

In the post-industrial era, current organization structures will become increasingly dysfunctional. If strategies of survival are to be developed, advanced societies, particularly the managers of their industrial and business organizations, will have to accept the obligation to examine existing assumptions and face the value issues regarding men and technology raised by the evolving environments.

Existing jobs and organizations will have to undergo reorganization to meet the requirements for a continuing high rate of change, new technologies and changing aspirations and expectations. These undertakings will be wrenching for institutions and individuals. Providing prescriptions would be presumptuous, but some organizations, joined by socio-technical researcher-consultants, seem to be well into the process.

REFERENCES

Ashby, W. R. (1960) *Design for a Brain*. Wiley.

Bell, D. (1967) "Notes on the Post-industrial Society: I and II." *Public Interest*, Nos. 6 and 7.

Bennis, W. G. (1966) *Changing Organisations*. McGraw-Hill.

Davis, L. E. (1957) "Toward a Theory of Job Design." *Journal of Industrial Engineering*, vol. 8, p. 305.

Davis, L. E. (1962) "The Effects of Automation on Job Design." *Industrial Relations*, vol. 2, p. 53.

Davis, L. E. (1966) "The Design of Jobs." *Industrial Relations*, vol. 6, p. 21.

Davis, L. E. (1970a) "Restructuring Jobs for Social Goals." *Manpower*, vol. 2, p. 2.

Davis, L. E. (1970b) "Job Satisfaction—A Sociotechnical View." *Industrial Relations*, vol. 10.

Davis, L. E., and Valfer, E. S. (1966) "Studies in Supervisory Job Design." *Human Relations*, vol. 17, p. 339.

Davis, L. E., and Werling, R. (1960) "Job Design Factors." *Occupational Psychology*, vol. 28, p. 109.

Doeringer, P. B. (1969) "Ghetto Labor Markets and Manpower." *Monthly Labor Review*, vol. 55.

Emery, F. F. (1967) "The Next Thirty Years: Concepts, Methods and Anticipations." *Human Relations*, vol. 20, p. 199.

Emery, F. E. (1969) *Systems Thinking*, Penguin Books.

Emery, F. E., and Trist, E. L. (1960) "Socio-technical Systems." in C. W. Churchman and M. Verhulst, eds. *Management Sciences, Models and Techniques*, vol. 2. Pergamon, p. 83.

Emery, F. E., and Trist, E. L. (1965) "The Causal Texture of Organizational Environments." *Human Relations*, vol. 18, p. 21.

Fromm, E. (1968) *The Revolution of Hope: Toward a Humanised Technology*. Harper & Row, ch. 5.

Galbraith, J. K. (1967) *The New Industrial State*. Houghton-Mifflin.

Herzberg, F. (1966) *Work and the Nature of Man*. World.

Katz, D., and Kahn, R. L. (1966) *Social Psychology of Organisations*. Wiley.

Lawler, E. E. (1969) "Job Design and Employee Motivation." *Personnel Psychology*, vol. 22, p. 426.

Lawrence, P. R., and Lorsch, J. H. (1967) *Organisation and Environment*. Harvard University Press.

Thorsrud, E., and Emery, F. (1969) *Moton ny bedriftsorganisasjon*. Tanum, Forlag, Oslo, ch. 6.

Trist, E. L. (1968) *Urban North America, The Challenge of the Next Thirty Years—A Social Psychological Viewpoint*. Town Planning Institute of Canada.

Trist, E. L., et al. (1963) *Organizational Choice*. Tavistock.

13
Technology and
Job Design (1976)
Louis E. Davis and James C. Taylor

A NEW APPRECIATION OF INTERACTIONS BETWEEN
TECHNICAL AND SOCIAL SYSTEMS

The present view of the relationship of technology to organization and job structure, carefully nurtured for the past 150 years, is that of technological determinism—and it is dangerously simplistic (Ellul, 1964). It holds that technology evolves according to its own inherent logic and needs, regardless of social environment and culture. Further, it holds that to use technology effectively and thus gain its benefits for society requires that its development and application be uninhibited by any considerations other than those that its developers—engineers or technologists—deem relevant.

Technological determinism has generally been invoked to support the organizational and institutional status quo of the industrial era. For example, the claim is made that organizational structure and behavior are predetermined by technology and unalterably locked into its needs. Doomsayers predict the impending doom of society as we know it given the negative consequences of a substantial number of technical developments. While it has been shown that there are some correlations between technology and organizational structure and organizational process (Woodward, 1958; Burns and Stalker, 1961), there are choices available based on social system values and assumptions. Additionally, it is part of our new learning that the determination of technological form and its unalterable application is both misleading and defeatist. It is well known that many technological alternatives are considered by technical system planners, of which only one form is put forth in an instance. The new learning alerts us to look at the design process of production technology itself to see which social system planning and psychosocial assumptions were considered in the design of various technical system alternatives. Further, we have learned that we need to have made explicit what economic and social as well as technical factors were included in the decision process of choosing a technological form.

In the design and development of technology, we are dealing with the application of science to invent technique and its supportive artifacts (machines) to

Excerpted and revised from Louis E. Davis and James C. Taylor, "Technology Effects on Job, Work, and Organizational Structure: A Contingency View." In Louis E. Davis and Albert B. Cherns, eds. *The Quality of Working Life*: Vol. I New York: Free Press, 1975, chapter 15, pp. 220–241.

accomplish transformations of objects (materials, information, people) in support of certain objectives. The invention of technique may be engineering to an overwhelming extent, but in part is also social system design. If, then, we look at work, we can see two sets of antecedent determinants that constrain the choices available for design of tasks and job structure. First, there are the social choices already contained within the technological design; second, there are the social choices contained within the organizational design undertaken to use the technology. Our present appreciation is that one rarely finds technological determinism in the pure sense of technological or scientific variables exclusively determining the design or configuration of a technical system. On the contrary, most frequently technical system designs incorporate social system choices, made intentionally or included accidentally either casually or as the result of some omission in planning. In this sense, engineers or technologists can be called social system engineers, and they are crucial to evolving new organization forms and job structure.

For the very same reason, we are led to the position that it is impossible at present to draw many cause-and-effect or even correlative conclusions about the causal effects of technology on the structure and process of organizations and jobs. Yet, today, in study after study, we are confidently offered such conclusions despite the fact that the researchers did not undertake appropriate analyses of the technological systems to ascertain incorporated psychosocial purposes and assumptions (Davis, *et al.*, 1955). There are innumerable instances in which psychosocial assumptions indirectly or subconsciously become part of a technical system design. It is unknown to what extent psychosocial requirements or assumptions are wholly ignored in the design or choice of a technical system (particularly a work system), except insofar as the designer inevitably carries with him and expresses the values and assumptions of his culture.

TECHNOLOGICAL ALTERNATIVES IN SOCIAL SYSTEM CHOICES

Cultural or subcultural values and assumptions held by the designers of the technical systems referred to above can be manifest in at least several ways. Table 1 shows the effects of technical systems on jobs as specific elements, or on organizations or systems at a broader level; the social system effects of technology are separated into those which were consciously considered from those not considered by the designers.

Thus, the table presents four different cases or effects: cell 1 contains psychosocial system effects of technology at the system level which were not considered by the designers; cell 2 shows psychosocial system effects at the system level which were considered; cell 3 effects are at the job rather than the system level and are considered; and in cell 4 these specific job and work effects are not considered. Some brief examples of each of these four conditions are given to describe the ways in which systems designers can affect psychosocial systems.

The case of cell 1 is illustrated in enlargement and relocation of a series of distribution terminals in the British trucking industry. In effect, such changes in

TABLE 1.

MANIFESTATIONS OF PSYCHOSOCIAL EFFECTS

		CONSIDERED	NOT CONSIDERED
Levels of Psychosocial Effects	System	2	1
	Job (Task)	3	4

size and location of terminals or depots are a direct function of the changes in size and speed of the motor vehicles involved. The effects on psychosocial systems were both unintended or not considered by the designers of the new terminal system, but were also very widespread because not only the jobs of the truckers, but their extra-work activities, their home, family, and leisure time activities were greatly affected. In fact, the connection between the changes in the terminal size and location and the subsequent changes in worker behavior was not realized for some time following the changeover.

An example of cell 2 is the case of the Norsk Hydro fertilizer plant in Norway, already documented, in which the systems of jobs and work and outside activities were considered in advance of implementing the technical design of the new factory (Thorsrud and Emery, 1969; Engelstad, 1972).

When technical systems designers do consider psychosocial system effects of technology, the outcome is not necessarily the enhancement of the quality of working life. Cell 3 is an example in which the systems designers' consideration of technical effects on humans, given their assumptions about people, leads to greater dehumanization of work rather than to its amelioration. A number of parallel operating, automated machines for filling and capping aerosol spray cans, with one operator attending each machine, are arranged far enough apart so that there is no communication among the operators. The most frequent human intervention in terms of sheer time and effort required is the insertion of a small plastic tube into a large hole at the top of the upright cans which pass on a circular conveyor belt in front of the operator. The second human intervention and the basic reason for the presence of the operator in the first place is to press a stop switch placed on a post directly in front of him. In the event of perceptible trouble anywhere in the machine, the operator is expected to shut off the machine and seek help to resolve the problem. In this case, the machine design did not include the needed sophisticated sensing devices requiring human intervention as a substitute for them. At the present time, however, it was clear that workers were designed into the system as human machine elements to perform the isolated, technologically unnecessary, and tedious task of inserting tubes which could be easily done by the machine. The decision is one in which the human task of inserting tubes into cans was developed simply because the primary task of sensing and diagnosing required human eyes and ears and, by hiring those, one also acquired a set of hands which were not to be left idle.

Cell 4 represents a situation where the psychosocial effects at the task level are not considered specifically in advance, one which in our estimation is most frequently found in industrial era organizations. On assembly lines the technological needs for material transfer are considered to the exclusion of the psychosocial task demands, which are monotonous and often unpleasant (Walker and Guest, 1952). The psychosocial assumptions about people working at repetitive, machine-paced jobs are present, of course, even if technical systems planners have not explicitly considered them. Indeed, there is a veritable folklore to the effect that repetitive assembly-line work is desired by some workers and suited to the limited human capacities and aspirations of most American workers. This belief accommodates comfortably the exclusion of other psychosocial alternatives in the design of such technical systems.

CHANGES IN TECHNOLOGY

Man once played three roles in any goods production technology, two of which can now be preempted by machines. His first role, as energy supplier, is now virtually nonexistent in Western industrial societies. His second role, as a guider of tools, is increasingly being transferred to machines as part of a continuing process of mechanization. Man's third traditional role is the only one that remains in existence in advanced technology or in automated work processes: that is, man as controller or regulator of the working situation or system and as diagnoser and adjuster of difficulties. Similar changes are taking place in service industries based on information technology.

CHARACTERISTICS OF THE NEW TECHNOLOGY

Technology as developed during the industrial era has had a powerful impact on the organization of work. This trend began about 150 years ago with a number of developments in England which led to the gradual replacement of human and animal power sources and which brought about the factory system and the coordination of man and machines, stimulating the movement to rationalize or streamline the utilization of labor—and the notion of division of labor (for economic purposes). The latter was made possible by the deterministic character of industrial technology; that is, what is to be done, how it is to be done, and when it is to be done are all specifiable factors.

Organizations evolving out of the design processes implied in the industrial era reflect both this deterministic technology and the values and beliefs of Western society. A new kind of specialization of labor emerged in which jobs were deliberately fractionated so that unskilled people could perform them (Babbage,

1835; Taylor, 1911). Under such organizational arrangements, management is reinforced in its belief that workers are unreliable, interested only in external rewards, and regard their work as a burden. This is largely a self-fulfilling prophecy because the more planning, control, and supervision management undertakes, the less is there for workers to be interested in and the less they are willing to accept responsibilities. Thus, they come to see their jobs only as an instrumental means to other ends.

The most striking characteristic of the new sophisticated (automated) technology is that it absorbs routine activities into machines rather than leaving them for people, which creates a new relationship between a technology and its embedded social system. Workers in automated systems are interdependent components required to respond to *stochastic*—not deterministic—conditions; they operate in an environment where the important events are randomly occurring and unpredictable raising needs for commitment and wide competence.

Once again, the table presented earlier can be considered in the context of this technology. That modern technology can have more varied effects on jobs and work and that the impacts on the psychosocial system may be different do not necessarily mean that those additional assumptions or alternatives will be considered by the designers.

In fact, the illustration provided for cell 3 indicates this situation rather clearly, a case of more advanced technology being coupled with industrial era assumptions about workers being considered rather directly by the designers of the equipment. Any potential for changes in human skills or demands for those skills in the illustration provided is totally ignored. As will be noted below, the new sophisticated stochastic technology requires skills related to regulation, skills in monitoring and diagnosing, skills in the adjustment of processes. These skills can be related more to group efforts and tasks rather than to individual jobs and tasks. In turn, these group activities can have an impact on organizational structure. However, referring back to the above appreciation, the designers of the technology and their implicit assumptions about people, mediate between the new stochastic technologies and their behavioral, job, or organizational effects (Davis, 1971). Unfortunately, there are instances of organizations and job structures evolved to suit deterministic technology being used with stochastic technology.

AUTOMATION AND SKILLS

Automated computer-aided production systems are bringing about crucial changes in the skill requirements of the job occupants. From the earliest studies of the effects of automation, shifts in skill demands have emphasized a reduction in requirements for the traditional high-coordination motor skills or craft precision skills, in favor of mental skills, perceptual skills in monitoring dials and gauges, as well as decision-making skills regarding machine adjustment or repair (Bright, 1958). Other studies have found it useful to consider increased responsibility, increased need for attention and decision-making discretion as, in fact, new skill demands. It can be concluded from this early literature that demands for traditional skills are reduced in part while demands for new skills are increased.

More recent studies of the effects of technology on skills strongly support earlier findings. The aptitudes required in advanced production technology as examined in 1969, 1970, or 1971 still include aptitudes such as close attention to work processes or instruments, rapid response to emergency situations, ability to stay calm in attention-producing environments, and early detection of malfunctioning or of conditions leading to it. In addition to these characteristics such as freedom for social contact, decision-making power and variation in tasks are associated with modern technology. However, these recent studies have also noted that control over the work methods or planning of work sequences is found to be no greater in process-monitoring tasks than it was in the repetitive work tasks of the industrial era (Hazelhurst, *et al.*, 1971; Wedderburn and Crompton, 1972).

Throughout the literature, although a number of studies deal with the white-collar area, few are concerned with jobs and skills. To summarize what is available, however, the following can be advanced.

Studies of white-collar work in computer-assisted work organizations tend to suggest that it is becoming more similar to blue-collar work of the industrial era. For example, much of this involves the replacement of manual clerks with keypunch operators (Faunce, 1968; Mumford and Sackman, 1975). Some longitudinal studies tend to suggest that job enlargement can take place in conjunction with white-collar automation (Mann and Williams, 1962). The authors of these results caution, however, that these changes may not necessarily follow in other cases, and that some of the positive effects of the present case were offset by negative demands such as shift work in white-collar organizations. Also, aggregate skill demands have increased slightly while the demand for man-hours is reduced rather remarkably with white-collar automation (Crossman and Laner, 1969).

WORKER AUTONOMY AND DISCRETION; AND THE REDEFINITION OF SUPERVISION

The issue of the effect of technology on supervision has been of interest for a good many years. More particularly, at issue is the continuance—or perhaps the resurgence—of coercive, close supervision in automated industries versus the opportunity to develop supervisory styles which are more participative. Evidence collected over the past decade can be presented in support of either side. It should be noted as well that there is also a body of literature on supervisory styles which tends to negate the technological influence entirely. In turn, in other sets of studies conflicting hypotheses are supported that differences in supervision and their effectiveness are a function of subcultural values: for example, differences between rural and urban upbringing and residence. Finally, there are data that go beyond the simple test of whether or not the effect of technology on supervision is manifest.

As early as the late 1950s, but more so during the early mid-1960s, a number of studies presented evidence in favor of the position that automation leads to close and coercive supervision (Dubin, 1965; Gruenfeld and Foltman, 1967). At the same time, other studies suggested that the reverse was true, namely, supervision was becoming more participative, open, and democratic with the introduction of automation (Blauner, 1964; Woodward, 1965). The studies pointing to increased closeness of supervision and increased punitiveness with advanced technology had an advantage in that they could explain at least some additional portion of the variance remaining after associating supervisory style with the subcultural position being advanced by Hulin and Blood, Turner and Lawrence, and others. This position, held rather strongly for a period of time, tends to support the position of managerial and engineering emphasis on industrial era values.

A number of isolated studies conducted during that period tended to suggest an absence of subcultural effects, while more recently other researchers have begun to hypothesize and test these effects more rigorously (Susman, 1972). They have concluded that if there were a difference between rural and urban workers as recently as ten years ago, that difference is disappearing. As there is now a period of massive realignment of values and urban centers are increasingly transmitting values to the rural areas, there may be a leveling of regional and rural-urban differences that were noted and assumed to be valid not more than a decade ago (Hulin and Blood, 1968; Turner and Lawrence, 1965).

A number of the above studies tend to show "negative" effects of supervision as a function of automation—that is, tend to emphasize the emergence of close supervision, and tend also to couple that phenomenon of close supervision with coercion. Though it is true that span of supervisory control can become smaller with automation, this shortened span of control in itself is not necessarily close supervision nor is close supervision by itself punitive (Thurley and Hamblin, 1963; Williams and Williams, 1964; Davis and Valfer, 1966).

If, in fact, a small span of control is to represent the production management of the future, it could follow that supervision becomes increasingly closer and more highly skilled until industry returns once more to the crafts notion, namely, that the supervisor is merely the most skilled of the workers—and, if work groups continue to decrease in size, they may eventually be considered as either leaderless work groups or autonomous groups of workers. This raises the question of difficulty in distinguishing supervisors from workers. The early literature, as noted above, cited evidence of changes in worker skills showing increased discretion and responsibility replacing motor skills and crafts. These new skills would seem to be more typical of supervisory than nonsupervisory employees in previous periods.

Given this, the findings relating technology to supervisory style can be roughly summarized as follows: With the coming of automation, better technically trained foremen are more frequently needed and the remaining nonsupervisory jobs are upgraded, which combines the element of worker skill with the phenomenon of close supervision and smaller supervisory control spans. It could well be postulated that higher skills in the sense defined earlier in this selection may be automation's new skill requirements of machine process supervision—supervision of machine systems by operators rather than supervision of workers by supervisors (Bright, 1958; Dubin, 1965).

Increasingly, however, the more recent literature describes a different role for supervisors, one that is basically a shift from controlling internal variances in the work group to controlling variances impinging on the work group from the outside; that is, coming from outside the unit or the organization as a whole (Gulowsen, 1971; Quale, 1967; Archer, 1975). Other results tend to suggest that although the supervisor may seem more concerned with technical aspects of the work process, such concern is characteristic of his role at the beginning or early in the introduction of a technological innovation and is in great measure eliminated later on (Thurley and Hamblin, 1963; Mann and Williams, 1962; Walker, 1957).

There is little direct evidence that the social system assumptions held by managers and engineers can modify the effects of technological sophistication and effects on supervision. An organizational design study conducted in Norway highlights the problem of assessing the technological effects on worker autonomy and supervision (Engelstad, 1972). It points to management's insistence on maintaining a newly developed foreman role with strong internal group controls, together with a design for creating greater worker discretion on the job. The change achieved some measure of success in creating worker autonomy and discretion, but the company itself decided to eliminate the foreman role for this type of work after four years' experience with the internal conflict it created.

AUTOMATION AND WORK GROUP BEHAVIOR

Several studies of the impact of technological change on supervisory style also looked at work group behavior (Mann and Hoffman, 1960; Walker, 1957; Marrow, et al., 1967). These studies tended to show that changes in the direction of more meaningful group cooperation and coordination developed in conjunction with changes in the technology.

There is some causal logic which can be used in describing technological effects on work group behavior, although it is not well supported by empirical studies. This logic suggests that stochastic technologies provide a functional synthesis of formerly separated occupations. This diffusion of roles makes for less separation or overlap, forcing more contact and cooperation among members than was previously the case (Herbst, 1962; ILO, 1966; Miller and Rice, 1967).

Another and larger body of data uses a more associative, empirical logic, which looks at the degree of success of implementing more participative democratic and autonomous group structure with changes in technology (Rice, 1963). These are not only important for the correlative evidence they provide, suggesting strongly that new types of work group behavior can be used to advantage in situations where technology is changed or changing, but they also furnish a link between the emerging needs of workers, as noted above, and greater responsibility and discretion on the job.

How far a work group is capable of responsible autonomy and can adapt itself to ongoing conditions indicates the extent to which its social structure is appropriate to the demands of the work situation. At least one researcher suggests that the difference between autocratic management and autonomous work organization lies not in the amount of control exercised by the supervisor, but in applying control to external factors affecting internal stability (Herbst, 1962). When technology makes it easier to evaluate results, it is then easier to supervise on the basis of results, and autocratic management of work activities is less likely (Woodward, 1965).

The effects of managerial discretion in job design decisions can be difficult to separate from the effects of the technology itself. Regardless of the validity of the statement that managerial discretion can intervene between technology and work group design it is perhaps more important to acknowledge that implementation of technical systems must involve psychosocial assumptions juxtaposed with technical efficiency. For instance Susman (1970, 1970) and Taylor (1971, 1971) note that in oil refining the tasks of control and regulation predominate and that the line between supervisor and worker is tenuous. Industrial relations officers in the petrochemical industry are proud of their "advanced and enlightened" personnel practices. These practices may indeed be described as such, but they were not adopted for the sake of their enlightenment. They were adopted because they were, and are, a necessary functional response to the demands of process technology.

Here is the point at which both the social and the technological forces can be seen working toward the same end, for "job characteristics that develop commitment." Thus requirements that promote the economic goals of the highly automated organization are exactly those beginning to emerge as demands for "meaningfulness" from the social environment: participation and control, personal freedom, and initiative.

Nor is this linking of the two threads confined to industries as highly automated as oil refining and chemicals. Most industries are neither all automated nor all conventional; they utilize a mix of the two modes of production. If an industry has some employees whose enhanced jobs were designed to meet the requirements of automated technology, then the enhanced quality of their work life is visible to all the employees of the organization and creates demands by all employees for better, more meaningful jobs. It becomes very difficult to maintain a distinction in job design solely on the basis of a distinction in technological base.

Some recent reports argue against the position stated earlier, that work in automated technology is shifting from single jobs to a set of jobs (or group of performed activities) (Goldthorpe, et al., 1968). One, a comparative survey of British companies representing several different levels of technological sophistication, concludes that in automated lathe operation, as well as continuous process operations, social interaction and group relations are less frequent than in more traditional industrial technology—as well as involving lower skill levels, as traditionally defined.

In view of the earlier discussion of the influence of social system assumptions on the design of a technical system, a possible explanation for the absence of any meaningful group structure in automated operations is the following: If the managers and technical system planners imposed job and organizational structures which flow from the assumption that people (or parts of people) are merely parts of the machine or work process, then whatever potential the technology could provide for formation of group activities would be negated.

It seems reasonable to speculate that whereas management may change some psychosocial assumptions toward higher individual worker responsibility in more automated systems, it is likely to offer more resistance to changing its assumptions about delegating authority and reducing supervision of worker behavior. In other words, it is an issue of imposing "managerial authority structure" regardless of the "work authority requirements" (Thorsrud, 1968).

In reviewing the impact of technological effect on organizational structure, the literature is divided into those studies that tend to show some effect of technology on organizational structure and those that tend to show little or no relationship between technology and organizational structure. In the former case, the studies can be separated again into two categories: In the first, it is concluded in general that positive involvement of the lowest level persons in the organization, coordination among work groups, and horizontal communication are required when the technical system becomes complex (Touraine, *et al.*, 1965; Thompson, 1967). Although the definitions of technological complexity vary from one study to another and, further, rely on a small amount of impressionistic data, it is interesting that the conclusions show a great deal of similarity.

In the second category are data that not only support the findings regarding communication and responsibility but tend to show more flexible organizational design as well (Burns and Stalker, 1961; Blauner, 1964; Woodward, 1958, 1965). Very tentative conclusions based on these studies and several others would affirm that more modern technologies are associated with feasible, adaptive, more formless organizations or with a bureaucracy based on a consensus and a sense of industrial community (Perrow, 1970; Harvey, 1969).

The other studies, showing that technology is slightly or not at all related to organizational structure, consider the structural effects of a number of variables, such as organizational size and technology (Pugh, *et al.*, 1963). Both are related to organizational structure in general, but size is a better predictor. Thus the empirical evidence for technological effects on organizational structure is not only conflicting, but in even greater disarray than the results presented earlier for effects of technology on job and group structures. This is not surprising, for at least two reasons: First, the available studies utilize fairly gross, unquantified comparative judgments of degree of technological sophistication at the organizational level (Burns and Stalker, 1961; Woodward, 1965; Thompson, 1967; Blauner, 1964). Such gross categorization of technological sophistication makes comparison difficult and replication impossible. Second, there seems to be considerable resistance to changing psychosocial assumptions operative at the system level. It was noted earlier that whereas management may be less willing to allow modification of group structural arrangements and more tolerant of individual job and task changes, it is likely to resist even more strongly any attempts at changing organizational form or control structure, since such modification comes even closer to touching the organizational life space of managers themselves.

SUMMARY AND CONCLUSIONS

Our review of technology in the organizational setting is based on a new appreciation that technology design implicitly or explicitly includes certain psychosocial assumptions. A wide range of studies provides some direct evidence of considerable flexibility in the design of technology in response to psychosocial assumptions, which challenges the widely accepted notion of technological determinism.

The position has been taken here that the psychosocial assumptions related to postindustrial technology are at present the most crucial (and the most useful) elements in meaningful change in organizations. This position translates into action in designing jobs and larger social systems in organizations by considering emerging values toward people and work together with extant potentials of the technology. This implies a recognition that nearly all technology is designed by exercising certain assumptions about people and work. In almost every case in the past, these have been the psychosocial assumptions of the industrial era.

This review has dealt with studies of technological effects on job and skill requirements, worker autonomy and supervision, effects on group relations, and, finally, impact on organizational structure. And, in going from the specific topics of jobs and skills to the more diffuse topics of organizational structure, agreement among results of studies has diminished. In the area of organizational structure, little direct evidence is available so far—there has been no specific effort to look for it—for establishing managerial discretion as an important variable conditioning the relation between technology and organization (Child, 1972; Child and Mansfield, 1972; Cooper, 1972).

The remaining studies reviewed have not directly supported the model of technological determinism or that of the decision-maker intervention model. In the former case, methodological limitations of measuring technology, at least, create enough inconsistency across studies to obviate any monolithic support for technological determinism. At the same time, these inconsistencies might themselves provide indirect evidence for the latter model as managerial discretion may account for some of the inconsistencies noted.

Evidence has been presented that, although vastly different social systems have been associated with similar technologies, these differences have typically been less than the differences among technologies. This, we reason, is probably as much a function of the dominant social values extant at the time of a technology's introduction as it is of the constraints of the technology itself. If, for example, designers considered workers to be "parts of machines" by virtue of the values of the culture at that time, then this would have an effect upon all the similar technological installations of the period. Dramatic changes in technology over the past twenty years have been associated with a general shift toward jobs, work, and organizations, which are different from those that preceded them and reflect the changing value patterns of society, as well as of technological designers specifically. Such value shifts occur slowly, however, and are by no means universal.

That many engineers and managers continue to operate with industrial era assumptions about people at work is obvious. One element evidencing the shift is the greater degree of agreement among results of studies reporting new individual worker skill-level demands of automation compared with lower agreement among results of associations between automation and psychosocial effects at the work group and organizational system levels. This, we believe, can be explained by greater tolerance on the part of managers, designers of technology, and operating systems for psychosocial changes affecting the lower levels of the organization and the individual worker, and by less tolerance for psychosocial changes with general effect on the organization as a whole or upon higher organizational levels.

Accepting that technology design also involves social system design, when psychosocial assumptions contained in the technology design are revealed, the conclusions drawn from a review of the existing literature make even more ambiguous the effects brought about by changes in technology. We have, therefore, weakened the cause-and-effect linkages previously stated by many authors.

Starting with the position that psychosocial assumptions are a part of technical system design, the effects of technology are seen in the light of a self-fulfilling prophecy. That is, the observed effects on workers and on organizations of technology reflect the assumptions held by the designers of the technological systems about men and social systems. Hypotheses held about the nature of man embedded within a technical system are operationalized in the design of the technical system. For example, when assumptions are held that a system is composed of reliable technical elements and unreliable social elements, then, to provide total system reliability, the technical design will call for parts of people as replaceable machine elements to be regulated by the technical system or by a superstructure of personal control. On the other hand, if the system designers' assumptions are that the social elements are reliable, learning, self-organizing, and committed elements, then the technical system will require whole, unique people performing the regulatory activities. Experience has shown that in the latter case such a technical system design produces effects markedly different than in the former.

We, therefore, have no alternative but to consider technical systems and social systems to be *joint* systems with elements of one system residing in the other. The consequence, then, is that in designing organizations or jobs, these two subsystems have to be jointly optimized if there is to be a mutually effective organization or job result.

The conceptualization of correlated sociotechnical systems has been supported by the experiences in action research where researchers are forced to accept the complexity of the field as an outgrowth of a triple responsibility, namely responsibility to the created system, to science, and to the greater social environment rather than merely the responsibility to science alone. Such researchers have been forced to accept the reality of how technology is designed, and of how designs of technological alternatives get to be made. From these experiences has developed the learning or appreciation that is central to this review. Future research must go beyond the limited focus of positivistic science, yet at the same time lend itself to the descriptions of the real world complexities long experienced in applied science. What is called for is an end to the acceptance of technology as given and of unidimensional concepts or effects. One important variable stressed in this report is the interaction of the decision maker's discretion both in the design of technologies and in the organization of jobs based on the assumptions about people. That the inclusion of this variable increases analytic complexity and reduces elegance in research design is accepted as necessary if we are going to develop useful causal models of organizational functioning and behavior.

OPPORTUNITIES PRESENTED BY NEW TECHNOLOGY

Technology is changing, and doing so at a very high rate. This is reflected in the rate of introduction of both new products and new processes or techniques which are growing in sophistication, that is, more highly science based. The high rate of change has consequences for organization and job structure. On the product side, frequent new developments are leading to the growth of shorter production runs with the resulting need for adaptability of organization and workers to more changes. On the production side, there is the phenomenon of more sophisticated machines and simpler manual activities embedded within automated complex production processes, which blurs the boundaries of jobs and organization units as conventionally conceived.

Advanced technology presents us with a number of opportunities to develop new, more humane organizational forms and jobs leading to a high quality of working life. First, although it poses new problems, highly sophisticated technology possesses an unrecognized flexibility in relation to social systems. There exists an extensive array of configurations of the technology that, within limits, can be designed to suit the social system's needs.

Second, the new technology both increases the dependence of the organization on individuals and groups and requires more individual commitment and autonomous responsibility in the workplace. These requirements for mutual dependence and independence provide opportunities to redress past deep-seated errors in social organization and member's roles. Such opportunities may now be at hand to overcome alienation and provide humanly meaningful work in sociotechnical institutions providing for both organizational needs and for the personal and social needs of those who work (Fromm, 1968; Emery, 1967). The development, over a period of nearly twenty years, of a body of theory concerned with the analysis and design of interacting technological and social systems permits a research-based examination of the organization and job design in complex environments. Advanced technology, and its mismatch with conventional industrial organization, have further stimulated this examination. The diffusion of knowledge about applications of these theories is itself changing the environment of other organizations (Emery and Trist, 1960).

REFERENCES

Archer, J. (1975) "Achieving joint organizational, technical and personal needs: the case of the Sheltered Experiment of Aluminum Casting Team," in L.E. Davis and A.B. Cherns and associates, *Quality of Working Life Cases*. New York: The Free Press.

Babbage, C. (1835) *On the Economy of Machinery and Manufacturers in Reprints of Economic Classics* (1965) New York: Kelly.

Blauner, R. (1964) *Alienation and Freedom*. Chicago: University of Chicago Press.

Bright, J.R. (1958) "Does automation raise skill requirements?" *Harvard Business Review* No. 36 (July):85–98.

Burns, T. and Stalker, G.M. (1961) *The Management of Innovation*. London: Tavistock.

Child, J. (1972) "Organizational structure, environment and performance: the role of strategic choice." *Sociology* (6):1–22.

Child, J. and Mansfield, R. (1972) "Technology, size and organizational structure." *Sociology* (6):369–393.

Cooper, R. (1972) "Man, task and technology." *Human Relations* (25):131–157.

Crossman, E.R.F.W. and Laner, S. (1969) "The impact of technological change on manpower and skill demands: case-study data and policy implications." Berkeley: University of California. Research Document Department of Industrial Engineering (February).

Davis, L.E. (1971) "The coming crisis for production management: technology and organization." *International Journal of Production Research* (9):65–82.

Davis, L.E., Canter, R., and Hoffman, J. (1955) "Current job design criteria." *Journal of Industrial Engineering* (6)2:5–11.

Davis, L.E. and Valfer, E.S. (1966) "Studies in supervisory job design." *Human Relations* (19):4:339–352.

Dubin, R. (1965) "Supervision and productivity: empirical findings and theoretical considerations," in R. Dubin, G.C. Homans, F.C. Mann and D.C. Miller (eds.), Leadership and Productivity. San Francisco: Chandler Publishing Co.

Ellul, J. (1964) *The Technological Society*. New York: Knopf.

Emery, F.E. (1967) "The next thirty years: concepts, methods and anticipations." *Human Relations* (20):199–235.

Emery, F.E. and Trist, E.L. (1960) "Sociotechnical systems," in C. Churchman and M. Verhulst (eds.), *Management Sciences, Models and Techniques*. Vol. II. London: Pergamon.

Englestad, P.H. (1972) "Sociotechnical approach to problems of process control," in L.E. Davis and J.C. Taylor (eds.), *Design of Jobs*. London, Baltimore: Penguin.

Faunce, W.A. (1968) *Problems of an Industrial Society*. New York: McGraw-Hill.

Fromm, E. (1968) *The Revolution of Hope: Toward a Humanized Technology*. New York: Harper & Row.

Goldthorpe, J.H., Lockwood, D., Bechhofer, F., and Platt, J. (1968) *The Affluent Worker: Industrial Attitudes and Behavior*. Cambridge: Cambridge University Press.

Gruenfeld, L.W. and Foltmann, F.F. (1967) "Relationships among supervisor's integration, satisfaction and acceptance of a technological change." *Journal of Applied Psychology* (51):74–77.

Gulowsen, J. (1971) *Selvstyrte Arbeidsgrupper*. Oslo: Tanum.

Harvey, E. (1969) "Technology and the structure of organizations." *American Sociological Review* (33):247–259.

Hazlehurst, R.J., Bradbury, R.J., and Corlett, E.N. (1971) "A comparison of the skills of machinists on numerically controlled and conventional machines." *Occupational Psychology* (43):169–182.

Herbst, P.G. (1962) *Autonomous Group Functioning*. London: Tavistock.

Hulin, C.L. and Blood, M.R. (1968) "Job enlargement, individual differences and worker responses." *Psychological Bulletin* (69):41–55.

I.L.O. (1966) *Automation Abstracts*, 93, no. 2 (February 1966) Geneva.

Mann, F.C. and Hoffman, L.R. (1960) *Automation and the Worker*. New York: Henry Holt and Co.

Mann, F.C. and Williams, L.K. (1962) "Some effects of changing work environment in the office." *Journal of Social Issues* 18(3):90–101.

Marrow, A.J., Bowers, D.G., and Seashore, S.E. (1967) *Management by Participation*. New York: Harper & Row.

Miller, E.J. and Rice, A.K. (1967) *Systems of Organization*. London: Tavistock.

Mumford, E. and Sackman, H. (1975) eds., *Human Choice and Computers*. Amsterdam: North-Holland.

Perrow, C. (1970) *Organizational Analysis: A Sociological View*. Belmont, California: Wadsworth. Also, London: The Tavistock Institute.

Pugh, D.S., Hickson, D.J., Hinings, C.R., Macdonald, K.M., Turner, C., and Lupton, T. (1963) "A conceptual scheme for organizational analysis." *Administrative Science Quarterly* (8):189–315.

Quale, T.U. (1967) *Etterstudier ved NOBØ fabrikker*. Trondheim, Norway: Institute of Industrial and Social Research.

Rice, A.K. (1963) *The Enterprise and Its Environment: A System Theory of Management Organization*. London: Tavistock.

Susman, G.I. (1970) "The concept of status congruence as a basis to predict task allocations in autonomous work groups." *Administrative Science Quarterly* (15):164–175.

(1970) "The impact of automation on work group autonomy and task specialization." *Human Relations* (23):567–577.

(1972) "Worker's responses to job enlargement by location of childhood and current residence." University Park, Pennsylvania: The Pennsylvania State University. Unpublished paper.

Taylor, F.W. (1911) *The Principles of Scientific Management*. New York: Harper & Row.

Taylor, J.C. (1971) "Some effects of technology in organizational change." *Human Relations* (24):105–123.

(1971) *Technology and Planned Organizational Change*. Ann Arbor, Michigan: Institute for Social Research.

Thompson, J.D. (1967) *Organizations in Action*. New York: McGraw-Hill.

Thorsrud, E. (1968) "Industrial democracy project in Norway 1962–1968." Oslo: Work Research Institute. Unpublished paper.

Thorsrud, E. and Emery, F. (1969) *Mot En Ny Bedriftsorganisasjon*. Oslo: Tanum.

Thurley, K.E. and Hamblin, A.C. (1963) *The Supervisor and His Job*. London. H.M.S.O.

Touraine, A., Durand, C., Pecant, D., and Willener, A. (1965) *A Worker's Attitudes to Technical Change*. Paris: O.E.C.D.

Turner, A.N. and Lawrence, P.R. (1965) *Industrial Jobs and the Worker*. Cambridge, Mass.: Harvard University Press.

Walker, C.R. (1957) *Toward the Automatic Factory*. New Haven, Conn.: Yale University Press.

Walker, C.R. and Guest, R.H. (1952) *The Man on the Assembly Line*. Cambridge, Mass.: Harvard University Press.

Wedderburn, D. and Crompton, R. (1972) *Worker's Attitudes and Technology*. Cambridge, England: Cambridge University Press.

Williams, L.K. and Williams, B.C. (1964) "The impact of numerically controlled equipment on factory organization." *California Management Review* 7(2):25–34.

Woodward, J. (1958) *Management and Technology*. London: H.M.S.O.

  (1965) *Industrial Organization. Theory and Practice*. Oxford: Oxford University Press.

14
Job Enlargement: Effects of Culture on Worker Responses
Gerald I. Susman

THEORETICAL AND METHODOLOGICAL ISSUES

Job enlargement, as defined by Hulin and Blood (1968), is "the process of allowing individual workers to determine their own pace (within limits), to serve as their own inspectors by giving them responsibility for quality control, to repair their own mistakes, to be responsible for their own machine set-up and repair, and to attain choice of method." The key issue raised by research on job enlargement, therefore, is whether job satisfaction and/or productivity increase on "enlarged" jobs—that is, jobs which allow workers more discretion and responsibility through redesigned technology, workflow, or increased delegation to the job holder. Ideally, resolving this issue requires evaluation of a worker's response to increased discretion on the same job. In practice, however, the typical methodology compares worker responses across jobs which are similar in all respects except the amount of discretion which they allow.

Although several studies concerned with the effects of job enlargement on undifferentiated worker populations have used one or the other of these methodologies, none of the studies testing for rural-urban differences has. Studies by Turner and Lawrence (1965), Blood and Hulin (1967), and Shepard (1970)

Excerpts from Gerald I. Susman. "Job Enlargement: Effects of Culture on Worker Responses." *Industrial Relations,* vol. 12, 1973, pp. 1-15.

compare workers on jobs from very diverse industrial settings. Although the jobs studied by Turner and Lawrence and Blood and Hulin were rated for differences in discretion (Blood and Hulin used a measure of job skill requirement which was rated by workers only), they compare jobs across industries which are likely to differ in work-flow patterns and in opportunities for promotion and social interaction. Since discretion is likely to vary positively with other industrial conditions attractive to workers, one should be cautious in drawing any conclusions about job enlargement from these studies.

Types of Worker Populations Investigated

Studies by Katzell et al. (1961), Turner and Lawrence, and Blood and Hulin defined rural and urban worker populations only by plant location. This definition, however, begs the question whether current residence influences work attitudes more than the place where primary socialization occurs. Dalton (1947) implies that childhood residence has a stronger influence than plant location on expectations toward work. Turner and Lawrence suggest a number of environmental conditions that may create work alienation among urban workers, but are vague as to whether these are learned in the present work situation or during childhood. The plant location vs. early socialization issue raises questions concerning the pervasiveness of the urban alienation described by Turner and Lawrence and Blood and Hulin. The rapid decline of farming in twentieth century America suggests that a sizeable percentage of middle-aged urban workers were raised in rural communities. If early socialization has a greater influence on work attitudes than place of current employment, alienation among urban workers is less frequent than supposed by the above researchers.

Turner and Lawrence's population was unusual in that the urban sample was 100 per cent Catholic. While it is true that more Catholics live in cities than in rural areas, the relative homogeneity of the urban population in their study limits the generalizability of their findings. The authors acknowledge this after finding that urbans of "mixed ethnic-religious background did not respond in the predicted direction . . . ethnic-religious homogeneity, whether Protestant or Catholic, was prerequisite for any clear response to the task in terms of job satisfaction. Given such cultural homogeneity, the direction of the response was determined by whether the plant was rural or urban" (p. 106). The possibility of other population biases exists also as the authors indicate that their data were collected at plants in both the United States and Canada. Most of the urban plants, it is suspected, were Canadian as the authors state that three of the four companies in urban settings had predominantly French-Canadian work forces. Recent Canadian history suggests that alienation of French-Canadians from values held by the Anglo-Protestant majority is likely the result of sources other than urban residence.

Job Satisfaction as a Measure of Worker Response

Job satisfaction, used by Turner and Lawrence and by Shephard as a measure of worker response to increased discretion, must be cautiously interpreted as it is an omnibus measure resulting from the worker's overall evaluation of his job.

Shepard mentions nine job factors previously listed by Herzberg et al. (1957) (e.g., job security, opportunity for advancement, company satisfaction, wages, intrinsic job aspects, supervision, social aspects of the job, communication, and working conditions) which might influence the relationship between discretion and job satisfaction, but he does not test for them. Turner and Lawrence test most of these as intervening variables but do not test for working conditions (although they collected such data). The present author, however, found Turner and Lawrence's measure of job satisfaction to be highly influenced by working conditions.

SAMPLE AND METHODS

The data analyzed here were collected as part of a large study concerned with worker attitudes in continuous process industries. The industries are petroleum refining, industrial chemicals and plastics, cement, electric power, beverages, gypsum, and glass. Twenty-six plants are included in the study; all but two are in Pennsylvania. Defined by rural (under 50,000 population) or urban population, 11 plants are rural and 15 urban; seven of the latter are located in the greater metropolitan areas of Pittsburgh, Philadelphia, and New York City.

Selection and Rating of Jobs

A questionnaire sent to the industrial engineering department (or their equivalents) of the 26 plants requested a list of jobs that (1) are directly concerned with manufacturing or transforming raw materials into finished goods, (2) do not involve manipulation of the product in any way other than as an operating adjustment to machinery, and (3) include at least 80 per cent machinery monitoring or adjustment activity. Respondents were also asked to classify the jobs by type of control (automatic or manual), type of transformation (continuous or discrete), and continuity of process (batch or nonbatch). The instructions were to classify a job as automatic if at least 50 per cent of all process adjustments under typical operating conditions were done by self-correcting devices, as continuous or discrete depending on whether raw materials were transformed through a continuous flow or by discrete units, and as batch or nonbatch depending on whether product changes which significantly altered job content occurred more or less frequently than once a month. This procedure yielded a set of 127 jobs which can be broken down in three different ways: 106 continuous process and 21 discrete, 82 automatic and 45 manual, or 86 nonbatch and 41 batch. Compared to the studies cited above, these 127 jobs are relatively homogeneous by type of technology and industry, and although differences in job attributes still exist in continuous process industries, the major sources of variance due to technology and industry have been eliminated.

Researchers made on-site ratings of each job on four dimensions mentioned in Hulin and Blood's definition of job enlargement. The dimensions are: (1) methods choice, (2) discretion in task assignments, (3) performance criteria which require direct supervisory observations, and (4) task sequence choice. On-site ratings were also made using Turner and Lawrence's scales for working conditions (e.g., lighting, fumes, temperatures, and cleanliness).[. . .]

Job Attitudes

General job interest was selected as a measure of intrinsic motivation because it has been found to be strongly associated with supervisors' ratings of employees on "concern for doing a good job" and with work attendance (Patchen, 1970).

Pride in job accomplishment was also included as a measure of motivation as it has been shown to be strongly correlated with attendance in a continuous process plant and positively correlated with general job interest.

Shepard developed a measure of instrumental work orientation based on Blauner's (1964) definitions of work alienation. This concept refers to "the pursuit of work as a means of achieving ends outside the work situation. One who is instrumentally oriented toward work does not experience work as intrinsically meaningful" (p. 212).

Situational Factors as Intervening Variables

Data were also collected on the following situational factors so that their influence on the main hypothesis could be evaluated: company satisfaction, management-worker communication, pay, working conditions, degree of automation, process continuity, and type of transformation. The questionnaire included five questions used by Turner and Lawrence to measure company satisfaction and two questions regarding management-worker communication.

The questionnaire requested information on age, seniority, education, length of time on current job, and religion. Pay data were provided for each job by plant management. Finally, procedures for data collection on working conditions, degree of automation, process continuity, and type of transformation have been explained above.

Distribution of Questionnaires

Five hundred sixty-one questionnaires were mailed to the homes of employees listed by plant managers as holding one of the 127 rated jobs. Three hundred twenty-nine (55 per cent) were returned of which 73 were eliminated due to job tenure of less than six months or incomplete responses. The remaining 256 questionnaires were from holders of 101 of the 127 jobs.

Determination of Urban-Rural Populations

Populations were determined by first separating the data by plant location (at 50,000 population) and further dividing them by response to the question, "In what size place did you live while you were from 10 to 20 years old?" Respondents could indicate a farm area, small town (under 5,000), small city (between 5,000 and 75,000), or a city (over 75,000). The urban population criterion for childhood residence was set at 5,000 to coincide with smaller populations during the childhood of workers between 40 and 65 years of age. The resulting sets of workers were: rural bred–rural resident (rurals, N = 77), urban bred–urban resident (urbans, N = 70), rural bred–urban residents (transitionals, N = 84), and urban bred–rural resident (N = 25). The latter group has been excluded from the analysis due to its small size.[. . .]

DISCUSSION

The results of this study do not confirm the hypothesis that only rurals react favorably to job enlargement while urbans react unfavorably. Rurals respond to greater discretion with increased pride in job accomplishment and lower instrumental work orientation. Urbans and transitionals, however, instead of responding unfavorably to job discretion, respond with greater general job interest.

These results also suggest that current residence has a stronger influence on responses to job enlargement than does childhood residence as the responses of urbans and transitionals, who are both current urban residents but differ in childhood background, are similar and the responses of both are different from rurals. Also, current residence does not appear to be a variable strong enough to create opposing responses to job enlargement as has been implied by previous research. Values in urban and rural communities, rather than determining workers' responses to job enlargement, may provide the medium by which workers translate their subjective reactions into terms which are understood and used within that context. Rurals relate to themselves and others their favorable responses to job enlargement in terms of the traditional work values which predominate in their communities; urbans and transitionals living in communities which hold work values more instrumental than those of rurals relate their favorable responses in terms of its direct consequences for boredom or involvement.

The hypothesis that workers of different cultural and individual backgrounds respond differentially to job enlargement is supported here, but it appears that rural and urban birth or residence is too crude a distinction in the American context to expect opposite responses to occur. This was demonstrated by Turner and Lawrence who were unable to find clear-cut differences between groups (using only one measure of worker response to job enlargement) unless they were further differentiated into homogeneous ethnic-religious subgroups. It is likely also that the development of national mass-media over the last three decades has weakened regional sources of attitude formation. Future studies require more refined distinctions between populations with an accompanying theory to predict positive or negative responses to job enlargement.

The question can be raised that, perhaps, the urbans in this study lived in cohesive middle-class communities and not in communities which Blood and Hulin described as "alienating." However, seven of the 15 urban plants were located in large metropolitan areas with a population of at least 1,000,000. Researchers visiting the plants observed that the seven large city plants were located in "inner-city" sections or in areas with deteriorating housing and neighborhoods. Although these observations are not as refined as the indices which Blood and Hulin developed for community integration, they do suggest that the plants were not located in middle-class communities.

A further point can be raised that workers do not necessarily live in the communities in which they work and might live in more cohesive communities than those where the plants are located. This criticism can be applied as well to Blood and Hulin who determined community residence by plant location. While it is possible that some urban workers live in cohesive communities, it is unlikely that enough do so to be the sole explanation for similar positive responses to job enlargement among both the urban and transitional groups.

This study eliminates a primary criticism of previous studies in that it controlled for inter-industry and technological effects. It is not likely that using only continuous-process industries to control for these effects severely limits the generality of these findings as there was broad representation of jobs with different degrees of automation, types of transformation, and process continuity. However, continuous-process industries have several characteristics which lead to initially favorable job attitudes among workers including opportunities for mobility, communications with management, high employee benefits, and job security. It can be speculated that only under good working environments such as these will job enlargement lead to positive worker attitudes. The relationship between discretion and pride in job accomplishment for rural workers only under high company satisfaction lends support to this contention. If this contention is correct, it suggests that positive responses to job enlargement are possible in those industries with good "hygienic factors" and that these are an important prerequisite for a positive worker response to job enlargement.

REFERENCES

Blauner, R. (1964) *Alienation and Freedom*. Chicago: University of Chicago Press.

Blood, M. R. and Hulin, C. L. (1967) "Alienation, Environmental Characteristics, and Worker Responses." *Journal of Applied Psychology,* Vol. 51, pp. 284-290.

Dalton, M. (1947) "Worker Response and Social Background." *Journal of Applied Political Economy,* Vol. 60, pp. 323-332.

Herzberg, F. et al. (1957) *Job Attitudes: Review of Research and Opinion*. Pittsburgh: Psychological Service of Pittsburgh.

Hulin, C. L. and Blood, M. R. (1968) "Job Enlargement, Individual Differences, and Worker Responses." *Psychological Bulletin,* Volume 69, pp. 41-55.

Katzell, R. A., Barrett, R. S., and Parker, T. C. (1961) "Job Satisfaction, Job Performance, and Situational Characteristics." *Journal of Applied Psychology,* Vol. 45, pp. 65-72.

Patchen, M. (1970) *Participation, Achievement, and Involvement on the Job*. Englewood Cliffs, New Jersey: Prentice-Hall.

Shephard, J. M. (1970) "Functional Specialization, Alienation, and Job Satisfaction." *Industrial and Labor Relations Review,* Vol. 33, pp. 207-219.

Turner, A. N. and Lawrence, P. L. (1965) *Industrial Jobs and the Worker*. Cambridge, Mass.: Harvard University.

15
Job Satisfaction and Quality of Working Life: A Reassessment
James C. Taylor

Job satisfaction as a concept has become an embarrassing ambiguity. For many investigators in the social sciences, an interest in job satisfaction frequently represents an interest in quality of working life and industrial humanism, and suggests a concern with improving the experience of people with jobs and work. Since the 1930s this interest has been concerned with monitoring the factory model of work design which has been diffused from manufacturing into the service and clerical sectors. It must be asserted, however, that much of what has passed for job satisfaction research has failed to study the job or the work itself (Davis, 1971). Job satisfaction research has historically been used to either support or attack the status quo—and the trend continues.

The embarrassment with respect to job satisfaction measurement is that surveys of American employees continue to show that extremely high percentages of those measured report "satisfaction" with their jobs, while at the same time the incidence of decreased worker commitment as expressed through increases in absenteeism, strikes (for other reasons than wages), and sabotage of product and plant is high and apparently becoming greater. Increasing public attention has been drawn to these issues of employee alienation. If public concern continues to grow for what is increasingly seen as employees' quiet desperation with work, then the pressures for a reconciliation between these facts and the carefully prepared, rigorous job satisfaction surveys will become inexorable.

The present paper is intended to address this reconciliation not in terms of reducing sampling errors, guarding against response set, or the use of more sophisticated statistical tests of satisfaction data as currently defined and measured, but in terms of a quite different mode of research. In so doing I do not seek to criticize the job satisfaction research per se, but rather to criticize the use of the variable in evaluating and attempting to improve the quality of working life. The particular research model proposed is an action research approach (Lewin, 1946; Davis, 1971)—a model of "democratization of job design" (Elden, 1976; Herbst

Excerpts from James C. Taylor. "Job Satisfaction and Quality of Working Life: A Reassessment." *Journal of Occupational Psychology*, vol. 50, 1977, pp. 243–252.

& Getz, 1975)—in which indicators of what would improve the quality of working life for employees in given work settings are applied with the involvement and commitment and in the language of those concerned.

The issue of what the job satisfaction statistics really mean has been previously approached from several points of view. The debates over unitary versus multiple measures of satisfaction with work has long interested investigators, beginning with the intrinsic versus extrinsic factors studied by Kahn and Morse (1951), and finding a forum most recently in *Work in America* (1973). The present position in that debate urges the use of new specific measures of various job characteristics, increasingly projective measures using hypothetical cases, or otherwise approaching the respondent more cautiously or with indirect questions because direct questions may be too threatening. This debate, although heated, remains largely unresolved, in spite of rigorous and carefully done studies such as the "Survey of Working Conditions, 1970" from the University of Michigan's Institute for Social Research (ISR) which undertook to compare the unitary and additive approaches to job satisfaction scales. In this ISR survey, "JOBSAT '70" (the additive measure) and "Overall Job Satisfaction" (the unitary measure) were found to be related to each other at surprisingly low levels (Herrick and Quinn, 1971).

Some other of the recent job satisfaction discussions totally avoid either definitional or measurement debates in favor of more direct appeals to the underlying social issues. For example, part of the support for industrial humanism has been generated by extrapolating the absolute numbers of American workers presumed reporting dissatisfaction based on the job satisfaction statistics currently available (Rosow, 1974). Using this doughnut vs. hole approach, dissatisfaction is defined as an important social problem because the workers who report displeasure with their work must number in the millions.

In spite of these reconceptualizations the supreme authority on the state of American workers still seems to be the overall percentages from job satisfaction indices. Whether these indices are the crude single item measures taken in Gallup or other national polls, or are the very sophisticated multiple item scales such as those already mentioned, the proportion of workers reporting satisfaction remains inexplicably high. The statistical fact is that, regardless of what degree of measurement sophistication is brought to bear, 80% or more of those Americans surveyed report being satisfied with their jobs. This is true whether the studies use data specific to workers in assembly plants or to national random samples.

A. A. Imberman, of the consulting firm of Imberman and DeForest of Chicago, reported a survey of 3,800 employees in five factories which revealed that 79% to 85% reported satisfaction with assembly line work (1972). Researchers at the Rutgers University Medical School reported that of 576 UAW members interviewed in 1968, 95% were satisfied with their jobs in an auto plant (Siassi, Crocetti, and Spiro, 1974). Although these investigators state that their sample was representative of an insured group of UAW members in a prepaid union health plan in Baltimore, it should be noted that their sample is characterized as white males, averaging 40 years of age, with about 13 years on the job, and earning $9000 or more annually.

These results are consistent with more carefully sampled national surveys reported from time to time. For example, a 1954 national survey of ½ million workers by Science Research Associates (SRA) of Chicago reported 81% of those polled were satisfied with their work. More recently the Gallup organization has reported 87% satisfied in a 1964 poll, and 77% satisfied in 1973. Very recent survey results, reported by the Survey Research Center at ISR, reveal fully 91% of male workers are satisfied with their jobs. These last results are as high as those reported in earlier surveys (which are summarized over the period 1958-73 by Kaplan, 1976).

These different studies all clearly suggest that an overwhelming majority of American workers report satisfaction with their work. These results also show little change (only four percentage points) over the 20-year interval between the boom years 1954-1973. It seems that under the range of most normal circumstances job satisfaction (or the absence of dissatisfaction) ranges from a low of about 79% to a high of 95%.

This pattern receives additional support from the examination of data systematically collected from some 20,000 employees at all levels (nonsupervisory to management) in a variety of different organizations. The Center for Research on the Utilization of Scientific Knowledge (CRUSK) at the University of Michigan collected these data between 1966 and 1970 from some 33 offices and plants in 15 companies nationwide (CRUSK, 1970; Taylor and Bowers, 1972). Although they were not systematically sampled, these organizations differed widely on dimensions like management philosophy, economic condition, as well as size, technology, collar color and the like. Overall, 85% of all 20,000 people reported being satisfied (or more specifically not being dissatisfied) with their jobs, while across these organizations the range of this statistic was quite narrow. An insurance office of 200 people topped the list of 33 organizations with 95% not dissatisfied. A paper mill employing 440 people set the low point among the 33 organizations with 76% reporting no dissatisfaction with their jobs. In spite of not being taken from a scientific sample of American organizations, this range of satisfaction reported is not unlike the national surveys already described. At the same time that we find this overwhelming proportion of employees in all of these very different organizations reporting they are not dissatisfied with the work, we find indications that this reliable measure of job satisfaction is not as highly or as consistently related to grievances, absenteeism, or turnover measures within those organizations as we might expect. Internally, if we are to look at differences among work groups within these organizations the causal relationships between satisfaction and organizational behavior are not very high (Taylor and Bowers, 1972; pp. 77-79, 89). These findings may be explained on the basis that regardless of how well we define work satisfaction and how many careful categories we separate and recombine it into we are still measuring more than perceptions of the work itself. We cannot expect to measure all that is important to workers or to get beyond their internal defenses or expectations with precoded questionnaire measures alone.

Reports of studies recently funded by the National Science Foundation (NSF) on satisfaction and productivity (Srivastra, et al., 1975; Katzell and Yankelovich,

1975) have found that the important link in improving both of these outcomes rests in improvements in a few work related variables. These variables (task variety, information feedback, work related communication among employees, participation in decision making, and technical characteristics of the jobs) are very similar to some of those proposed by other investigators and action researchers seeking to improve quality of working life (e.g., Thorsrud, 1972). Thorsrud however points out that these concepts must be incorporated in job design (for example in recognizing and measuring them) to create a self-fulfilling hypothesis or "Hawthorne Effect" of their own in order to replace the self-fulfilling hypothesis of work design of older industrial models which have shaped their human occupants to expect little learning, little challenge, and little participation on the job. An action research approach to studying job satisfaction has been proposed (Davis, 1971; Thorsrud, 1972) which would break the vicious circle of the existing self-fulfilling hypotheses, currently exemplified by high levels of job satisfaction coupled with absenteeism and other signs of worker distress. Such an approach undertakes building expectations for the sort of job characteristics described in the two NSF studies above as related to both satisfaction and productivity.

Ample evidence exists to support the position that something dramatic is happening to the American work ethic. Persuasive reports such as *Work in America* (1973), and those articles reprinted in *Man Against Work* (Zimpel, 1974) document the rates of negative worker behavior observed during the late 1960's and early 1970's. This includes increased absenteeism and turnover, increased sabotage of product and plant, and a decreasing willingness to accept supervision without question. In spite of a recessionary economy, and the pressures that such a situation places on employees to accept work as given, recent absenteeism rates (especially part-week rates) reported by the Bureau of Labor Statistics show no changes from the high levels of 1971 when worker discontent seemed at its peak. This is in revealing contrast to voluntary turnover figures for the same period which show a marked decline by 1975. Employees are staying with their jobs while the job market is tight, but they continue apparently to take off for long weekends as a way of improving the quality of their lives. Other signs of continued employee response include reports of college educated youth entering corporate positions in greater numbers—but increasingly unwilling to accept the corporate philosophy as given.

The question is no longer whether the reported high levels of job satisfaction make sense, but rather why they don't relate to the other findings noted above. A number of studies based on interviews with workers gives some insight into why employees might report satisfaction in a given situation. A quotation from *Work in America* (cited from George Strauss, cf., p. 14, footnote 32, Chapter I) suggests, as we all know, that we tend to answer idle questions dealing with ourselves or our health in an offhand way. It is simply culturally acceptable to answer "How are you?" or "How's your job?" with the response "Pretty good." Further questioning in Strauss' case revealed that "good" really meant " . . . an O.K. job—about as good as a guy like me might expect." Other descriptions of what a "good job" is results in a whole variety of answers. A personal example of the author's came up in an informal interview with an autoworker who indicated that a "good job" was one where autonomy (even in minute quantity) makes a difference. This man described the job of driving ("hiking") completed cars from the storage yard to railway cars, and transport trailers as a "good job" because he could take work breaks when he wanted them simply by losing ignition keys, discharging batteries, or flooding carburetors in ways that he remained blameless.

It is not merely the richness of such data that is important, although collections like *Working* (Terkel, 1972) surely contribute significantly in that respect, but the fact that talking with workers (at all levels and collar colors) and watching what they do, helps in an important way to explain job satisfaction as a construct by basing the analysis on their own "language." Meissner (1976) has summarized this distinction nicely and from his analysis we can conclude that much will be learned from basing studies on what is communicable by employees in the "Language of Work"; these data cannot be obtained from them by more formal methods presented in an alien form of expression. As Davis (1971) has pointed out, information about values, concerns, fears and ambitions cannot be obtained at arm's length. It is privileged information and as such requires a collaborative and trusting relationship between the worker and the investigator.

The danger is great of assuming at this point that precoded satisfaction measures can be modified into other more understandable or communicable versions, or otherwise smoothed to counter nearly any methodological objection. However attractive this strategy may seem, the variety and nature of the possible internal weakness of these measures are simply too great to use in understanding what can be done for improving quality of working life in a particular setting, or for communicating the state of worker response to that work life to others.

In the following discussion, these weaknesses in precoded instrumentation will be classed as definitional and methodological. The former class notes the differences in treating satisfaction as fulfillment of human needs or wants, while the latter deals with the effects of such problems as changing expectations, unknown norms, alternative goals, and cognitive dissonance between evaluations of self and job.

The definitional argument follows Schwab and Cummings (1970) in distinguishing between defining satisfaction as the fulfillment of "needs" (or innate, unlearned characteristics) versus the fulfillment of "wants" expressed as an attitude towards the job as an object defined by society. The more narrow of the two, the need fulfillment model, ties fixed human needs (such as those in the Maslow hierarchy) to statements of satisfaction with the job as it presumably fulfills them.

The broader model of attitudes toward a variety of specific job activities and characteristics deals with employee likes and dislikes. This definition of satisfaction of wants is more ambiguous because it relies on the fact that we can like or dislike only what is known. We cannot want something (therefore allowing the opportunity for dissatisfaction or frustration) until we know about it or until we know it is available. Expectations of what is "out there" differ with education, exposure to alternatives, and with much more. If two workers hold knowledge about the same aspect or outcome of a job activity, they can still differ one from another in their assessment of the potential availability, and of the importance of these expectations to each of them. In addition, the awesome task of guaranteeing that all aspects of the work place which are potentially important to job occupants are included in precoded measurement makes this want-satisfaction approach even more general and ambiguous than was implied above. In this light, using concepts like attitudes and wants seems to lead investigators not to measures of what work and jobs are like, but more toward the vagaries of what is known or is seen to be available, or to the norms or standards that the respondents to job satisfaction studies bring with them. These issues are methodological, but result from the improper, or at least incomplete definition of satisfaction.

There are other methodological problems in measuring and interpreting measurement of satisfaction as well. Satisfaction can also be seen as a function of one's ability to adjust to a given work situation, or to modify that situation to one's needs. In other words workers may report satisfaction with a job to which they have adjusted their needs or requirements, irrespective of the real quality of that job or of their working life. If these employees see no avenues of escape and if they have made a suitable adjustment, then they could well see their work (whatever it is) as satisfactory. When this kind of adjustment satisfaction is measured, it may or may not be measuring a stable characteristic. A most destructive as well as unstable personal adjustment mechanism is on-the-job drinking or other narcotic use. To the degree that this characteristic is an unstable one, satisfaction is a less reliable measure of quality of working life.

On the other hand, people can adjust jobs and work to suit themselves instead of adjusting themselves to the job. Recent examples of such adjustment range from the harmless or even "helpful" acts of using room deodorizers and incense, or "banking" or "sandbagging" work (to be able to control work pace); to more "negative" acts such as soldiering on the job, and sabotage of product or plant which also represent workers' attempts to modify the job or workplace in order to satisfy some feeling of distress. As illustrated above in the example of the car hiker in the auto plant, a frustrated worker might say that the job is satisfactory or satisfying if he or she can exert some control over the work or workplace, even if that control results in "negative" behavior.

There is a special case of the personal adjustment mechanism. Let us call this methodological issue the problem of cognitive dissonance. We find that the job satisfaction usually increases for people who stay on jobs over a period of time, and is higher for people with longer time in job or grade. For example, job satisfaction where people have held jobs for five to ten years is usually lower than satisfaction with similar jobs in the same organization for people who have held those jobs 15 to 20 years, or longer. This result is frequently explained on the basis that "we become what we do." The longer we spend on a job the more we may come to define ourselves in terms of that job, while at the same time the less likely it is for us to change that job so that we come to identify more with the job and confuse assessments of the job with assessments of ourselves. Therefore if we are asked to report the level of satisfaction for a job, and we have been at that job for a long time, with little chance that we will move from that job, then we are more likely to say that job is satisfactory. To say that it is unsatisfactory or that it is a bad job at that point has more of a direct impact on what we are and what we see ourselves to be.

Methodologically job satisfaction measures are always relative measures. They are an assessment of one's state relative to something else: "I am satisfied with this job because my needs are more fulfilled." "I am satisfied with this job because my wants are properly seen to." "I like this job because this job is better than other jobs I have known, or than other jobs in this plant." "I am satisfied with this job because I have adapted to it and am thereby able to tolerate it better," or, "I like this job because I have changed this job and thereby make it more tolerable." Thus, measures are always implicitly relative to something else. When we use specific satisfaction measures (specific, that is, to particular needs or wants) we can obtain a long list of "satisfaction" with certain elements. We are still measuring each one of those specific questions relative to some norm or standard against which to say it is "satisfactory" or "satisfying"—simply because it is better than something else.

This is in the nature of attitudinal measurement. When we are talking about jobs and work, however, we are talking about certain phenomena that exist in more absolute time and space—something that can be measured in a behavioral way, something for which behaviors are undertaken. Job satisfaction measures, however, are attitudinal rather than behavioral. They are not measures of on-the-job behavior. They are not perceptions of that on-the-job behavior. And in fact they are not even opinions about certain behavioral facts of the job. An opinion is an interpretation or report on facts stated in a way that attitudes come into play. If you like the kind of work you do (an attitude), your opinion of the variety or challenge for this job may be more favorable (because of your attitude in general) than it might be for someone else whose attitude toward that kind of work was lower (that is for someone who disliked it in general). But purely attitudinal measures of general job satisfaction do not even measure this sort of opinion. They are always measuring likes or dislikes of the job generally relative to some unmeasured object or event.

These are not the only limitations to definition or measurement of satisfaction. Meissner (1976) and Davis (1971) have criticized survey measurement schemes more generally in terms of distance of the investigator from the subject whether in terms of social class or personal concern. How much, they ask, can any worker be expected to tell middle class researchers by answering precoded questions framed by the latter? Their implicit answer is that workers cannot tell us as much as they or we would like. A concluding point before leaving the critique itself must include the question not frequently asked—what is the meaning of a survey to a worker who doubts whether the quality of his or her working life can really be improved by such means? One conclusion is that the "offhanded" question of the objective investigator receives the "casual" answer from the respondent.

The argument to be made, it follows, is not for a better measure of job satisfaction even if it could be defined, but for some indicators of what would improve the quality of working life for given workers in given settings. In order to overcome the various methodological limitations described above, measurements should reveal the values of those being measured, should reinforce expectations regarding the ability to change, should provide a wide range of alternatives to present conditions, and should highlight dissonance between self and job to ensure a more human integration between them. To overcome the limitations (namely resistance and suspicion) to the application of those data for improving the quality of working life, questions must be communicable and believable to those involved. Employees and managers alike are cautious in their acceptance of survey results. In order to overcome this caution the product of research should be of interest to all of those involved in organizational change, and not only to other academics or to policy makers. The typical programmatic control in contemporary America is to compare objective data collected against standards in order to punish violators—withholding government funding, or imposing fines are examples. That this approach will find its way into the application of job satisfaction data is a real possibility. Based as it is on such problematic measures, this outlook is embarrassingly like that of "Wonderland" for Alice. Satisfaction data can, and should, be used for improving quality of working life rather than merely establishing its absence or presence. Such data can be used not only for creating improvements in the workplace, but for rewarding and reinforcing those changes, once they are in place.

Survey feedback or its derivatives (Mann, 1957; Bowers and Franklin, 1972) are one method of involving those who are measured by conventional surveys, in the process of analyzing the results of those surveys and designing improvements based on those data. This approach is an authentic development of the action research ideas of Kurt Lewin (1946), and it has been used with considerable success for many years. The respondents are directly involved in making sense of the grouped summaries of their own answers to questions in order to make improvements based on them. In spite of this respondent participation in analysis, certain limitations imposed by the structure of this method serve to make it inappropriate for our purposes as stated above. Because the survey questionnaire is developed in advance by the "experts," it is necessarily narrow in its sampling of items (e.g., employee needs or wants) used to reveal disparities in employee fulfillment. No hope can be held that a questionnaire can include all elements of importance to all employees, either over time or over organizations. Survey feedback, since it relies on initial work group structure for the feedback process, also limits the perspective (if not the opportunities) for alternative organizational structures to be considered. Finally the precoded survey used for analysis is also used for monitoring results of change. Since the survey measures usually remain unmodified (for purposes of comparison) they will not usually be specific enough to a given situation to permit continued reward and support to those involved—to do so these results would need the continued "translation" or interpretation by group members, which cannot always be guaranteed. Unfortunately the reverse is not true and "negative" aspects in the uninterpreted, standardized results can continue to be used as punishment, or worse yet, proof of failure by those elsewhere in the system.

Experience with even more pervasive models of democratizing research measurement is just beginning to accumulate. Although action research models are not uncommon, most have not involved the "subjects" of the research in the measurement. Only isolated examples of employee participation in measurement of satisfaction and quality of working life can be found over the past few years (e.g., Hesseling, 1970; Elden, 1976; Herbst & Getz, 1975; Taylor, 1976). What there is suggests that participation involvement in measurement is not necessarily technically inferior to measurement carried out by experts (Herbst & Getz, 1975).

It is evident that measures designed jointly by managers, workers, and social scientists stand a better chance of measuring such research and action questions as: What is wanted by organizational members? What can the technology be made to do? What kind of social arrangements are needed? and What new systems are people ready for? Such measures, designed and modified for both research and action interests, can also be specifically created to change expectations and to generate their own "Hawthorne Effects" to reward and reinforce the new behaviors. Systematic experience with this degree of "democratized" job and work design is too short to establish the power of such a model for stabilizing change. To observers interested in accounting for discrepancies between high levels of reported job satisfaction, and conflicting signs of worker distress, the model of more collaborative measurement is beginning to replace the use of the "oft told anecdote" or the "passing comment."

REFERENCES

Bowers, D. G. and Franklin, J. L. "Survey-guided Development: Using Human Resources Measurement in Organizational Change." *Journal of Contemporary Business,* 1972, 1, 43-55.

CRUSK, *"Survey of Organizations'* Statistical Standards (All Company Figures): Updated for June 1, 1970." Unpublished paper. Center for Research on the Utilization of Scientific Knowledge, Institute for Social Research, Ann Arbor, Michigan.

Davis, L. E. "Job Satisfaction Research: The Post Industrial View." *Industrial Relations,* 1971, 10, 176-193.

Elden, Max. "Bank Employees Begin to Participate in Studying and Changing Their Organization." A paper presented to the Conference of Workers' Participation at the Shop Floor. Dubrovnik, Yugoslavia, February 1976.

Herbst, P. G. and Getz, I. "Work Organization at a Banking Branch: Toward a Participative Research Technique." Unpublished paper. Oslo: Work Research Institute, Doc. 77/1975.

Herrick, N. Q. and Quinn, R. P. "The Working Conditions Survey As a Source of Social Indicators." *Monthly Labor Review,* 1971 (April), pp. 15-24.

Hesseling, P. "Communication and Organizational Structure in a Large Multinational Company." In G. Heald, ed. (1970) *Approaches to the Study of Organizational Behavior.* London: Tavistock.

Imberman, A. A. "Is It True What They Say About Assembly Line Workers?" Address given before The Industry Convention, Doral Country Club, Miami, Florida, November 10, 1972. Available through Imberman and DeForest, Management Consultants, Chicago, Ill. 60604.

Kahn, R. L. and Morse, N. C. "The Relationship of Productivity to Morale." *Journal of Social Issues,* 1951, 7, 8-17.

Kaplan, H. R. (1976) "Is There an American Work Ethic?" Unpublished Paper, Sociology Department, State University of New York, Buffalo.

Katzell, R. A. and Yankelovich, D. (1975) *"Work, Productivity and Job Satisfaction."* New York: The Psychological Corporation.

Lewin, Kurt. "Action Research and Minority Problems." *Journal of Social Issues,* 1946 (November) 2, pp. 34-46.

Mann, Floyd C. "Studying and Creating Change: A Means to Understanding Social Organization." *Research in Industrial Human Relations.* Industrial Relations Research Association, Publication No. 17, 1957.

Meissner, M. "The Language of Work." In R. Dubin, ed. (1976) *Handbook of Work, Organization and Society.* Chicago: Rand McNally.

Rosow, J., ed. (1974) *The Worker and the Job.* Englewood Cliffs, N.J.: Prentice-Hall.

Schwab. D. P. and Cummings, L. L. "Theories of Performance and Satisfaction: A Review." *Industrial Relations,* 1970, 9, pp. 408-450.

Siassi, I., Crocetti, G., and Spiro, H. R. "Loneliness and Dissatisfaction in a Blue Collar Population." *Archives of General Psychiatry,* 1974, 30, 261-265.

Srivastra, S., et al. (1975) *Job Satisfaction and Productivity.* Cleveland: Department of Organizational Behavior, Case Western Reserve University.

Taylor, J. C. "Employee Participation in Sociotechnical Work System Design." 36th Annual National Meeting of the Academy of Management, Kansas City, Missouri, August, 1976.

Taylor, J. C. and Bowers, D. G. (1972) *Survey of Organizations, A Machine-scored Standardized Questionnaire Instrument.* Ann Arbor: Center for Research on Utilization of Scientific Knowledge, Institute for Social Research.

Thorsrud, E. "Job Design in the Wider Context." In L. E. Davis and J. C. Taylor, eds. (1972) *Design of Jobs.* Harmonsworth, Middlesex: Penguin.

Work in America. Cambridge: M.I.T. Press (1973).

Zimpel, Lloyd. (1974) *Man Against Work.* Grand Rapids, Michigan: Wm. B. Eerdmans Publishing Co.

Part 4

JOB CENTERED STUDIES

Introduction

16. Orthodox
Job Enrichment (1977)
—Frederick I. Herzberg

17. New Leads
in Job Design:
The Philips Case (1977)
—J. Friso den Hertog

INTRODUCTION

Job-centered approaches are at present probably the most popular reforms in work organization. The two papers in Part 4 report the extent of the approaches. The major concepts of job-centered approaches essentially have remained unchanged over the past five years, with the exception of job structuring as described by den Hertog (reading 17). Job-centered approaches share the crucial limitations of not seeking to connect the job to the larger work system and of not taking into their purview technical system variables. These limitations impede the usefulness of job-centered approaches in sophisticated or high technology settings. Even in conventional settings they very frequently render marginal any opportunities for change. The implied basis of job-centered approaches—that the "problems" are located at the worker-job level rather than at the organization structure level or with the design of technical systems—may restrict unnecessarily the opportunities for reforms in work organization.

Herzberg (reading 16) reports on a large-scale application of what he calls "Orthodox Job Enrichment" which is a work motivation program based on his motivation-hygiene theories, and may be recognized as his conventional job enrichment approach.

Den Hertog (reading 17) reports what is probably the most extensive and continuing work reform endeavor in a firm, having begun at Philips in the early 1960s. Although this reform concentrates on jobs, continuous application over the years has led to extension beyond jobs themselves. Work structuring differs significantly from job enrichment by entering into the design of the production process and by the high degree to which workers participate in making changes.

16
Orthodox
Job Enrichment
Frederick I. Herzberg

While productivity is a function of both technology and human motivation, maximum productivity isn't achieved by simply increasing one or the other. Social scientists have written relentlessly about how motivation and productivity are related, but have erred in attempting to manipulate their instruments to produce a relationship that simply does not reflect the psychological and organizational realities of many institutions. A more fruitful task for applied behavioral scientists is to develop programs that provide a link between an individual's satisfaction and productivity on the job. To do so, an optimal balance must be obtained between technology, which includes worker competence—to be efficient—and worker motivation—to be human.

Such a formula has been implemented by an Orthodox Job Enrichment (OJE)[1] program at the Ogden Air Logistics Center (ALC), Hill Air Force Base (AFB), Utah. By taking an approach that concentrated directly on the work itself, the

Excerpts from Frederick I. Herzberg. "Orthodox Job Enrichment." *Defense Management Journal,* vol. 13, no. 2, 1977, pp. 21-27.

[1] Registered trademark, Herzberg and Associates.

project increased productivity, effected significant cost savings, and increased worker satisfaction with their jobs.

HISTORY

In 1973, military commanders like many other managers were searching for the means to accomplish more within the limits of their shrinking resources. Major General Bryce Poe II,[2] then commander of the Ogden ALC, and later his successor, Major General Edmund A. Rafalko, directed the Ogden staff to research and analyze much of the scientific literature, federal and industry programs, and even past Ogden ALC programs for answers to this managerial dilemma. By May, a conceptual plan for developing applications for a motivation enhancement program had been approved. In September, further authorization was given to develop various elements of the program. I was contacted by members of the Ogden ALC staff charged with the development of motivation applications. In January 1974, I agreed to begin implementation of Orthodox Job Enrichment, the work motivation program based upon my motivation-hygiene theory (Herzberg, 1966, 1976), which deductively suggests that productivity is a function of efficient technology and human motivation.[. . .]

The Hill OJE program was initially in conjunction with an Air Force Logistics Command productivity development effort called Pacer Owl. One of the intents of Pacer Owl was to initiate behavioral science experiments to enhance command-wide productivity and then to encourage the proliferation of the successful techniques at each installation. In early 1974, the Commander of Hill AFB, his staff, and members of my staff noted the problems historically incurred in implementing diverse forms of change into an organization. Such changes were often at cross-purposes and placed employees in a double bind. The intent at Ogden was to methodically implement a single, theoretically consistent sequence of management-initiated changes to enhance productivity while simultaneously increasing the humanness of work life at Hill Air Force Base.

KEYMEN TRAINING

In January 1974, an OJE office was set up and training of the first group of 16 management personnel (called keymen) began. Each of the ALC's five directorates named keymen from their organizations to participate in a 3-week training program on motivation-hygiene theory and Orthodox Job Enrichment. The keymen were selected on the basis of current managerial skills, broad knowledge of their organization, and a history of success.

---

[2] Presently Lieutenant General Bryce Poe II is Commander, Air Force Acquisitions Logistics Division, Wright-Patterson Air Force Base, OH.

This training process continued outside the classroom for an additional 8 months and included guidance as the keymen worked on projects assigned by their directorates. This guidance concentrated on two essential aspects of the projects if they were to be successful. The first was avoiding the inclusion of job changes that were either basically of a hygiene nature or would only horizontally load the job. The second major area of guidance was assuring that the keymen were developing appropriate measures of the effectiveness of the job enrichment efforts. The objective was to inaugurate projects that would impact on areas of fragmentary jobs and heavy workload requirements typified by low job satisfaction and low productivity. The keymen operated as internal consultants and coordinators of OJE training in their divisions. To do this, each directorate organized two task groups—one for implementation and the other for coordination.

The implementating group, which generated changes that would create more satisfying jobs, consisted of the supervisor of the job to be enriched and other supervisors from related functional areas. The coordinating group, which served as a review board for the pilot projects, consisted of middle-level managers who borrowed on the expertise of managers from other divisions.

Within this structure the keymen thus catalyzed job changes by helping the supervisors generate the changes and by eliciting support from middle management. In addition, concise overviews were given to an executive review group of upper-level managers so that they were kept well informed and support of the project was generated from the top down.

PILOT PROJECTS

The first 16 keymen selected 11 pilot projects involving distribution, materiel management, personnel, civil engineering, transportation, data automation, procurement, and maintenance. Over 350 direct-labor workers were involved, including mechanics, warehousemen, service people, and a variety of administrative and office personnel.

Auditing the results of these first pilot projects yielded the data in Figure 1. The bulk of investment costs was for salaries paid to keymen and management personnel. The data used to derive the return included materials, fuel, increased units of production, and reduced personnel costs.

In July 1974, Major General Edmund A. Rafalko, Ogden ALC Commander, reviewed the status of the pilot OJE projects. Impressed by what he saw and the enthusiasm of those involved in the projects, he became in his own words "a skeptical believer" and authorized the establishment of an organization designed to accelerate the expansion of success. Thirty full-time positions were staffed by the most qualified personnel available and organized as shown in Figure 2. The number of projects was quickly increased from 11 to 29. Hill AFB estimated that more than 1,000 employees in a wide variety of jobs were directly involved with over 260 managers trained in OJE during the first year.

Figure 1. Return on Investment from OJE

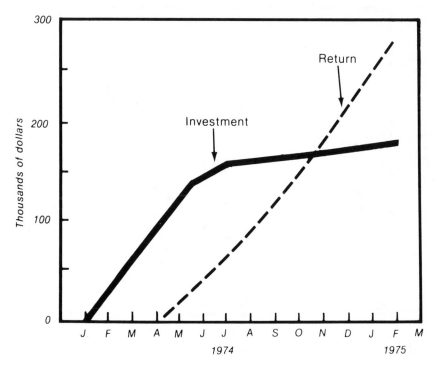

Figure 2.

ORGANIZATION FOR EXPANSION

Commander

Plans and Programs

1 Administrative Keyman
2 Lead Keymen

Herzberg & Associates

	Keymen	Positions
Maintenance	8	7500
Base Commander	9	2600
Distribution	4	2500
Materiel Management	5	2300
Procurement	2	400

Figure 3. Cost-Benefit Analysis of 29 Mature Projects

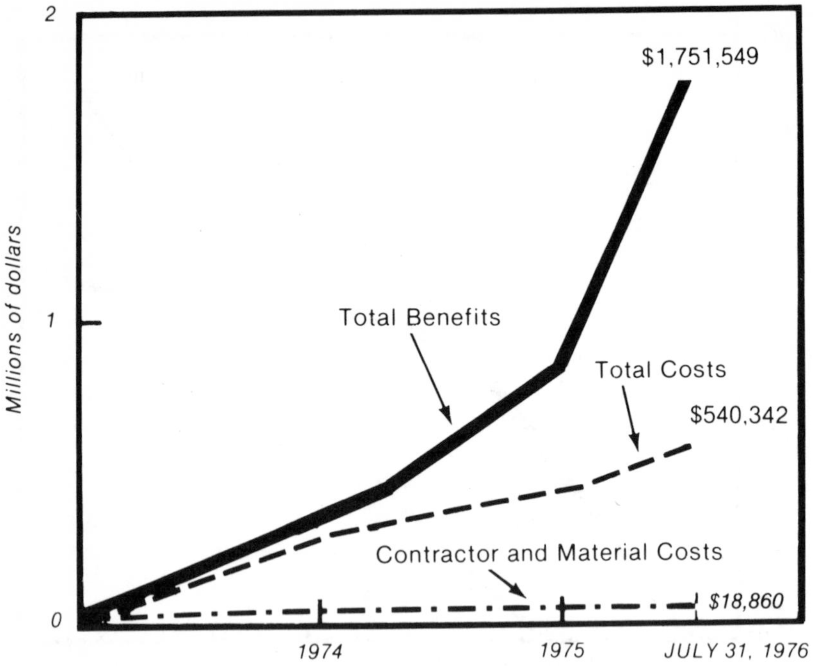

The results were dramatic: a $1.75 million savings in 2 years on 29 projects that had matured to the point where careful auditing of savings was possible (see Figure 3). The dollar benefits accrued from reduced sick leave, a lower rate of personnel turnover, less overtime and rework, a reduction in man-hours, and material savings.

The cost of implementing the 29 OJE projects was some $500,000, over 95 percent of which consisted of one-time expenditures for salaries of keymen during their initial training. Thus, these costs required no increase in the command's budget.

Results of the 29 mature projects turned General Rafalko from a skeptical believer into a skeptical base-wide implementer. To date, OJE techniques have been introduced to 74 different projects at the Ogden facility.

MORALE SURVEYS

The measurement of job attitudes (some of the softer measures of the social scientists) was largely deemphasized during the initial test phases of this project. The Ogden ALC needed hard productivity data to justify its costs, a requirement in line with the OJE perspective that attitudes are the "fallout" of performance, not the reverse.

To measure this fallout in terms of worker attitudes, employees are asked what has changed in the satisfaction they get from their work. Events precipitating change provide the primary data on their satisfactions and dissatisfactions. Unlike rating scales, this sequence-of-events method obtains the significant events from the workers themselves and not from the test items produced by behavioral scientists. Justification of such rating scales has come mainly from the laws of large numbers, with the consequential loss of human meaning and utility in research. Much evidence shows that workers' "ratings" on such scales represent their rationalizations, not their motivation to work (McCormick, 1965).

It was determined that a case study assessment of employee perceptions would furnish qualitative insights into the psychological effects, the long-range mental health benefits, and the potential hazards caused by changes in job design.

Both quantitative and qualitative information were obtained by face-to-face interviews. Interview data from 13 projects that had now been completed showed job-enriched personnel reporting markedly higher job satisfaction than pre-OJE employees (see Figure 4) (Herzberg and Zautra, 1976).

Clearly affected by the OJE efforts were five of the six motivators: achievement, work itself, responsibility, advancement, and growth. That one motivator, recognition for achievement, did not follow the trend and appeared unaffected by the OJE changes was anticipated, because recognition is a low-yield motivator that accompanies hygiene-oriented programs as well as job enrichment efforts.

Thus, there was substantial evidence that the OJE program would continue to provide increased efficiency and improved worker morale. Corroboration of this view came from a visiting team of approximately 50 personnel from the Department of the Navy and a smaller visiting team from an interested major industrial corporation. A study was then made on the efficacy of the process itself, with in-depth interviews being conducted with all the keymen and top executives in each of the directorates.

The survey results confirmed that the essential process was quite workable and had more strengths than anticipated. A particularly desirable outcome revealed in these interviews was that the OJE process was in itself an effective management development medium. The managers began to better comprehend many of the managerial concepts that they had been taught in isolated training programs. Classroom management teaching and "hands on" changes in operations were coalesced by OJE.

The surveys also disclosed many problem areas and barriers that were not too unexpected; these were then fed into the training programs to further enhance the process and eliminate much of the agony that people endure during a rather drastic organizational change. The major problem areas uncovered were proper selection of keymen, a need for a more in-depth understanding of the conceptual framework of OJE by the managers, and the need for less stereotyped views of measurement. With respect to the measurement problems, older "index games" persisted in the minds of many rather than the view that more valuable measures could now be attempted because of new job designs and responsibilities.

Figure 4. How Employees Reported Changes in Job Satisfiers

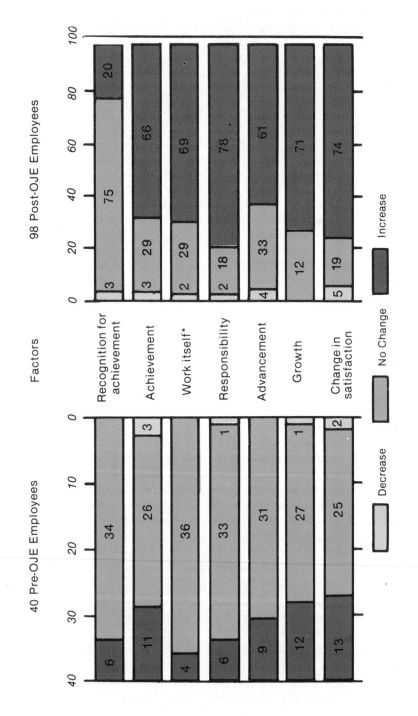

*Two post-OJE employees reported an increase in one type of job and a decrease in another.

Each of the problem areas was followed up by review of the process of keyman selection and a procedure for rotating keymen back to line operations after the completion of their projects. The desire was to expand the OJE concepts by this practice of rotation beyond the realm of an experimental effort to a continuing managerial procedure. Also, follow-up reviews of motivation-hygiene theory and OJE principles were given to appropriate personnel by the central OJE staff. A review of the whole measurement problem was made in order to prevent this problem from being used as an excuse to avoid pursuing agreed-upon job changes.

CONCLUSIONS

Productivity improvement through redesign of work for personal worker satisfaction would seem to be rather restricted in a bureaucratic and authoritarian military setting. The great significance of the Hill AFB project is its validation of the workers' positive response to intrinsically rewarding activity, in spite of all barriers that sophisticated organizational wisdom would suggest.

Also significant is that the Air Force program did not concentrate on eliminating all of the pains that people experience due to working conditions; instead, it concentrated on the development of the talent of Air Force personnel and the opportunity through job enrichment to use that talent. Through OJE the emphasis was on productivity that emanated from the individual's desire to prove to himself his value as a productive human being. The essence of the program is that motivated productivity will lead to increased morale.

Other personnel programs were also facilitated by the OJE concentration on the redesign of work. The minor personnel problems that OJE created in the hygiene area were more than offset by the employees' and managers' better understanding of the hygiene difficulties that beset the military.

APPENDIX*

A detailed look at 4 of the first 11 projects may help illustrate the dynamics of Orthodox Job Enrichment in providing managerial effectiveness. Not all the projects have been unqualified successes, however, and some comments on the problems will also highlight the difficulties in managing change.

Avionics Project

The avionics project is one of the most successful in terms of cost savings, as estimated by the Hill Air Force Base staff. The responsibilities of avionics are to test and repair all navigational equipment on the F-4 aircraft scheduled for maintenance.

---

*These excerpts are taken from Frederick I. Herzberg and Edmund A. Rafalko, "Efficiency in the Military: Cutting Costs with Orthodox Job Enrichment," *Personnel*, November–December 1975 (New York: American Management Association).

TABLE A
OJE CASE STUDY, AVIONICS REPAIR PROJECT

Before OJE	After OJE	Ingredients of a good job involved
Avionics technicians separated into production-line and flight-line groups	Consolidation of flight-line and one-third of production-line technicians	Own expertise, learning function
Flight-line groups corrected all avionics defect	Each avionics technician handles own defects	Personal accountability, responsibility for work
Only flight-line group communicated with pilots	Each avionics technician works with pilot testing his aircraft	Direct feedback, client relationship with pilot

The maintenance activity is separated into three production lines, each with an avionics section followed by a separate avionics flight-test section. Before Orthodox Job Enrichment, the avionics personnel on the production lines checked the 19 navigational systems on their assigned aircraft before flight test and then began work on another aircraft. Any defects found subsequently were analyzed and repaired by flight-test personnel.

Wing-Slat Project

The wing-slat project was concerned with another maintenance function of the F-4 aircraft. This time the work involved a modification of the aircraft as a means of improving its maneuverability. For this particular job, a three-piece steel strip has to be fastened to the bottom side of the aircraft, wing tip to wing tip, with over 600 fasteners.

Before Orthodox Job Enrichment, there were 217 separate tasks, and the work was scheduled by the foreman and checked by him or a quality officer. When a quality error was found, the foreman reassigned the job to another machine. Table B shows the strategy of job redesign. The implementing group, as in avionics, chose one of the four production crews and had the mechanics begin to work directly with quality inspectors. Foremen began checking only some of the aircraft, and any defects in workmanship were the responsibility of the mechanic who made the error. In addition, the total job on an aircraft was assigned to crews, overlapping on shifts, and the crews began scheduling their own work. The result was an increase across the board on the ingredients of a good job.

Warehouseman-Driver Project

The distribution division at Hill Air Force Base provides the supply support for the maintenance of the aircraft and other weapon systems, both on base and worldwide. Yet the executive planning for storage utilization and internal supply

TABLE B
OJE CASE STUDY, SHEET-METAL WING MODIFICATION PROJECT

Before OJE	After OJE	Ingredients of a good job involved
217 separate tasks	1 job	Own expertise, learning function, resource control
No coordination between mechanics at shift change	Crews paired between shifts to facilitate turnover of work	Personal accountability, direct communications
100% foreman inspections	Selected foreman inspections	Direct feedback, personal accountability
No mechanic inspections	Selected mechanic inspections	Scheduling, personal accountability
Quality inspectors worked with foreman	Quality inspectors work with mechanic	Direct feedback, personal accountability, recognition
Foreman scheduled defect work	Mechanic fixes own defects	Learning function, personal accountability

functions is often dependent upon the efficiency of the warehousemen who handle the goods. Because of productivity and quality problems in the warehouse, a pilot project was initiated in the installation equipment division to see how Orthodox Job Enrichment could benefit the supply functions.

Essentially, the job consisted of locating and delivering equipment to other divisions. The warehouseman-driver would receive his orders from a scheduler-planner, find the equipment and deliver it to the customer. Receipts on delivery were handed to an inspector, who then checked to see if they had done their jobs correctly.

The implementing group decided to give more responsibilities to the warehouseman-driver. As Table C shows, the employee was assigned specific customers, allowed to schedule his own work, and given his own vehicle and the responsibility for budget control and maintenance of that vehicle.

Magnetic Tape Library Project

The magnetic tape library supplies all the computers within the Data Automation Branch at Hill Air Force Base, with approximately 41,000 reels in storage. The major problems that made this function a good pilot project was a problem with missing tapes. Several tapes a month would be lost, requiring a slowdown in computer processing and extra time spent on locating or reconstructing those tapes. Somewhere within the tasks of filing, pulling, and erasing tapes, as

TABLE C
OJE CASE STUDY, WAREHOUSEMAN-DRIVER PROJECT

Before OJE	After OJE	Ingredients of a good job involved
Scheduler-planner assigned work	Employees have own customer area of responsibility, schedule own work	Scheduling, client relationship, own expertise
Vehicle usage controlled by scheduler	Employees given responsibility for own vehicle, including maintenance	Personal accountability, resource control
Inspectors checked all work	Training provided in inspection, and some employees carry out own inspection	Learning function, direct feedback

scheduled by the supervisor, the librarians were misplacing tapes. Since the programmers and operators also had access to the library, the librarians could not be held solely accountable.

TABLE D
OJE CASE STUDY, MAGNETIC TAPE LIBRARY PROJECT

Before OJE	After OJE	Ingredients of a good job involved
Separate tasks as assigned	Total systems responsibility, filing accountability	Responsibility, customer relationship, accountability
Pulled tapes and delivered them to meet delivery schedules	Meeting customer demand, scratching, cleaning	Customer relationship
Scratched and cleaned tapes in period-end batches	Individual feedback system on errors —must correct own errors	Feedback

The implementing group, after considerable debate, decided to initiate the changes in the job shown in Table D. The librarians were given more responsibility for each customer order, and they improved location accuracy and followed through with additional quality services.

REFERENCES

Herzberg, F. (1966) *Work and the Nature of Man.* New York: Thomas Crowell Co.

Herzberg, F. (1976) *The Managerial Choice: To Be Efficient and to Be Human.* Illinois: Dow Jones-Irwin.

Herzberg, F. and Zautra, A. (1976) "Orthodox Job Enrichment: Measuring True Quality in Job Satisfaction." *Personnel,* September-October issue, p. 54.

McCormick, E. J. and Tiffin, J. (1965) *Industrial Psychology.* Englewood Cliffs, New Jersey: Prentice-Hall.

17
New Leads
in Job Design:
The Philips Case
J. Friso den Hertog

THE DUTCH CONTEXT

The context in which work structuring has developed in the Netherlands is typical for most western industrialized countries. A central factor in this development is the gap between the qualitative level of work, on one hand, and the rising level of education and, hence, capacities, on the other. Studies conducted within Philips 14 years ago showed that the capacity level of workers in a number of assembly plants as measured by selection tests were out of balance with the very simple level of the jobs offered (Arends, 1964). Recent studies by the Dutch Labour Office (*Nota*, 1975) show that this gap between capacities and possibilities is widening. In a few years, we will have more college and university graduates than unskilled workers, which will result in a rapid change in values and expectations with regard to the quality of life.

Recent survey research in Holland (*Social*, 1976) indicates that in the last 10 years Dutch people have become much more satisfied with their income and the social security laws. However, at the same time, they have become much less satisfied with the quality aspects of life, for example, work and marriage. Thorsrud (1972) states, in this respect, that there has been a shift from the quantitative to qualitative aspects of life.

Changes in the sociotechnical situation accelerate this development. Social security laws make people less dependent upon work organizations because they have more posibilities to withdraw from the work situation. The rising level of absenteeism is one of the negative effects. Hofstede and Kranenburg (1974) conclude on the basis of their research in a large factory in Amsterdam that more and more unemployed people prefer staying unemployed to accepting dull and meaningless work. Very supportive of this conclusion are the outcomes of survey research among Dutch unskilled unemployed and exunemployed (Table 1).

Table 1 shows that (ex)unemployed people are very critical in accepting jobs offered by employment agencies. They would rather accept heavy and dirty work and work around noise than to earn their money working on an assembly line. In production organizations, the effects of the bad fit between the worker and the job become manifest in the rising level of labour turnover, absenteeism and deteriorating work commitment. In this context, programs were established in a number of

Excerpts from J. Friso den Hertog. "The Search for New Leads in Job Design." *Journal of Contemporary Business*, Vol. 6, No. 2, 1977, pp. 49-66.

TABLE 1

PERCENT OF RESPONDENTS WHO WOULD (DEFINITELY) BE PREPARED TO ACCEPT THE TYPES OF WORK LISTED BELOW

Type of Work	Time Registered at Employment Exchange						Total
	0-3 Months		3-6 Months		More than 6 months		
	Ex-employed	Un-employed	Ex-employed	Un-employed	Ex-employed	Un-employed	
Irregular working hours	30	31	35	29	35	33	32
Assembly belt	7	5	8	6	3	7	6
Shift work	20	19	22	18	18	15	6
Heavy work	35	34	41	40	26	30	35
Work in noise or smell	14	14	15	12	16	10	13
Work outside own trade or profession	42	38	38	33	30	45	39
Indoor work	61	63	59	69	66	63	63
Outdoor work	75	69	80	70	73	73	72
Sedentary work	28	39	26	36	27	34	33
Temporary work	32	42	37	53	45	51	43

*Nota Inzake Werkgelegenheid (Den Haag: Dutch Labour Office, 1975).

Dutch companies to improve the quality of working life (QWL). The Dutch government supports these activities by subsidization, which, in 1975, amounted to a sum of $30 million.

In the past, Dutch unions did not play a dominant role in the field of job design. However, today the unions are preparing their own programs.

Work Structuring at Philips

At Philips, the problems just sketched became manifest during the late 1950's and early 1960's. At that time the company was in a period of enormous expansion; pressure on production was high and management became aware of the negative consequences of the growing gap between expectations and capacities, on one hand, and the quality of work offered, on the other. This created the problem of "attracting and holding workers." At the same time, it was becoming clear that the traditional production systems and line/staff relations were limiting the organization's ability to respond adequately to the environmental demands. In this process research on absenteeism, labour turnover and job satisfaction by Philips' Psychology Department played an important role. As a result, a number of organizational renewal projects which differed in scope and content were started in various plants. Work structuring is one of the main areas in which these efforts were undertaken and still are taking place. According to its formal definition, work structuring is aimed at: "The organization of work and work situation in such a way, while efficiency is maintained or improved, job content accords as closely as possible with the capacities and ambitions of the individual employee."

In 1970 the president of Philips pointed out that work structuring was a central element of company policy. In practice, work structuring consists of a set of elements. (See Table 2.) The local production unit has to find for itself the most appropriate form of work structuring. A rough estimate shows that in the last 15 years, some 4,000 people have been involved in approximately 60 projects. In the development of work structuring within Philips, a number of phases can be identified.

First discoveries. In the first phase, projects were started in different places on an incidental basis. They showed that the effectiveness of traditional scientific management approaches could be questioned. A characteristic experiment for this phase is described by van Beek (1964) at length.

Van Beek proposed forming subgroups in a long assembly line ($N = 100$), introducing buffer stocks between the subgroups and integrating the quality control function in the subgroups, which were quite successful; waiting times diminished and quality level and worker morale improved. Like other projects in this phase, it fulfilled the function of "discovery" that there were alternatives beyond the existing system and showed how large the impact of "the human factor" was on the qualitative and quantitative performance of the production system. Finally, these first experiments made clear how useful the contribution of behavioral scientists could be in solving production problems.

The experiments were started upon the initiative of individual production managers and were not based upon a common philosophy or common policy. In

Table 2

ELEMENTS OF WORK STRUCTURING

1. Job enlargement (horizontal load): The work cycle is enlarged by adding more tasks of the same level; the work becomes a module, with a certain identity; the number of people working in a group can be reduced.

2. Job enrichment (vertical load): Job enrichment refers to the qualitative change in the job; work formerly done by the foreman and by people from staff and auxiliary departments are brought to the shop floor.

3. Job rotation: Group members take over each other's jobs for a certain period of time; they learn more tasks and rotate in accordance with a roster or by mutual arrangement.

4. Feedback on quality and output: Inspection of their own work and short feedback loops create conditions in which workers learn; the workers are given an opportunity to see the process as a whole.

5. Small product groups: Production is organized in small stable groups, each making a product that is complete in itself.

6. Job consultation: Job consultation is a very central element of work structuring; once every 2 or 3 weeks the workers and their supervisors meet in groups to discuss the problems of the last period and possibilities for improvement.

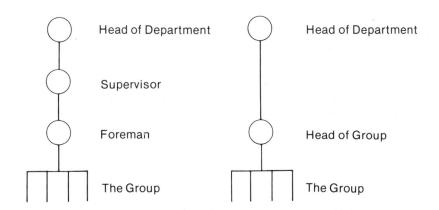

7. Deverticalization: The shortening of the organizational hierarchy makes it possible to delegate responsibility to the production workers. The most usual deverticalization is illustrated above; the head of a group has a supporting rather than a controlling function.

most projects the approach adopted was somewhat limited; only single or a combination of very few work structuring elements were introduced. The emphasis was on factors such as job rotation, formation of smaller groups and abandonment of man- or machine-pacing.

Experimental phase. About 1965 the importance of work structuring became more officially recognized at the corporate level. The initiative of individual production managers was stimulated, and on the level of central staff departments capacity was made for research, consultancy and training. In essence, job design experiments began to flourish.

In the beginning little attention was given to the process of coaching and change; initiative still came from individual department heads and consultants from staff departments. Again, only a few elements were implemented, mostly on a very small scale, and workers had little actual "say" in the project design. At the end of this experimental phase (1968-72), projects became more integrated, coaching and preparation improved and there was more of an effort made to evaluate the projects. Gradually the practical action became more influenced by the theoretical notions and ideas.

The theoretical framework was eclectic in character; ideas from different schools such as the orthodox job enrichment school, the sociotechnical system approach and the organizational development school were included. However, in most cases, work structuring was born out of the practical situation and theory only played a role afterwards in explaining the outcomes and in integrating experiences. Short-cycled assembly work and machine operating were the typical fields for experimentation. Two examples, which are characteristic of this phase, are given below.

Semiautonomous groups in bulb assembly. "Special miniatures" are small bulbs made for special purposes (dashboards, telephones, etc.) in fairly small batches. The production process of these items is partly automated, but the finishing process is performed manually by the workers. In this department, there were many problems, for example, the precalculated production norms were not being achieved and the proportion of rejects was high.

The production process, as a whole, was difficult to control. Workers showed very little interest in the (short-cycled) work itself and in the results of their units. After consultation with representatives of the workers and the management supervisors, management made the decision to experiment with a new setup. The most important elements of the new work system are listed below:

1. Formation of small groups of four instead of fourteen workers
2. Performance of four operations instead of one by every worker
3. Job rotation
4. Elimination of the foreman or "assistant fore(wo)man" supervisor on short production lines
5. Delegation of the foreman's duties to work groups
6. Group consultation
7. Rapid feedback

Both in the economic and the social sense. this program was a success. The proportion of rejects dropped from 9 to 5 percent; productivity increased to 10 percent above the precalculated norms. None of the workers was willing to go back to the old lines, and even people working short distances away from the experimental groups wanted to join the experiment. After the experimental phase, the project was expanded to the whole assembly section of thirty workers.

Integration of functions: operators and setters. This experiment was carried out in a department of a metal parts factory where automatic presses were operated by twenty men. The operators fed in metal strips and the presses stamped or pierced components in large numbers. The operator's tasks were to watch the machine, take samples of the product, supervise the input to the press and take particular care of the dies, which are very expensive. Every operator was in charge of one press.

Once every 24 hours the dies were changed by semi-skilled workers called setters who were recruited from the best operators and learned their job by spending work time with an experienced setter. The status of the setter's job was apparently higher than that of the production workers and operators; flexibility of the department was low because of its highly specialized jobs. Multiple Moment Analysis showed that much time was lost by poor coordination among the operators, setters, quality-controller, foreman and supervisor. Operators often had to wait a long time before the setter could change the die. Management also wondered who would be willing to do this simple work in the future. Enrichment of the operator's job could make it more attractive, and finally it was integrated with the setter's. For this purpose, almost all the operators attended a full-time training course that lasted 6 weeks. At the outset, management had grave doubts about the success of the project. The risk of damage to machines was high and it was not certain that every operator was fit for the new job.

After the job restructuring, waiting times were reduced considerably. Most employees now were operating more than one machine without difficulty, less time was spent on coordination and the quality level remained the same.

Six months after the experiment began all the people involved were interviewed.* The interviews showed that the workers now perceived their jobs as being more interesting, challenging and meaningful. They enjoyed much more freedom to talk and move about; in essence, their work had acquired more importance because it had more responsibility connected with it.

Self-criticism. The year 1972 was a turning point in the development of work structuring. After 10 years of experimentation, there were more and more indications that work structuring was in a very critical phase. The Central Workers Council at Philips started a critical investigation into the diffusion and quality of the projects. They arrived at a conclusion, stated in the following unmistakable terms: "It must be concluded that work structuring has scarcely got off the ground, or not at all, it must not be forgotten that there are people who have expended great efforts in order to achieve something good."

---

* Editors' note: see J. F. den Hertog, *Work, Work System, Work System Design* (Eindhoven: Philips, 1975).

The Council's criticism was directed chiefly at the limited extent of the projects. Only 3.5 percent of Philips' workers in Holland had until than been involved directly in a work structuring project. In a number of very large units, the percentage of involvement had been zero. The Council argued that in the majority of projects, work structuring remained restricted to a small experimental group or section, isolated from the organization around it. A plea was made to approach the organization as a whole and to have "preventive work structuring." This means that in the design of new production systems, new plants and technologies, work structuring criteria had to be considered. The Council also concluded that until then work structuring too often was regarded as a "new technique" or a "standard solution." It was argued that work structuring is not just a set of recipes; rather, it is a constant occupation with mutual relations, communications and arrangement of the work organization. Finally it was noted that the workers themselves were given scarcely any opportunity to exert influence on the design of the programs. The report advocated involvement of workers at the earliest possible moment.

On the central staff level, the awareness grew that the promotion of ideas and the support from the central organization were far from adequate. It was concluded that the central research, promotion and consulting resources should be structured in a more effective and goal-directed way. Self-critical comments also were heard at the local level. In a number of production units, management and staff tried to formulate or to reformulate a work structuring policy.

Current Developments

Since 1972 the search for new leads has become more and more intensive on different levels of the organization. We will discuss some of these current developments briefly.

Social marketing: diffusion from the concern centre. Within the Philips organization the product divisions are, to a large extent, autonomous. Central staff departments, like Central Personnel and the Central Organization Department, have a both supporting and stimulating task in the field of quality of work life. In their relations with product divisions, the link between central activities and local needs is of paramount importance.

Work structuring within Philips is based on a very broad and general philosophy about the relation between the worker and the job. Central in this philosophy is the normative balance between social and technological factors within the organization.

When it comes to concrete action and the development of change programs, the initiative and design, for example, are left to the local units. This means that in practice each project becomes *"customer fit"* because every situation is so different. For the gathering of know-how and the exchange of experiences, this customer-fit approach represents a major problem.

It is very difficult to derive more general notions about work structuring on the basis of case material. Situational variance is one of the barriers. Field experiments and evaluation studies lack a common basis for integrating knowledge and experience.

Broad general and superficial ideas, on one hand, and customer-fit practical projects, on the other, do not form a very solid ground for development of concepts and frameworks that can be useful in practice. There is a need for a level of analysis in between: one that would bundle together the experiences and research for a number of important segments that can be distinguished within the organization—segments with specific problems that call for specific solutions.

A scenario has been worked out to optimize the link between local needs and central ideas and services. Kotler's social marketing approach proved to be a very useful guideline. Social marketing can be defined as

> The design, implementation and control of programs seeking to increase the acceptability of a social idea cause or practice in target groups. It utilizes market segmentation consumer research, concept development, communications, facilitation, incentives and exchange theory to maximize target group response (Kotler, 1975).

The first stage in the scenario has been the differentiation of *"market segments"* on the basis of interviews, literature and analysis of field projects. Segmentation of the market was achieved on the ground of agreement on the three following points:

1. The *pain* in the organization, that is, the problem involved in the relationship between the worker and the work
2. The *therapy,* or the forms of work structuring which are most suitable solutions of certain problems
3. The *roadblocks* encountered when finding solutions.

Segmentation on the basis of these points corresponds to segments in the technology of production (Table 3).

In the second stage, these channels and media for diffusion of ideas and services were developed: (1) the creation of networks of staff and line people, (2) the creation of internal newsletters and publication series and (3) the forming of a consultancy group. In the third stage, research, which we recently have entered, exchange and training programs are set up to tackle specific problems and solutions. The first experiences with this program aspect are very promising.

Approaching the organization as a whole. In a number of plants, management realized that work structuring and related QWL matters do not stand on their own but have to be integrated into planned change of the whole organization. In this respect, the word "organizational renewal" is used; it is aimed toward optimization of the total sociotechnical system.

Programs implemented in three machine and tool factories (600, 300 and 250 employees, respectively) are good illustrations of this approach. Management of these factories was confronted with a number of serious problems: (1) pressure from internal and external clients for higher flexibility, lower prices and shorter delivery times, (2) difficulties in controlling the manufacturing of very complicated, high-technology products which demand high coordination among specialists from different disciplines and crafts and (3) worker dissatisfaction and low commitment. It became clear that the existing functional organizations with their

TABLE 3

MARKET SEGMENTATION AT PHILIPS: A PROVISIONAL ELABORATION

	Type of Technology					
	Mechanical Workshops	Manual Assembly, Small Batch	Manual Assembly in Mass Production of Large Products	Manual Assembly in Mass Production of Small Products	Semimechanized Mass Production	Fully Mechanized (process) Industry
Products (exemp)	Machines, tools	Data and medical systems	White goods	Mixers, shavers	Components, lamps	Fluids, components, lamps
Tasks	Metal work, machine operating	Nonpaced, long-cycled	Paced, short-cycled	(Paced) short-cycled	Materials handling, filling, emptying	Process control, maintenance, setting
Pain	Delivery times, flexibility, worker morale ("the craftman problem") dropping production norms	Control of complex and fast-changing production processes, need for (semi) skilled people scarcely available for this kind of work	Attracting and holding people for unskilled, monotonous work, rigidity of the system, balancing and system losses, quality control, stress on the line	Attracting and holding people for unskilled, monotonous work, rigidity of the system, balancing and system losses, quality control, stress on the line	Attracting and holding people for very short-cycled machine-paced work in shifts, bad ergonomical conditions, process control: the process often calls for high attention and commitment	Disturbances occur suddenly and require fast and adequate interventions, disturbances are hard to predict, attention and commitment often drops rapidly, shiftwork

Therapies	Product lines, integration of work preparation and control in direct tasks,- integration of various metal-cutting jobs in autonomous groups, deverticalization	(Little experience is gathered in this segment) project/ matrix setup, small product groups, test work in assembly groups; no rotation or enlargement of tasks	Abandoning the line by buffers and production "islands" small groups, deverticalization, longer cycle times	Individual assembly jobs, deverticalization, control work in the assembly task supply and transport by production workers	Preventive work structuring: taking into account the autonomy, variety and freedom of the operator already in the design phase, mechanization, integration of setting and maintenance tasks in the operator's job	Integration of control and maintenance functions, deverticalization, preventive work structuring, ergonomics, direct contacts with maintenance, technologists, team-building
Roadblocks (or "key systems," which have to be tackled)	Planning system, job classification, lower management, training	Main emphasis on R & D often leaving little attention for production, which has little autonomy, signals for change remain often under the surface	Materials management, floor space traditional Tayoristic climate	Labour content is often very small	Handling functions primarily left over because they are so difficult to mechanize we lack know-how in preventive work sructuring; often a good relation between manufacturer and machine designer is lacking	Dominance of the technological process, extra training is needed

traditional patterns of management, large-scale operations and high specialization, were badly equipped to meet these problems. The programs were based upon the idea of *factory in the factory,* in which there is an attempt to create relatively autonomous and "complete" subunits within a larger organization, in order to return to the use of small workshops within the larger organization.

The basic elements of these projects were:

1. The creation of *product groups* (different functions are integrated)
2. The transfer of *staff functions* such as work preparation, maintenance or production control to these product groups
3. The formation of *management teams* in each product group (the product group leader now has its own staff of supervisors and specialists)
4. The creation of *semiautonomous groups* of craftsmen within the product groups
5. The redesign of *control systems,* fitted to the new structure
6. The integration of production work and elements of *planning* and *control* (job enrichment) in the craftsman's job
7. The development of a *consultation* structure
8. The shortening of hierarchical lines, or *deverticalization*

These projects are set up in an intensive consultation procedure with craftsmen, staff and line.

Preventive work structuring. Work structuring becomes real the moment the production process enters the design phase. For example, recent developments in a Dutch TV assembly plant reinforce this concept. The factory has a long history in the field of work structuring, and since 1961 a large number of projects have been started. On a micro level these projects have been rather successful, but in 1973 a work structuring project was stopped for planning reasons. The experiment with two semiautonomous groups received enormous attention in the international press. Confronted with the end of this small-scale experiment ($N = 14$), management and staff realized that a new approach was needed because such projects were not easy to implement. In 1973 a middle management task force was formed to create conditions for the implementation of work structuring on a wider scale in the factory. The group made it very clear that the experimental stage was no longer applicable; they preferred taking smaller steps over a broad front to implement far-reaching changes in an isolated corner of the factory. The first decision the group made was to discuss within the group each design for a new production line in terms of work structuring. Second, there was an effort made to tackle the structural conditions for work structuring, such as materials management, layout and production equipment. They worked towards a flexible "building block system," which would allow as much freedom as possible to arrange and rearrange the layout. Recently, in say the last 4 years, much has changed. In addition to a renovated work environment, production groups are much smaller than they were 4 years ago. At that time, there were still color TV lines employing 100 people; now the largest group has only 24 members. Mean cycle times have increased from 3 or 4 minutes to 15 minutes or more. More people are able to work at two or three positions instead of one, and most workers can control their own work pace instead of being only one part of a much larger system. Finally, job consultation has been introduced in almost every group.

The development described herein is situated in a mass assembly environment with a relatively low level of mechanization. In a heavily mechanized environment, the *design* of machines and tools is the central entry for work structuring. Especially in the manufacturing of electronic components and lamps there are many short-cycled, repetitive jobs. On a central level, in 1976 a task force was installed to study how QWL criteria could be introduced in the design process. The task force worked out a plan which consisted of the following elements:

1. Training designers on sociotechnical aspects of the design
2. Developing a routine procedure in the budget inquiry for mechanization projects describing the QWL aspects of the plan
3. Starting pilot studies in large mechanization projects.

Participation. As stated before, one of the critical points in the development of work structuring is the amount of input that workers have in the design and implementation of change programs. In the past, some projects created more room for participation than others. However, on the whole line, having a real say was more of an ideal than a reality. If we look at the present situation, we can see some promising changes. First, there is the development of job consultation on a large scale in the company. In change projects this direct form of consultation between supervisor and work groups is used to involve the workers in the programs. The three change projects in machine factories described above are good examples of projects in which intensive consultation structures were set up to involve the workers in factory redesign. In a limited number of departments, job consultation was the impetus for discussion of the structure of work.

The second trend originated from the consultation on the plant and company levels. In the Dutch Philips organization, each plant has its own Works Council; each product division has its own division Works Council and, on a company level, there is a Central Works Council (totaling 116 Works Councils in the Netherlands). These Works Councils are becoming more and more involved in the issue of work structuring and job consultation. The Central Works Council organized networks of members of local councils in the Netherlands. In this way, there is an attempt to exchange information and understand management policy regarding work structuring matters.[. . .]

REFERENCES

Arends, G. (1964) *Research Note on Labour Turnover*. Eindhoven: Philips.
Hofstede, G. H., and Kranenburg, R. J. (1974) "Work Goals of Migrant Workers." *Human Relations*, Vol. 27, pp. 3-14.

Kotler, P. H. (1975) *Marketing for Non-profit Organizations*. Englewood Cliffs, New Jersey: Prentice-Hall.

Nota inzake Werkgelegenheid (1975). Den Haag: Dutch Labour Office.

Social Cultureel Rapport 1976. Den Haag: Dutch Ministry of Social and Cultural Affairs.

Thorsrud, E. L. (1972) "Job Design in the Wider Context." In L. E. Davis and J. C. Taylor, eds. *Design of Jobs* [first edition]. London: Penguin.

van Beek, H. G. (1964) "The Influence of Assembly Line Organization on Output, Quality and Morale." *Occupational Psychology*, Vol. 38, pp. 161-172.

Part 5

WORK SYSTEMS STUDIES

Introduction

INTRODUCTION

The readings in this section report empirical demonstations of the beneficial effects of designing or redesigning jobs as work roles which are parts of work systems. The analytic concept of *role* rather than *job* reflects the importance of all aspects of the organization, which are viewed as job environment. The first two papers show both the range of applications for which the sociotechnical concept has utility and the means by which technology can be analyzed for organizational and job design purposes.

Davis and Trist (reading 18) review some of the more important studies of work reorganization that apply sociotechnical systems concepts. The studies show the continuing transition from studies of job content to those of role content and from jobs to systems and organizations. The now classic early British studies conducted by the Tavistock Institute are not included simply because they are widely available, but the studies reported by Davis and Trist were strongly influenced by the earlier British developments. These recent empirical studies deal with the emerging issues in development of role designs as part of larger work systems or organization designs: i.e., sophisticated process technology, job design and quality of working life, and organizational change.

Engelstad (reading 19) clarifies sociotechnical systems analysis with a well-developed case study. Specifically, he demonstrates the usefulness of the *matrix of variances* or the *variance analysis matrix* as a potent method for analysis of technical systems for the purpose of organization and job design.

Gulowson (reading 20) contributes to our understanding of autonomous work groups in industrial settings by providing characteristics that distinguish such groups from others.

Björk (reading 21) shows the complexity of the participative process for making changes even in a relatively small work system. The outcomes of this small experiment in work reorganization are exceedingly complex and present difficult evaluation and measurement problems to researchers.

18
Improving the Quality of Working Life: Sociotechnical Case Studies
Louis E. Davis and Eric Trist

Briefly, sociotechnical theory rests on two premises. The first is that in any purposive organization in which men are required to perform activities (when work is to be done and human beings are required as actors in it) the desired output is achieved through the actions of a social as well as a technical system. These systems are so interlocked that the achievement of the output becomes a function of their joint operation. The important concept is "joint," for it is here that the sociotechnical idea departs from more widely held views—those in which the social system is thought to be completely dependent on the technical. "Joint optimization" is also crucial to this theory: It is impossible to optimize for overall performance without seeking to optimize jointly the correlative but independent social and technological systems.

The second premise is that every sociotechnical system is embedded in an environment that is influenced by a culture, its values, and a set of generally acceptable practices. This environment permits certain roles for organizations, groups, and the individuals in them. To understand a work system or an organization, one must understand the environmental forces that are operating on it. This emphasis suggests, correctly, that sociotechnical theory falls within the larger body of "open systems" theories. Stated simply, this means that there is a constant interchange between what goes on in a work system or an organization and what goes on in the environment. The boundaries between the environment and the individual systems are highly permeable. What goes on outside affects what goes on inside. When something significant occurs in the general society, it will inevitably affect the organizations within it. There may be a period of cultural lag, but sooner or later the societal tremor will register on the organizational seismographs.[. . .]

EXPERIMENTS IN TRADITIONAL PRODUCTION METHODS

Primary Work Group Reorganization

The earliest of the long-term, empirical sociotechnical studies began in 1948 (Trist et al., 1963) in an English colliery and continued for ten years. It is unique in that mining technology and physical environment sharply display the effect of organizational design on sociopsychological relations—an effect which in other technologies is frequently masked by compensatory management action. Quite aside from mechanical devices, individual skills, and wage payment systems, the design of the work organization and its effect on all participants stand out as a major factor contributing to system performance and personal satisfaction.

For economic reasons it was necessary to reintroduce longwall working into a particular area of the coal mine under study. For some time, this area had been worked with short faces where "composite" work groups customarily shared all

Excerpts from Louis E. Davis and Eric Trist. "Improving the Quality of Working Life: Sociotechnical Case Studies." In James O'Toole, ed. *Work and the Quality of Life*. MIT Press, 1974, Chapter 11, pp. 246-280.

tasks. Improved roof control made longwalls feasible, but the men did not want to go back to the one-man, one-task jobs traditional on longwalls. While union representatives and management arrived at a settlement regarding wages, the workers arranged a scheme whereby they could share tasks and shifts among themselves. Goals were set for the performance by the overall group of the entire three-shift cycle, and inclusive payments were made to the group for the completion of all the required tasks, plus an incentive for output. Such payment placed responsibility on the entire group for all operations, generating the need for individuals performing different tasks, over interdependent phases of the cycle, to interrelate positively rather than negatively, as they had done under the conventional mode of organization. Equal earnings required equal contributions from the cycle group's members, which led to the spontaneous development of self-directed interchangeability of workers according to need. Interchangeability required multiskilled face workers (which most were from their shortwall experience) and permitted a sharing of the fund of underground skill and identity.

Work was arranged to maintain task continuity. Each shift picked up where the previous shift left off, and when an activity group's main task was done, it redeployed itself to carry on with the next task to prevent "cycle lag." Teams worked out their own systems for rotating tasks and shifts, thereby taking over regulation of deployment and affording the opportunity for equalizing good and bad work times. Each team was large enough so that enough men were available to perform the tasks that arose on the shift.

The autonomous cycle group thus integrated the differentiated activities of longwall mining by internal control through self-regulation. By contrast, the integration practices used in conventional longwall mining were those of indirect external control through specialization of tasks with fixed assignments, wage incentive bargaining for each task, and unsuccessful attempts at direct supervision.

Some objective indicators of the appropriateness of composite organization for longwall mining were positive changes in absence rates, cycle progress, and productivity. Face work puts many stresses on miners, particularly when difficulties arise; changing tasks, shifts, or workplaces helps to reduce these stresses. Table 1 shows the variety of work experience possible under each method of organization. When changing or sharing difficult tasks was not possible (under the old method), there was high withdrawal and absence from work. Table 2 shows the difference in absence rates under the two systems. It may be inferred that absence rates had an effect on cycle progress and productivity, which are shown in tables 3 and 4.

As so frequently happens with innovations before they become "ideas in good currency," the new organizational design did not spread. It threatened existing arrangements by being too productive for unions and requiring management to make radical changes in organizational form and supervision.

Assembly-Line Modification

A manufacturing department producing a line of small plastic medical appliances in a unionized West Coast firm was the setting of the first controlled

TABLE 1. VARIETY OF WORK EXPERIENCE (AVERAGES FOR WHOLE TEAM)

Aspect of Work Experience	Conventional Longwall	Composite Longwall
Main tasks	1.0	3.6
Different shifts	2.0	2.9
Different activity groups	1.0	5.5

Source: E. L. Trist et al., *Organizational Choice* (London: Tavistock, 1963).

TABLE 2. ABSENCE RATES (PERCENTAGE OF POSSIBLE SHIFTS)

Reason for Absence	Conventional Longwall	Composite Longwall
No reason given	4.3	0.4
Sickness and other	8.9	4.6
Accident	6.8	3.2
Total	20.0	8.2

Source: Trist et al., *Organizational Choice.*

TABLE 3. STATE OF CYCLE PROGRESS AT END OF FILLING SHIFT (PERCENTAGE OF CYCLES)

State of Cycle Progress	Conventional Longwall	Composite Longwall
In advance	0	22
Normal	31	73
Lagging	69	5
All cycles	100	100

Source: Trist et al., *Organizational Choice.*

TABLE 4. PRODUCTIVITY AS PERCENTAGE OF ESTIMATED FACE POTENTIAL

	Conventional Longwall	Composite Longwall
Without allowance for haulage system efficiency	67	95
With allowance	78	95

Source: Trist et al., *Organizational Choice.*

experiment on the shop floor to manipulate the configuration of technology (as interpreted in task design and assignment) as jobs (Davis and Canter, 1956). The specific purpose of the experiment was to explore the conditions under which improvement in productivity could be expected from changes in job content. The major criteria used to evaluate the effectiveness of the modifications were quantity and quality of output; worker attitudes and satisfaction were also measured. Modifications were introduced through the department manager. Two experimental job designs were compared with the existing assembly-line job design: (1) Group job design. The conveyor and pacing were eliminated, and workers rotated among nine individual stations using a batch method of assembly. Other conditions were the same as for the existing design. (2) Individual job design. All nine operations, final inspection, and securing of materials were combined into one job and performed by workers at individual work stations.

The experiment showed that greater variety of tasks and responsibility for methods, quality, pacing, and product completion led to higher productivity, quality, and satisfaction. Under the group job design (no pacing by conveyor), the productivity index fell to an average of 89, compared to the assembly-line average of 100, while quality improved. Defects fell from an average of 0.72 percent to 0.49 percent per lot. Under the individual job design, after only six days the average productivity index rose slightly above the original line average. Quality improved fourfold, with defects per lot falling to 0.18 percent.

Interviews with assembly-line workers and a survey of their attitudes and expectations before any changes were introduced indicated that they were satisfied with their jobs, management, and the company and considered the lack of responsibility a positive feature. They were dissatisfied with pacing, the repetitiveness of the work, and the lack of opportunity to do higher-quality work. The identical interviews and survey after individual job design was operating indicated that the same workers were satisfied with their composite jobs and were eager for more responsibility and the opportunity for self-regulation. When asked to compare the composite with the previous assembly-line jobs, they indicated that they would leave the company before going back to the old methods.

Another experiment in assembly-line modification is the enlargement of assembly-line jobs undertaken by a midwestern home laundry manufacturing firm which sought to improve workers' attitudes and increase output and quality (Conant and Kilbridge, 1965). The company felt it might have gone beyond the "optimum" division of labor on its assembly lines, so that increased costs of nonproductive work and line-balance delay exceeded the savings of fractionation. To this company job enlargement meant providing jobs that involved an increased number and variety of tasks, self-determination of pacing, increased responsibility for quality, increased discretion for work methods, and completion of a part or subassembly. For a number of years the company had pursued a deliberate program of transferring work from progressive assembly lines to single-operator work stations; this transfer permitted study of the effects of enlarged jobs on workers' performance and attitudes.

The results indicate that there may indeed be an optimum division of labor on assembly lines. The authors make a case for job enlargement based on reduction of costs of nonproductive work and line-balance delays. Greatly improved quality of output and increased worker satisfaction were obtained—gains perhaps otherwise unobtainable—along with savings in labor costs and greater production flexibility.

Total Departmental Reorganization

The impact of the organizational component of job design on the productivity of work groups is illustrated by a field experiment conducted in a textile plant in India that had recently installed automatic looms (Rice, 1958). The looms had been studied intensively by engineers for the purpose of laying out equipment and assigning work loads based on "careful" time measurements of all of the job components. Yet the new methods failed to produce quantity and quality levels equal to those when nonautomatic looms were used, let alone attain the improvements expected.

The work to be done in a weaving shed containing 240 looms was divided into twelve one-task jobs:

- A weaver tended approximately 30 looms.
- A battery filler served about 50 looms.
- A smash hand tended about 70 looms.
- A gater, cloth carrier, jobber, and assistant jobber were assigned to 112 looms.
- A bobbin carrier, feeler-motion fitter, oiler, sweeper, and humidification fitter were each assigned to 224 looms.

These occupational tasks were highly interdependent. The utmost coordination was required to maintain continuity of production. However, the worker-machine assignments created organizational confusion. Each weaver had to relate to five-eighths of a battery filler, three-eighths of a smash hand, one-fourth of a gater, one-eighth of a bobbin carrier, and so on. The jobbers who carried out on-line maintenance reported to shed management through a separate supervisory channel from weavers, and there were no criteria to establish whose looms should have priority when breakdowns and other trouble occurred.

To meet these problems, internally led work groups were organized so that a single group became responsible for the operation and maintenance of a specific bank of looms. Geographic rather than functional division of the weaving room produced interaction patterns that made for regularity of relationships among individuals with interrelated jobs. They could now be held responsible for the production of their teams. This reorganization was suggested by the workers themselves as the result of discussions held by the social science consultant with them and the shed supervisors and manager. The consolidated loom groups reported to a single shift supervisor who in turn reported to an overall shed manager.

As a result of these changes, efficiency rose from an average of 80 percent to 95 percent, and damage dropped from a mean of 32 percent to 20 percent after sixty working days. In the adjacent part of the weaving shed, where job design changes were not made, efficiency dropped for a while to 70 percent and never rose above 80 percent, while damage continued at an average of 31 percent. The whole shed was then converted, and the improvements were permanently maintained. When it became clear that there was improvement, a way was found to introduce consolidated loom groups throughout the large number of nonautomatic sheds. A third shift, which had been previously resisted by the union, could then be introduced. Within loom groups, status differences were reduced; the less skilled were given opportunities to learn the roles of the more skilled, so that a promotion path was created. Wages were increased as substantially as costs were decreased.

EXPERIMENTS IN NEW PRODUCTION METHODS

The Sheltered Experiment

As a novel and valuable strategy for making changes in existing organizations, the sheltered experiment was developed in the Canadian aluminum industry (Chevalier, 1972; Archer, 1975). The experiment lasted twelve months and was sheltered by agreement from management rules and union contracts so that both parties could see concrete results. A growing number of industrial studies reflect the impact of sophisticated automated technology on organizational structure. The semiprocess technology normally used in continuous aluminum casting generated randomly spaced responses by workers. The sheltered experiment called for the introduction of semiautonomous work crews. Within each crew there was interchangeability of tasks, so that roles became larger than jobs. The crews also assumed responsibility for deciding who would perform a certain task and when it would be performed.

The results were: (1) high satisfaction of workers with new roles and the new skills learned; (2) demonstration of a new organizational form (the self-regulated work team); and (3) increased ability of the work crew to meet emergencies. Production of the casting unit increased 12 percent, and productivity attributable to the experiment showed a net gain of 7 percent. The cost per ton of production was reduced by $2.35 compared to the previous period.

New Technology as an Impetus to New Organization

In addition to the sheltered experiment, another project was carried out in the same Canadian aluminum firm which resulted in the formation of a large number of autonomous work groups to look after some 3000 smelting furnaces (or pots) (Gagnon and Blutot, 1969). The project shows what adaptive social change can accomplish when a new technology essential for cost-effective operation in an intensely competitive worldwide industry renders obsolete the traditional forms of work organization.

The new technology involved the substitution of solid-state in place of mercury arc rectifiers, increasing the amperage in the pots and leading to higher productivity. The higher amperage required a different level of continuous quality control, made possible by the introduction of on-line computers. The greater heat and frequency of certain operations made it necessary to mechanize a large number of tasks of the pot line operation. Control of the traditional French Canadian work force, whose older members were poorly educated and rural in outlook, had been achieved through close external supervision and a rigid hierarchy of narrow one-man jobs. This form of organization could not handle the new technology.

The divisional management was trained in sociotechnical concepts and analysis at UCLA by the authors. This management, in consultation with supervisors and key workers (after agreement with the union), whom they in turn trained, worked out a new form of organization in which primary, internally led groups of six workers were responsible for a line. In addition, there were extensive changes in the service and maintenance departments. Because the new work organization required considerably fewer men and supervisors, acceptance of the plan was not immediate. Alternative employment had to be found for some; early retirement was given to others. Great care had to be exercised since unemployment in the region was high.

A recent communication from the personnel manager states that the new groups have done well, improving during their two years of existence. Quantitative records of the results are still awaited. This and related experiments have led to similar work arrangements in two new fabrication plants and have attracted wide attention in Canada because of the firm's standing as a leading Canadian enterprise.

The Plant as an Evolving Learning System

Continuous development of all workers in a department can be achieved by moving men and groups to a semiautonomous condition as part of a company-wide program, as was demonstrated at an oil refinery in England (Burden, 1975; Hill, 1971). The variety of changes introduced included widespread participation in decision making and the development of new competencies through on- and off-the-job training.

Each machine operator was given a complete subprocess unit to control, including an instrument panel in the main control room. Jobs in the shift teams were flexible, and operators learned each other's units and assisted each other in times of upset. Time clocks were removed, and flexibility of arrival, departure, and time away from work was allowed. (Men were able to make arrangements with the senior operator for competent replacements.) Training was provided in the plant and at a local technical college. Operators covered for each other to take time off for training. Senior operators were given authority to alter plant conditions in order to meet a weekly plan and became able to run the plant safely and efficiently without management intervention.

Everyone participated in planning changes, including redesign of the routing of pipelines. This redesign removed considerable operating problems for the men, and the costs saved paid for the modifications in less than a month. The men were given complete responsibility for test runs and routine testing. As a result, the life of equipment was extended significantly—before repair shutdown and off-plant testing was reduced by 75 percent. Supervisors and foremen had complete discretion about expenditures within the department budget.

The results indicate increased job satisfaction and more effective operations. The sickness-absence rate fell from 5.4 percent to 2.8 percent, and the promotion of senior operators to foremen doubled over the three-year period of the experiment compared to the previous year. Output in the first unit increased by 35 percent and in the finishing unit by 40 percent because of technical improvements suggested within the department. The second and third units, whose outputs limit total plant output, increased by 100 percent because of improvements in manual operations. The entire process plant department achieved a steady operation requiring little management intervention. The men became more satisfied with their jobs and with management.

The Redesign of Maintenance Roles

Modification of job content and of the organization units of general maintenance was undertaken by a West Coast branch plant of a national industrial chemical manufacturing company (Davis and Werling, 1960). Local management was seeking to improve productivity, to eliminate jurisdiction disagreements among various crafts, and to respond to worker demands for more creative activities and opportunities for closer identification with the job. Crucial to the entire undertaking were the presence of a strong industrial union and a long history of mutual trust and respect in union-management relations.

Maintenance crews consisting of broad-spectrum repairmen for general maintenance were assigned to each operating department. Centralized shops, having conventional single-craft jobs, supported the departmental crews by doing work requiring heavy or costly machinery. The jobs of the newly designated maintenance repairmen were enlarged to include general welding, layout and fabrication, pipe fitting, boilermaking, equipment installation, and dynamic machine repair. The additionals skills were acquired by means of a formal on- and off-the-job training program. Jobs were then reclassified and wages increased accordingly. To support the crews, two specialist classifications were introduced. Workers in these classifications performed certain special types of welding and machine repair.

The changes in organization and enlargement of jobs produced positive results in a number of criteria of operational effectiveness: quantity and quality of output, lowered costs, and personal relationships and reactions. Before the changes were initiated, the company's total maintenance labor costs had moved upward, paralleling the national index. After reorganization and job enlargement, the labor costs index fell from 130 to 110 in two years (the index was 100 in 1954), while the national index continued to rise, from 110 to 120. The labor costs of the enlarged group of maintenance repairmen, considered separately, fell from an index of 90 to 65 over the same period. When the index of performance (output divided by direct labor costs) was examined, the production departments showed no change over the period, while the maintenance repairmen showed an increase from 150 to 230.

Total employment in the firm was reduced from an index of 100 to 95. The ratio of complaints about product quality and packaging to orders shipped, an indirect measure of quality, fell from an index of 100 to 55 over the same period.

Workers with enlarged higher-skill jobs were concerned with the importance of their jobs, control over job content and work methods, variety of assignments, special training, responsibility for quality, and performance of preparatory activities. The responses of this group indicate that they were concerned with matters to which management attaches great importance, possibly foreshadowing the development of identity in objectives between management and workers holding enlarged jobs. Workers indicated that they wished to make contributions to improvements in operations. They related company success to their own and their own advancement to better skills and performance. They identified learning of new skills as a positive value of the job and indicated readiness to accept additional duties to help improve their own and group performance.

The Upgrading of Supervisory Roles

It is difficult to design supervisory roles because there are few good models to follow. These jobs are often complicated by the supervisor's conflicting objectives vis-à-vis workers and management and by conflict between the supervisor's management objectives and his superior's. In addition, supervisors are often uncertain about the behavior required for effective leadership, the implied threat to their status and effectiveness inherent in the authoritarian-participation conflict, and the ambiguity that exists over the discharge of their responsibilities. For purposes of designing supervisory jobs, there is a paucity of information and data apart from generalities concerning leadership behavior.

Two modifications in supervisors' jobs were introduced separately into a number of experimental aircraft instrument shops in the U.S. (Davis and Valfer, 1965). (Control shops were selected that parallel these in terms of type of work, style of supervision, worker skills, and past performance.) The changes were undertaken in the industrial facility of a West Coast military aircraft overhaul, repair, and test station. Except for senior executives, all 5900 employees were civilians. The modifications were as follows: (1) *Product responsibility.* The redesigned supervisor's role involved responsibility for all functions required to complete the products processed in the shop. This changed two experimental shops from functional to product organizations, requiring the acquisition of additional knowledge and skills by supervisors and workers. (2) *Quality responsibility.* Inspection was added to the supervisor's functions, including authority for final quality (authority to accept or reject a product). (Some time after the quality control inspectors were withdrawn the supervisors transferred the authority to key workers.)

The objective performance of the supervisors improved. Supervisor behavior became more autonomous and more oriented to the technical problems of producing the product and to worker training. The modifications shortened the quality and process of information feedback loops to workers and concentrated dispersed functional authority. As supervisors moved toward technological aspects of management, giving more time to planning, inspection, control, etc., they had less time to manage the men, who to a much greater extent managed themselves. This change in management style was acceptable to the workers, as judged by their positive attitudes. The attitudes of supervisors were also enhanced in the experimental shops, indicating that the changes satisfied personal needs and helped to develop individuals who were contributing to the organization's viability or health.

IMPROVEMENTS AT THE PROFESSIONAL AND TECHNICAL LEVELS

Complexity and Interface Negotiation

Several of the leading U.S. aerospace firms have made use of behavioral science concepts and methods to improve interpersonal relations, but few have gone on to employ them to change work organization. A recent report, however, describes an action research project in one of the most sophisticated of these firms which took such a step to improve its project and matrix organization (Kingdon, 1973).

The "workers" were engineering analysts (with Ph.D.'s) and computer programmers (with M.S.'s) producing software. The interaction between these two groups was too complex to be managed from outside. Status differences and mutual distrust had to be overcome before it could be managed from inside. Moreover, this could not be fully accomplished until new relations had been worked out with the technical supervisors and heads of the functional departments and with the project manager. This set of relations comprised the "nuclear system."

The high degree of uncertainty characterizing the work and the many unanticipated problems encountered led to crisis management that was prodigal in the expenditure of resources without containing cost overruns.

Key groups were often shut up together for several weeks, working overtime, in a place known as the "bat cave" from which they would emerge only when a critical problem had been solved. Correspondingly, project managers could hire any talent they wanted from other departments or from outside on short notice to catch up after delays. They could then dismiss these men as they were no longer needed. This practice was called the "job shop."

The research showed that these customs could be replaced by regular and open dialogue among all concerned. Group meetings were organized that helped develop a shared "cognitive map" of everything that had to be done, and flexible monitoring was initiated which permitted continuous adaptive planning. In fact, a new type of control system was evolved that increased learning and personal satisfaction, while improving results.

Professional Career Development

A leading U.S. aerospace firm was suffering from large cost overruns and time delays in meeting contract requirements for the design and testing of aerospace devices (Davis, 1970). The nature of the devices (and the contract) called for state-of-the-art design, i.e., invention of new designs along with the use of existing parts or subunits. The firm's management felt the designers were recalcitrant, at worst (or unrealistic perfectionists, at best), spending too much time and money in doing their work.

Analysis determined that these highly skilled and privileged aerospace engineers were rejecting existing designs and proceeding to design *de novo*. In the aerospace industry could they be expected to behave otherwise? Those working in the industry have learned to relate more to the industry as a whole than to the individual firm. As contracts changed, engineers and scientists would move to new contracts, usually in other firms. The crucial aspect in this interim movement is the state-of-the-art capability of the scientists and engineers. This is what the firms are looking for and what makes for the difference in value (and income) of the engineers. It is the touchstone of continued employment.

When management understood the basis of the behavior, a solution that embodied both jobs and career needs was developed. Management began to consider how immediate contract needs could be met for the organization while the individual maintained his state of the art. This was accomplished when immediate work was viewed as an intersection in time between two tracks. The first track consisted of a series of tasks or jobs required by the organization; the second track consisted of experiences that advanced or supported an individual's capabilities. This is the same concept as professional career development, and is, of course, essential to the concept of human resource management.

The career needs of the individual and production needs of the organization were considered jointly. This required that management guarantee, through planning, that an individual has career-advancing assignments soon and frequently, although at any one time he may be engaged in more routine assignments. This program provided a new base for the organization and its members to satisfy their different but related needs.[. . .]

Corporate Strategies for Sociotechnical Change

In the early 1960s the refining side of Shell Oil in Britain experienced severe problems of overmanning, chronic difficulties in labor relations, and increasing management frustration. The company decided to make an all-out effort to bring about changes that would make possible a higher level of motivation and commitment to company objectives on the part of all its employees, leading to an enhanced level of performance. The results of this project have been reported by Paul Hill (1971), who led the internal team that developed and implemented the program (which is still in operation). The following paragraphs are condensed from his summary.

A small team was set up to study the company's long-standing motivation problem on a full-time basis and to propose long-term plans for solving it. A collaborative relationship was established between outside social science resource people from the Tavistock Institute and internal resource people from the company. One result was a considerable transfer of knowledge and skills into the organization.

A document was produced that stated explicitly the objectives the company would work toward and the management philosophy, or values, which would be used to guide decision making in pursuing them. Key features of the document were a reconciliation of the company's economic and social objectives and the adoption of the principle of joint optimization of the social and technical systems.

At a residential off-site conference, the top management team of the company, led by the managing director, committed itself to the objectives and philosophy and to seeking commitment to them throughout the organization. The top management team met under similar circumstances at critical decision points in the program to decide and guide the general course it should take. In order to secure this wider commitment a complex dissemination program was developed. Through numerous conferences at each location, large numbers of employees at all levels were able to test the objectives and philosophy for themselves. The remaining employees had an opportunity to do this at departmental meetings; eventually all the employees in the company were included. The dissemination process was dynamic, not stereotyped. Different methods were tried out, and each location developed programs that were best suited to its own refinery situation. The dissemination process achieved considerable success in securing a widespread understanding of, and commitment to, the company's objectives and philosophy. It also produced quite a number of highly enthusiastic employees. They represented the critical mass who led the process of implementation.

With few exceptions, trade union representatives, both outside officials and internal shop stewards, reacted very favorably to the company's intentions and offered their support. The dissemination program developed new skills in many people and created a climate in the company that permitted and encouraged trying out new ideas. Although not all the experiments fully achieved their purpose, they contributed to the overall learning and development and provided a stepping-stone to the next move forward. An important example of this type of innovation was the setting up of joint management-union working parties, whose new role and new frame of reference were accepted by the majority of the shop stewards and by all of the trade union officials. Although they did not fully complete their tasks, the work they did made a valuable contribution to the productivity bargains that followed.

The outcome of the productivity bargaining, after the expenditure of much time and effort, was also very successful. More important than the content of the bargains—significant as that was—was the manner in which they were decided. Both management and union representatives were dedicated to the bargaining's success and shared to a greater extent than ever before the same frame of reference. The level of participation on the part of the shop stewards in the formulation of the bargains and the level of effective communication with the shop-floor employees was exceptionally high. The result was commitment to the content and the spirit of the deals, not merely a collection of unenforceable agreements. A more general result of the new climate and the new collaborative working relationships between shop stewards and management was a vast improvement in the industrial relations situation at Shell Haven, where they had been exceedingly bad. General morale improved accordingly.

The other major field where innovation took place was in the design of jobs. Here again, partial success in one venture did not stop progress, but led to the start of another. The process was again dynamic. The pilot projects at Stanlow Refinery created great opportunities for learning and indicated good possibilities for improvement in performance levels. The introduction of two simplified methods of analyzing existing systems provided another great learning experience, in which many people in the company were involved. The application of the methods at Stanlow showed good and promising results. As with the earlier pilot projects, they demonstrated how shop-floor employees could contribute significantly to these results. The nine-step method of sociotechnical analysis was also found valuable, both as a training tool and in its practical application in places outside the company.

The largest-scale application of the philosophy was in the design of the social system at Teesport, the new highly automated refinery. The principle of joint optimization of social and technical systems was consciously and carefully applied, with highly successful results. A wide variety of other implementation measures were all undertaken within the framework of the philosophy. They included changes in the staff appraisal system and in manpower planning, job enrichment projects, and so on.

The development program was subjected to many countervailing pressures, some internal (such as the retirement or transfer of key people, both in management and among the resource people), and others external (such as the disruption of crude supplies by war and the pressure felt at the Teesport refinery to regress to old norms).

Local Experimentation

It is often asserted that effective sociotechnical changes cannot be introduced without the commitment of top management. A number of cases demonstrated that this is not always the case. Small changes can get under way in particular departments, the success of these convincing others, until finally top management conducts a review and becomes convinced enough to give them a "blessing." If good results continue, management may then decide to back the new way of doing things as affirmed corporate policy.

A remarkable case of this kind has been reported from Corning Glass Works (Beer and Huse, 1972). One or two innovations in the research and development department of one plant developed from experimental sociotechnical change with the assistance of behavioral scientists. Other departments were impressed with their success and tried out changes for themselves. Since then, widespread corporate support has been obtained for work redesign based on sociotechnical research.

NATIONAL SOCIOTECHNICAL CHANGE

Collaboration between Employers and Unions

The first country to attempt the redesign of work on a nationwide basis is Norway (Emery and Thorsrud, 1969). The program specifically directed at enhancing the quality of working life, the Norwegian Industrial Democracy Project, has given a new dimension to sociotechnical studies by relating them to the crucial questions of value change in society as the postindustrial era is brought nearer by the technologies of the second industrial revolution.

The project began in 1961 and is still proceeding. It grew out of a crisis between the Norwegian Confederation of Employers and the Norwegian Confederation of Labor over a sudden increase in the demand for worker representation on boards of directors of firms, which was proposed as a way of reducing alienation and increasing productivity. It was remarkable that the two confederations (later joined by the government) requested the assistance of social scientists to gain a better understanding of what ordinarily would have been treated as a political problem. A group directed by Einar Thorsrud was established to undertake research relevant to the problems of the two confederations. The group, the Institute of Work Research, drew from the beginning on the Tavistock Institute Human Resources Centre as a collaborating organization.

Another remarkable feature of the project is the extent to which research plans have been drawn up in conjunction with representatives of the sponsoring confederations. This was a necessary condition for success, since the objective could not be limited to undertaking isolated sociotechnical experiments. The purpose was first to secure in the leadership of both sides of Norwegian industry an understanding of the relevance of sociotechnical philosophy of work to problems at the national level, and then to establish the conditions that would allow this philosophy to diffuse throughout Norwegian industry.

The first phase of the project consisted of a field study of what actually happened in the five major firms where workers were represented on the boards of directors. These government owned or partly owned enterprises were obliged by law to have workers' representatives. The results showed that very little happened except at the symbolic and ceremonial level. There was no increase in participation by the rank and file, no decrease in work alienation, no increase in productivity. The overall state of industrial relations being stable within a stable framework of political democracy, little was accomplished simply by adding a workers' representative to the executive board of directors. However, the inclusion of such representatives in trustee boards representing the public interest in Norwegian industry proved invaluable. (A recent law, May 1972, has replaced these boards with bodies exercising wide powers, introducing in all concerns, except the smallest, a political element with consequences impossible to foresee). These results, which were compared with experiences in other countries, were widely discussed in both confederations and in the press. The discussions opened the second phase of the project, to search out ways for securing improved conditions for personal participation in a man's immediate work setting as constituting "a different and perhaps more important basis for the democratization of the work place than the formal systems of representation." This led to the idea of sociotechnical experiments in selected plants in key industries, which, if successful, could serve as demonstration models for diffusion purposes. The selections were made by the members of the two confederations serving on the research committee in consultation with sector committees of the industries concerned. No pains were spared in developing both understanding and acceptance, at all levels, of the experiments in the proposed plants. The plants were selected on the grounds that they were respected organizations which possessed both influence and prestige. They were seen as foreshadowing the future direction of Norwegian industrial development without being too far ahead of the field. To obtain this breadth and depth of sanctioning and centrality of societal positioning was regarded as essential. Its absence in other contexts had prevented the spread of successful innovations.

The first experiment was carried out in the metal-working industry (Thorsrud and Emery, 1970), a sector regarded as critical but one which required considerable rehabilitation. A rather dilapidated wiredrawing plant in a large engineering concern was chosen on the grounds that if improvements could be brought about there they could be brought about anywhere. Productivity increased so much that the experiment was suspended; the workers concerned had begun to take home pay packets in excess of the most skilled workers in the firm. Thus a very large problem had to be sorted out. Although the experiment confirmed earlier findings regarding what could be accomplished when alienation is reduced, it also revealed, for the first time, the magnitude of the constraints embedded in the wage structures and agreements negotiated according to the norms of the prevailing work culture. The difficulty of changing such a structure, which enjoys an enormous historical accumulation, accounted in considerable measure for the failure of earlier pilot experiments to spread.

The second experiment was in the pulp and paper industry (Engelstad, 1970),* also regarded as a critical sector, but where the problem was not so much to upgrade performance with old technologies as to gain control over new ones. The sophisticated chemical pulping department was selected in one paper mill where the basic work was information handling—the core task in the technologies of the second industrial revolution. The requisite skills are perceptual and conceptual; the requisite work organization is capable of handling the complex information flows on which controlling the process depends. To do this requires immense flexibility and capability for self-regulation. In the experimental department a number of key process variances were not being controlled by the social system, nor had some of the most important ones been identified. The research team had to engage those concerned in evolving a form of organization that brought as many of them as possible under the control of the primary work groups. After much resistance and many setbacks, a process of continuous learning was established and maintained as improvements were effected first in one area, then in another.

The model of an action group was established, which consisted of the operators concerned actively using supervisors, specialists, and managers as resources, rather than passively responding to them simply as bosses. This model was then taken up by Norsk Hydro, the largest enterprise in Norway, which manufactures

---

*Editors' Note: See reading 19.

fertilizers, chemicals, and metals for the world market. The model was used first to refashion an old plant and then to develop the entire organization and operating procedures for a new one.

The success of the Norsk Hydro experiments was publicized widely throughout Scandinavia. It marked the beginning of the third phase of the project, which concerned the diffusion process itself. The joint committee that originally sponsored the project was transformed into the National Participation Council, and the new Parliamentary Commission on Industrial Democracy was formed. In Sweden similar developments have recently taken place at the national level, but it will be some time before a critical mass of concrete experience with the new methods can build up. Meanwhile, in Norway, the most significant recent developments have taken place in the shipping industry in the manning of bulk carriers (Herbst, 1975).

Undoubtedly there are features in the culture and the industrial situation of the Scandinavian countries, particularly those of Norway, which have enabled them to act as the world's laboratory in developing a new concept of industrial democracy based on sociotechnical theory. In larger, more authoritarian countries, where the first industrial revolution has left a deeper imprint or the culture is more fragmented, much greater difficulties are to be expected.

The Spread of a Grass-Roots Movement

A remarkable movement involving a new philosophy of work has been spreading in Japanese industry over the last ten years. There is special emphasis on improving product quality by increasing worker involvement and participation in decision making at the shop floor level and encouraging the worker's personal development. This represents a dramatic break with the traditional culture of the Japanese factory and the imported Taylorism which was recently added.

Sony has been a leading exponent of the new philosophy. This company attributes a significant role in its remarkable growth to this philosophy, particularly with reference to the ability of its work force to cope with the rapid technological change in its products. Juran (1967) concludes that "the Japanese are headed for world quality leadership" through the development of these methods, and provides the first account in English of the Quality Control Circle (QCC) movement. QC circles can best be described as groups of workers and foremen who voluntarily meet together to solve shop-oriented production quality problems. John Hird (1971) has published a report of recent QCC experiences and S. Kobayshi (1971) reports the QCC developments at Sony.

The first social innovation is that status in terms of age is in the process of being eliminated. The older generation and the younger generation are beginning to merge into a kind of senior-junior, teacher-pupil relationship performing closely associated jobs in which they assume joint responsibility for the work.

This relationship also extends to the scientist-technician and to people with differing backgrounds and academic disciplines who are brought together to solve problems across technical, business, financial, and political boundaries. In these respects Japanese social structure is beginning to develop into a series of collective partnerships, involving deep relationships and effective teamwork, supported by free-flowing information, responsible judgment, and youthful zeal.

The second social innovation is the mechanism of the teamwork itself. The bulk of the teamwork is carried out through the QC circles, which aim at improving daily work and human relations through what the Japanese describe as the "mutual development of the participants."

Since June 1962, when the first three circles were officially registered with the Union of Japanese Scientists and Engineers, the QCC movement has grown fantastically. The members of the Fourth QC Circle Team that toured the United States in September 1970 reported that there were over 400,000 circles (with over 4,000,000 workers) operating within Japanese industry.[. . .]

The QC circles are active not only when there are particular production quality problems to be solved but continue regularly throughout the year. The QC circles provide for the progressive development of each individual's native intelligence and shrewdness and allow him to gain recognition and prestige for himself through the successes achieved by the group.[. . .]

A recent survey by JUSE has shown that 32 percent of QC meetings take place during working hours and 44 percent outside, while 24 percent meet under both conditions. When meetings take place outside working hours, compensation in various forms is offered in 71 percent of the cases. While 35 percent of the circles meet once a month, 65 percent meet more often; 80 percent of the meetings are for an hour or more (35 percent for two hours or more).

Of 1566 companies surveyed, 1424 (91 percent) were using QC circles. These industries produced chemicals, electronics, textiles, general machinery, wood products, and consumer products. The big driving force behind the QC movement is top management, who have placed heavy emphasis on quality control education at all levels in their companies. (This account is based on Hird's report, which also emphasizes the extent to which the Japanese lay stress on a philosophy of happiness and creativity in work.) [. . .]

CONCLUSIONS

Autonomy, Personal Growth, and Participation

The cases we have reviewed indicate that types of organization structure, management methods, and job content can be developed that lead to cooperation, commitment, learning and growth, ability to change, high work satisfaction, and improved performance. When responsible autonomy, adaptability, variety, and participation are present, they lead to learning and behavior that improve the organization and enhance the quality of working life for the individual.

By autonomy we mean that the content, structure, and organization of jobs is such that individuals or groups performing those jobs can plan, regulate, and control their own work worlds. Autonomy implies a number of things, among which are the need for multiple skills within the individual or within a group organized so it can share an array of tasks; and self-regulation and self-organization, which are radical notions in conventional industrial organizations. Under the principle of self-regulation, only the critical interventions, desired outcomes, and organizational maintenance requirements need to be specified by those *managing,* leaving the remainder to those *doing.* Specifically, situations are provided in which individuals or groups accept responsibility for the cycle of activities required to complete the product or service. They establish the rate, quantity, and quality of output. They organize the content and structure of their jobs, evaluate their own performance, participate in setting goals, and adjust conditions in response to work-system variability.

The studies indicate that when the attributes and characteristics of jobs are such that the individual or group becomes largely autonomous in the working situation, then meaningfulness, satisfaction, and learning increase significantly, as do wide knowledge of processes, identification with the product, commitment to desired action, and responsibility for outcomes. These findings supported the development of a job structure that permitted social interaction among jobholders and communication with peers and supervisors, particularly when the maintenance of continuity of operation was required. Simultaneously, high performance in quantity and quality of product or service outcomes was achieved. This has been demonstrated in such widely different settings as the mining of coal, the maintenance of a chemical refinery, and the manufacture of aircraft instruments.

The content of jobs has to be such that individuals can learn from what is going on around them and can grow, develop, and adjust. Slighted, but not overlooked, is the psychological concept of self-actualization or personal growth, which appears to be central to the development of motivation and commitment through satisfaction of the higher-order intrinsic needs of individuals. The most potent way of satisfying intrinsic needs may well be through job design. Too often jobs in conventional industrial organizations have simply required people to adapt to restricted, fractionated activities, overlooking their enormous capacity to learn and adapt to complexity. (Such jobs also tend to ignore the organization's need for its workers to adapt.) In sophisticated technological settings, the very role of the individual is dependent on his adaptability and commitment. With nobody around at a specific instant to tell him what to do, he must respond to the situation and act as needed. The job is also a setting in which psychic and social growth of the individual should take place. Blocked growth leads to distortions that cost the individual, the organization, and the society. Where the sociotechnical system is designed so that the necessary adaptive behavior is facilitated, positive results in economic performance and personal satisfaction has occurred at all levels in the organization.

Man surely has always known, but only lately has it been demonstrated, that part of what a living organism requires to function effectively is a variety of experiences. If people are to be alert and responsive to their working environments, they need variety in the work situation. Routine and repetitious tasks tend to dissipate the individual. He is there physically, but not in any other way. Psychologists have also studied this phenomenon in various "deprived environments." Adult humans confined to stimulus-free environments begin to hallucinate. Workers may respond to the deprived work situation in much the same way—by disappearing (getting them back is another issue). Variety in industrial work has been the subject of study and controversy for fifty years. Recently, considerable attention has focused on the benefits to the individual and the organization of enlarging jobs to add variety.

Another aspect of the need for variety is less well recognized in the industrial setting today, but will become increasingly important in the emergent sophisticated technological environment. Cyberneticist W. R. Ashby (1960) has described this aspect of variety as a general criterion for intelligent behavior of any kind. To Ashby, adequate adaptation is only possible if an organism already has a stored set of responses of the requisite variety. This implies that in the work situation, where unexpected things can happen, the task content of a job and the training for that job should match this potential variability.

Participation of the individual in the decisions affecting his work, in development of job content and organizational relations, as well as in planning of changes, is fundamental to the outcome of many of the cases. Participation plays a role in learning and growth and permits those affected by changes in their roles and environments to develop assessments of the effects.

Systemic Properties

Beyond these considerations is the total system of work. We notice that in the cases where tasks and activities within jobs fell into meaningful patterns reflecting the interdependence between the individual job and the larger production system, then enhanced performance, satisfaction, and learning took place. In sociotechnical terms, this interdependence is most closely associated with the points at which variance is introduced from one production process into another. When necessary skills, tasks, and information were incorporated into the individual or group jobs, then adjustments could be made to handle error and exceptions within the affected subsystem: failing that, the variances were exported to other interconnecting systems. Conversely, in "deterministic" systems, the layers on layers of supervisors, buttressed by inspectors, utilitymen, repairmen, and so on absorb the variances exported from the workplace.

Implications and Action Requirements

The most important research on the quality of working life has implications for leaders of business and industry, unions, and government. Some of these will not be easily accommodated, for they require fundamental rethinking of the roles of people in organizations and concomitant modification in organizations, management, labor contracts, and government regulations.

Some of the tentative conclusions are directly contrary to cherished beliefs held at all levels of our society. Widely held beliefs cannot be undermined rapidly— another reason for the slow progress to date. The most significant conclusions and implications can be stated as follows:

- Productivity or efficiency versus the quality of working life is in itself an inappropriate concept. Productivity and quality are not opposite ends of a continuum, but are on two different scales. Enhancing one does not necessarily diminish the other. Under appropriate organizational structure and job design, experience shows that the two are directly related, i.e., both increase together.

- Coercive regulation and control by management beget more coercion. Planning and measuring to achieve and maintain coercive or repressive regulation and control of an organization's members trap both management and unions. They are forced into dead-end situations, with no options for developing suitable social or technical organizations. Urgently required are new ways of measuring outcomes where the social system and its members are considered as resources as much as the technical system and its parts are now. At a national as well as company level, the incompleteness of economic theory and supportive accounting systems relegates these concerns to externalities, removing them from organization design and the management decision process. The effect has inhibited considerations of the quality of working life.

- Regarding flexibility of technology, the indicators are that the opposite of technological determinism is the reality. Results of sociotechnical design of factories with sophisticated technology indicate that there is more than enough flexibility on the technological side to suit social system requirements for a high quality of working life. Of course, there are limitations, but the full constraints are not known because almost everywhere engineers are asked to look at and design the technical system independently of any other considerations.

- Self-regulation and control at the workplace through autonomous or semiautonomous jobs and groups yield high levels of satisfaction, self-development, and learning and high performance in output and quality. They form the basis for further organizational design to reduce the repressive and coercive character of organizations and resulting worker alienation.

- In all instances where substantial enhancement of the quality of work life has taken place, it was preceded by a rethinking of management ideology, about how organizations and individuals work. The ideology of the first industrial revolution regarded man as unreliable, unmotivated, and responding only to economic inducements. Men were spare parts in organizations and society. This ideology has had to be reassessed and changed. Though spurred on by the requirements of the second industrial revolution, this reassessment is a slow process and a large undertaking.

Support is required at a nationwide level to produce demonstrations, allow sheltered experiments to take place, and disseminate results. Government should aid in these efforts by supporting a new paradigm for productivity; relaxing (under controlled conditions) wage and hour laws; permitting experiments to be undertaken; providing national social indicators on the quality of working life; and not least, as an employer, beginning to redesign its own organizations.

REFERENCES

Archer, J. (1975) "Achieving Joint Organizational, Technical, and Personal Needs: The Case of the Sheltered Experiment of the Aluminum Casting Team." In L. E. Davis and A. B. Cherns, eds. *The Quality of Working Life: Cases and Commentary*. New York: Free Press, pp. 253-268.

Ashby, W. R. (1960) *Design for a Brain*. New York: Wiley.

Beer, M. and Huse, E. F. (1972) "Systems Approach to Organization Development." *Applied Behavioral Science,* Vol. 8, pp. 79-109.

Burden, D. W. (1975) "Participating Management As a Basis for Improved Quality of Jobs: The Case of Microwax Department, Shell U. K., Ltd." In L. E. Davis and A. B Cherns, eds. *The Quality of Working Life: Cases and Commentary*. New York: Free Press, pp. 201-215.

Conant, E. H. and Kilbridge, M. D. (1965) "An Interdisciplinary Analysis of Job Enlargement: Technology, Costs, and Behavioral Implications." *Industrial and Labor Relations Review,* Vol. 18, p. 377.

Davis, L. E. (1970) "TRW Systems, Design Test Engineering." Unpublished report.

Davis, L. E. and Canter, R. R. (1956) "Job Design Research." *Journal of Industrial Engineering,* Vol. 7, p. 255.

Davis, L. E. and Valfer, E. S. (1965) "Supervisor Job Design." *Ergonomics,* Vol. 8, no. 1.

Davis, L. E. and Werling, R. (1960) "Job Design Factors." *Occupational Psychology,* Vol. 34, p. 109.

Emery, F. E. and Thorsrud, E. (1969) *The Form and Content in Industrial Democracy*. London: Tavistock.

Engelstad, P. H. (1970) *Teknologi og Sosial Forandring pa Arbeidsplassen*. Oslo: Tanum Press.

Gagnon, J. J. and Blutot, E. (1969) "Autonomous Groups in Aluminum Reduction." Unpublished report.

Herbst, P. G. (1975) *Socio-Technical Design*. London: Tavistock.

Hill, P. (1971) *Toward a New Philosophy of Management*. London: Gower Press.

Hird, J. (1971) *Professional Engineer,* December issue.

Juran, J. M. (1967) *Industrial Quality Control*. New York: McGraw-Hill.

Kingdon, D. R. (1973) *Matrix Organization*. London: Tavistock.

Kobayshi, S. (1971) *Creative Management*. New York: American Management Association.

Rice, A. K. (1958) *Productivity and Social Organization: The Ahmedabad Experiment*. London: Tavistock.

Thorsrud, E. and Emery, F. E. (1970) *Mot en Ny Bedriftsorganisasjon*. Oslo: Tanum Press.

Trist, E. L., et al. (1963) *Organizational Choice*. London: Tavistock.

19
Sociotechnical Approach to Problems of Process Control

Per H. Engelstad

SYNOPSIS

The Industrial Democracy Project in Norway is a long-term research sponsored jointly by the Confederation of Employers and the Trades Union Council. The field experiment reported took place in the chemical pulp department of an integrated papermill as one of a series of four experiments carried out in different industrial settings. Extensive task fragmentation and bureaucratization in modern industry have produced widespread feelings of alienation in the work force, owing to an increasing mismatch between technologically based task requirements and human needs. Emerging theories of socio-technical systems, including a list of psychological job requirements, offer a frame of reference for understanding these problems. Previous experience suggests that full commitment to productive aims can be achieved only under conditions that allow for a high level of self-regulation and learning. In process technology (including pulp and paper), the dependence relationships among the state characteristics of the materials form a complex network. In the present case, this resulted in uncontrolled variations being transmitted along the process. Having identified the optimum unit for experimentation, individual jobs were redesigned in order to facilitate group learning, which would permit the work groups to increase their control of the process. Results of the socio-technical analysis before and after the experiment are reported and reference is made to the *variance matrix* technique.

INTRODUCTION

This paper describes a concrete experiment conducted by a team of social scientists in the Hunsfos pulp and paper mill during 1964–67 under the supervision of the author. This is part of the research team's complete program for which Professor Einar Thorsrud (Work Research Institutes, Oslo) and Professor Fred E. Emery (Human Resources Centre, Tavistock Institute of Human Relations, Lon-

Excerpts from Per H. Engelstad. "Socio-technical Approach to Problems of Process Control." In F. Bolam, ed. *Papermaking Systems and their Control,* British Paper and Board Makers Association, 1970.

don) have been responsible. The study is one of the four experiments carried out in different industries under the so-called Industrial Democracy Project, an action research program sponsored jointly by the Norwegian Federation of Employers (NAF) and the Trades Union Council of Norway (LO) (Thorsrud and Emery, 1969).

The primary objective of this program was, through a systematic redesign of jobs, to improve the conditions whereby men could exercise more discretion and have greater influence over their own work situation. To achieve these goals, however, neither party was willing to sacrifice the rising standard of living resulting from economic growth in industry.

Existing evidence indicated that one could reduce the feeling of alienation and release human resources in the company if jobs could be constructed either in accordance with the well-known principle of job enlargement or with the more promising model of partly autonomous work groups. The changes required were expected to be primarily related to the type of technology involved, taking for granted that the changes were in accordance with basic constraints imposed by the psychological needs of job-holders (see the next section and Appendix 1).

The research task was conceived of as twofold. Firstly, to give practical demonstrations of new principles of job design and, secondly, to encourage the diffusion of possible results that were found useful. In the following, we shall confine ourselves to the first task in general and to the experiment at Hunsfos in particular.[1] Consequently, it should be noted that, although this one field experiment might properly illustrate the socio-technical approach as such, a full evaluation of the results achieved by this research program requires the four field experiments to be considered as a whole.[. . .]

THE SOCIO-TECHNICAL APPROACH

Improved production control in industry has hitherto very much been looked upon as a question of finding the best technical solution to the problem, whereas organizational factors were not taken so much into consideration, particularly during the design phase. This takes for granted that people, within their physical capacities, will be able to cope with and adapt to whatever type of task structures and variances they are left with. This procedure has led to a compartmentalization of the organization. Hence, many of the artificial segregations of crafts advocated by the trades unions are also reflections of traditional management practices. To our mind, it appears evident that these procedures must have resulted in sub-optimum solutions for the socio-technical system as a whole, since the reliability of the total system in this case will be decided by its weakest link. It should be noted that, with the general development towards automation, the location and

---

[1] The other field experiments were carried out in a wire-drawing department at Christiania Spigerverk, Oslo, in a department for assembling electrical panels at Nobo, Trondheim and in a fertilizer plant at Norsk Hydro, Porsgrunn.

character of the socio-technical interface will change, though such an interface will always persist at some level of an enterprise. Furthermore, in a period when almost everyone in society receives an increasingly higher education, it appears to be a paradox that the jobs, in particular at the lower levels in industry, still tend to be rigidly delineated, offering little scope for variation, learning and joint problem solving and decision-making.

The socio-technical approach is based on organizational thinking that, within the unavoidable constraints of the technology, encourages as far as possible local initiative and responsible autonomy.

In our terms of reference, enterprises and their subsystems are considered as open socio-technical systems. Hence, like other living systems, they are open to matter–energy–information exchanges with an environment. Without trying to go more deeply into any of the principles that are a consequence of the open system characteristics of the enterprise, the following may be listed as being of particular relevance to the present project.[2]

1. The primary task of a manager is to control the boundary conditions of his unit.
2. The goals of an open system can be understood only as special forms of interdependence between the system and its environment.
3. The goal state has the characteristics of a steady state, which requires (a) a constancy of direction and (b) a tolerable rate of progress.
4. Steady state can be achieved only through leadership and commitment.
5. The basic regulation of open systems is self-regulation.
6. As individuals have open system properties, the enterprise must allow its members a sufficient measure of autonomy.

It is well known that motivations and attitudes of job-holders are decided not only by external rewards and sanctions but also by certain intrinsic characteristics of the tasks. Hence, empirical evidence suggests that workers prefer tasks (Emery, 1959):

1. Of a substantial degree of wholeness (that is, which shows a strong *gestalt*).
2. Where the individual has control over the materials and the processes involved.

These requirements have been further translated into a set of psychological job requirements (Appendix 1).

The co-existence of a social and a technical system involves a coupling of two part-systems, each independently governed by its own laws, towards a common goal. As the contributions of these systems are essentially complementary, special attention must be paid to the interdependence between them.

---

[2] For a condensed presentation of the principles of systems theory referred to, see the Introduction in Emery (ed.) (1969).

The two systems are primarily coupled through the reciprocal allocation of tasks to work roles, each of which is able to form systems of a higher order. Existing evidence shows that, when units' tasks were small, job enlargement has been a useful organizational model (Thorsrud and Emery, 1969). In the English coal mines, where a number of tasks exceeded the one man/one shift unit, it appeared that technological requirements as well as human needs could be adequately met by an autonomous work group (Herbst, 1962; Trist, Higgin, Murray and Pollock, 1963). The same principles of job design have later been applied also in the textile industry (Rice, 1958). In these cases, the problem of identifying naturally bounded areas (in the sense that they had a high potential for self-regulation) was relatively easy. This task is considerably more difficult in an integrated pulp and paper technology where:

1. The dependence relationships of process variables form a complex network along the process.
2. The continuity of production, the level of throughput and the restricted buffer capacities in the process, to be effective, require that the disturbance control sequences be operated at appropriate speeds.

In order to identify units that would optimally meet these requirements, a method of analysis based on task structure has been developed. The so-called *matrix of variances,* which is based on the dependence relationship between state characteristics of the material, has been useful in identifying natural clusters of variances that are to be allocated within the same organizational unit (Appendix 2).

Finally, conditions for self-regulation can be improved by various changes in the social and the technical systems. This is best illustrated by our case material.

HUNSFOS PULP AND PAPERMILL

This account is an abstracted and rewritten version of a much more detailed report on the Hunsfos experiment, 1964–5, written for another purpose (Engelstad, Emery and Thorsrud, 1969). Further reference to this report will not be made in the following.

The Hunsfos mill is situated in a small community, about ten miles north of the industrial seaport of Kristiansand, in the very south of Norway. The rural surroundings as well as the tidiness of the workplaces contribute to the general impression of a friendly atmosphere when one is visiting the site.

Since the end of the last century, the company has been the major employer in the community and, even in 1963, employed almost 50 percent of its adult male working population. About 80 percent of the Hunsfos labor force of 900–1000 had close links with the community and the mill through their families, often employed by Hunsfos for three generations. The personal relationships at work are stable and closely linked to the religious, political and economic life of the community. The workers and foremen have been recruited mainly from the local district; the managers and most of the technical staff have moved in from other parts of the country. Hunsfos has a strongly professional management, respected both within the industry and within the plant, also a local union leadership with effective working relations with the central union headquarters in Oslo.

The company is one of five integrated papermills in Norway that offer the full range of the major technologies—mechanical pulping, chemical pulping and papermaking. Of the approximate total of 80 mills in the country, Hunsfos ranks fifth in terms of total sales. In 1964, the mill converted 200,000 m³ of timber to 20,000 tons of mechnical woodpulp and 34,000 tons of chemical pulp. This again resulted in a total output of 65,000 tons of paper. The production covers a wide range of qualities within the sectors of magazine, packaging and fine papers. Total sales, of which 85 percent were exported, came close to 80 million N.Cr.

The economic situation of the pulp and paper industries in Norway has been difficult for years, and Hunsfos during the last ten years, in order to meet the challenge, has carried out two large reconstructions and investment programs.

In 1959, the company, as the first one in Europe, introduced the magnesium bisulphite process in order economically to exploit the firs and hardwoods that, combined, are more prevalent than spruce in the south of Norway. Soon afterwards, fully continuous running, based on a four-shift schedule, was introduced to maximize plant utilization. A number of technical improvements have been effected, including the reconstruction of some of the paper-machines. This has allowed the company gradually to change its paper grades toward qualities of a higher converting value.

SELECTION OF THE CHEMICAL PULP DEPARTMENT FOR EXPERIMENTING

In September 1964, the management and the trades union at Hunsfos agreed to have the research team find a suitable area in the plant to introduce new principles of job design experimentally. From a research point of view, sites would be acceptable only in so far as they would have:

1. Process technology characteristics.
2. A high potential for diffusing possible results to the company as a whole.

Initially, this left us a choice among wood preparation, mechanical and chemical pulping, stock preparation and papermachines. Interviews with employees covering all levels of responsibility in these areas of production provided a detailed picture of the role system and how the technical interdependencies were coped with by role interrelations. The attitudes expressed by the employees were taken as clues to the fit or lack of fit of the social and technical systems.

A matrix of variances, based on the dependence relationships between state characteristics of the materials in different parts of the process, was constructed in close cooperation with some of the process technologists. Our focal concern, unlike that of the design engineer, however, was with those variances arising from the technical system that required responses from the organization of individuals if the production goals were to be achieved. The matrix helped us to identify where these variances arose in the technological process and where in the subsequent stages of production they could be identified, communicated or acted upon. The matrix was worked out in close cooperation with technologists in the company. Our analysis also entailed working over historical records of plant operations, estimating cost/benefit ratios for possible changes in different parts of the mill and collecting labor force statistics that would indicate social costs incurred by different departments.

It was agreed to start the experiment in the chemical pulp department. Taking into consideration such factors as the dependence structure of the variances in the materials, the spatio-temporal aspects of the process, potential input/output measurements and certain variables in the social system, this department appeared to be a naturally bounded socio-technical unit with a relatively high potential for self-regulation. It appeared also to be an optimum choice, because:

1. The department showed an opening for significant improvement in that some of the variances in the timber, if not coped with in the chemical pulping, could be met in the papermaking only by downgrading the quality (and economic value) of the paper. (To a much lesser extent, mechanical pulping had the same effect.)
2. Located in between the wood preparation and the papermill, changes in the mode of chemical pulp operations would exert maximum leverage on these parts.
3. Local leadership on the management as well as on the union side appeared to be sufficiently capable and willing. This we expected would offset the resistance to change that might be expected from the senior operators (ten out of fifteen of whom were over fifty years of age) and from some of the men who were apt to stick to their viewpoints or to seek isolation.

TASKS ARISING FROM THE TECHNICAL SYSTEM

The Chemical Pulp Process

I shall describe only those aspects of the technology that were found to be of particular importance for this experiment.

The technical system of the chemical pulp department consists of five converting processes carried out in different, but adjacent areas—boiling, screening and bleaching and the preparation of boiling acid and of bleaching liquids. Chips of spruce, fir and hardwood are boiled separately in large digesters with acid magnesium bisulphite. (In the wood, the two major components of lignin and cellulose form a rigid three-dimensional structure.) Under the right conditions of acid concentration, temperature, pressure, time, etc., the lignin is dissolved and the cellulose fibres are released. The fibres, together with other undissolved material, are washed and prepared for further separation in the screening section; the lignin and the used boiling liquid go to waste.

Fresh acid magnesium bisulphite is drawn from a buffer tank, to which acid is continuously fed after it has been prepared from magnesium oxide and sulphur dioxide in a separate section.

A complex system of screens raises the homogeneity and purity of the fibres by removing unboiled wood particles (knots, splinters, etc.), small fibre fragments (fines), as well as sand, bark, resin and other impurities. From the screening section, the spruce pulp goes to buffer storages as unbleached pulp, whereas the fir and hard wood are transferred to the bleaching floor.

The bleaching liquid, prepared from chlorine and sodium hydroxide in a separate section, is used mainly to dissolve residual lignin still attached to the fibres and coloring them. The three pulps together with the mechanical woodpulp constitute the major imputs to the papermill.

Variances in the Technical System

The following groups of variances arising from the system's technology were of particular relevance to be controlled by the social system:

1. The use of fir as one of the raw materials had led to serious pitch problems, which were only partly brought under control. Whenever sticky resin accumulated on the screens or in the bleaching equipment, extensive cleaning was required.
2. Since the growing and storage conditions of the timber vary a great deal, some of these input variances would be transmitted along with the flow of materials and, if not controlled, would reduce the paper quality.
3. The conversion of spruce, fir and hardwood batches in the same equipment induced additional variances, owing to pitch contamination one with the other and the mixing of fibres of different wood species.
4. The variances resulting from mechanical breakdowns had been extreme during the period after the introduction of the bisulphite method, but, by 1965, they had been reduced to a near-normal level.

Key Characteristics of Operator Tasks

These are:

1. The individual part-processes were by themselves relatively complex and demanding. Spatially separate from each other, the present level of their performance could be sustained with a limited number of contacts with other areas. Hence, they appeared to form a strong *gestalt* by themselves.
2. In addition to the cluster of internal interdependencies, however, a number of important relationships still existed between the part-processes and across shifts. For example, the boiling and the bleaching

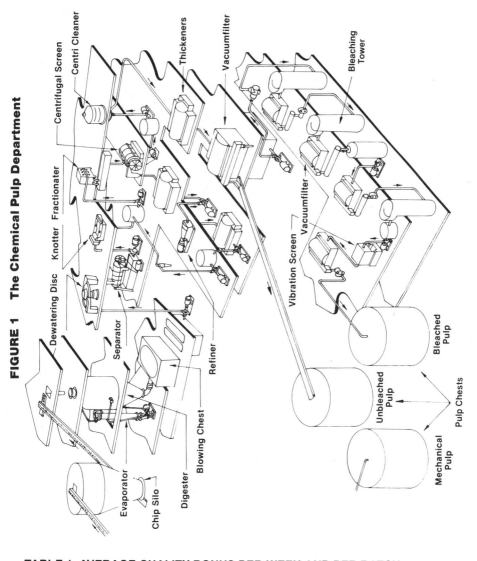

FIGURE 1   The Chemical Pulp Department

TABLE 1 AVERAGE QUALITY BONUS PER WEEK AND PER BATCH ACROSS ALL TYPES OF TIMBER RELATED TO HALF-YEAR PERIODS OF THE EXPERIMENT

Period	Average/week	Average/batch
First half-year	100 per cent	100 per cent
Second half-year	145 per cent	140 per cent
Third half-year	124 per cent	137 per cent
Fourth half-year	124 per cent	123 per cent

operations were interdependent in terms of removing the lignin from the fibres, and the sixteen-hour cycle between filling and emptying each of the four boilers required close cooperation and contact across shifts. Hence, the naturally bounded unit tasks clearly exceeded the traditional one man/one shift type of work role.

3. Finally, it became evident in this case, as in others, that the requirements of the technology were not fully known and predictable. As previously indicated, the pitch problem was far from being fully understood and the variances in raw material made it impossible to predict what problems the operators at any time would have to tackle. Moreover, the properties of the technical equipment would change somewhat over a period. This implies that the designated process control standards were arbitrary ones based on current knowledge. Hence, they ought to be adjusted to the extent that the changing properties of the technical system caused a relocation of the optimum point for some of the process variables. For example, the evolutionary operation technique is based on this fact (Box, 1957).

THE RESPONSE RESOURCES IN THE SOCIAL SYSTEM

Formal Organization

The department organization included seven shift positions and four shift teams, plus one daytime worker preparing the bleaching agents. A senior operator was charged with the responsibility for each of the other four-part processes. These men belonged to the highest of two formally recognized status levels. There were also a boiler assistant, a screener assistant and a reserve on each shift who, together with the daily worker, made up the second grade of operators.

In supporting roles outside the department were two laboratory technicians providing data for process control. In case of mechanical breakdowns or pitch troubles, the operators had to rely on maintenance men and cleaning people being called in from other areas by the foreman. Special contact man positions had been set up to facilitate communications between maintenance and operations.

Four shift foremen (plus one assistant foreman to cover absentees) were responsible for the chemical and mechanical pulping, even though the two processes were not technically interdependent. The levels above the shift foremen included the general foreman, the production engineer, the pulpmill manager and the general manager.

It should be noted that the number of operator positions is strictly prescribed in the central agreement between the employer and the trade union. This arrangement, having a long tradition in the Norwegian pulp and paper industry, is specific to this industry. This had undoubtedly added to the tendency of a strict delineation of work between individual job-holders, a well-known result of traditional job design in industry. Being of crucial importance to the problems of self-regulation and process control in this kind of technology, this point will be further explored in what follows.

Wages and Bonus

The total wage of the operator includes hourly pay, shift allowances, regular overtime, additional hours and production bonus. Generally speaking, the complexity of this arrangement makes it difficult for the average man to see any direct connection between his efforts and his wage packet.

In accordance with this, the production bonus was based on the number of batches produced, even though the papermachines used to be the bottleneck in the production line. Thus, by leaving out the quality aspects of the pulp, which the operators could influence and by which alone *they* could facilitate the production of the papermachine, the production bonus, though paid out on a group basis, could not in fact function as a group goal. This is of particular significance, since management (at that time, extremely anxious to build up the quality reputation of the company in the market) could through a quality bonus have effectively translated such a quality-oriented policy into operational terms at the lower levels in the organization.

Of particular interest also are the additional hours, a form of extra pay earned by the men for odd jobs done in addition to their permanent tasks and within their regular working hours. This exemplifies one of the measures used by management in order to cope with the lack of flexibility on the shop floor, to be considered in the following section.

Segregation of Operator Jobs

Since 1961, the total manning had been gradually reduced through natural turnover, the major part of which used to occur in the spring. Recruitment was done mainly therefore through the annual intake of holiday reserves for the summer months. Operator training was, in keeping with the tradition in the industry, limited by the notion of one man/one job. Hence, when a man had been permanently selected for one department, further advancements would be confined to the more recognized jobs in the same area.

The segregation of jobs and lack of overlapping skills in the permanent shift teams had made the work organization increasingly unable to cope with the existing variances as the number of stand-ins in the general manpower pool was gradually reduced. In the chemical pulp department, for instance, one multi-skilled reserve had been introduced on each shift in order to stand in for absentees and otherwise to help out with odd jobs. Even if it had functioned, however, this arrangement would probably have proved inadequate to solve the flexibility problem on the shop floor. As it was, the lack of balance between the higher skill requirements for this key position in the shift groups and, on the other hand, the pay, security and working conditions offered, resulted in a disturbingly high turnover among the reserves.

Traditionally—and not only in the pulp and paper industry—management has seen apparent advantages in strict delineation and specification of individual jobs. The time needed for training is short and the supervisory control is strengthened through a clear definition of what each worker is accountable for. The workers for their part will tend to react to this system by interpreting the job specification as the maximum they owe rather than the minimum.

Beyond the first line of defence established by the union, the men make out of the job specification and customary practice a second line of defence against management. Moreover, within the welter of expectations about what is mine and what is yours, the men create a pecking order among themselves based on who gets the cosier jobs and who gets the less attractive ones.

Consequently, while the individual jobs may be lacking in intrinsic satisfaction, because of this rigid definition and segregation, they gain psychological significance because of what are merely relative advantages. As the men come to base their judgement of themselves and others on their ability to seize these relative advantages, they become stronger defenders of this system of job design than would be warranted by the built-in limitations for self-fulfilment.

As an example of this insidious trend, our *post hoc* analysis of the records revealed that one of the four digesters was a particularly good piece of equipment for pulping a certain wood. This we found was not public knowledge. In discussion, however, we found that one of the boilermen had already discovered this long ago and kept it to himself. This suggested to us at least that the lack of learning in the department was due not only to a *laissez-faire* attitude or feeling of uncertainty among the men, but that the system failed to encourage the men to share self-acquired knowledge, as they did not regard themselves as integrated members of a group.

Operators Responses to Task Requirements

Our analysis of tasks and attitudes showed that, among the first three psychological requirements (Appendix 1), these jobs lacked mainly in the interest, excitement and self-enhancement that comes from being able to learn to do one's task better. Knowledge of results appeared adequate so long as learning was inhibited. The degree of variety and demand and the scope for personal control were higher than is usually found in industrial jobs and felt to be so by the operators.

This explained the relatively high level of job satisfaction expressed in interviews with senior operators and older workers, who had little reason to want to change in order to participate in a more comprehensive learning process that might disturb some of the privileges they had obtained. The more dependent nature of the assistant jobs and the particular situation of the reserves explain the lower level of satisfaction expressed by the second grade operators.

Interaction of Operator Roles with Foreman and Management Roles

The position of the shift foreman in the chemical pulp department was introduced as a management response to increasing variances and planning problems arising after the changeover to the magnesium bisulphite method. This was in accordance with the traditional approach to organizational problems on the shop floor. These include such measures as specifying individual jobs in more detail, strengthening the hand of the supervisor, calling in specialists, introducing a new level in the organization, etc. In this case, a short-term solution was achieved at the cost of a more serious long-term problem.

Recruited from among the best operators, the foremen would only with extensive training succeed in forming a leadership and planning position clearly ranking above and essentially complementary to the operating group. Familiar with operator work and lacking the means and self-confidence to lift himself to a new level, the foreman tended to focus his attention primarily within the work group rather than on controlling its boundary conditions. Hence, the foreman had developed the practice of being constantly on the move as a troubleshooter within the department; he would then do most of the unpredictable tasks that the operators were reluctant to carry out without special compensations (see remarks on additional hours), perceiving such tasks as falling outside their own strictly defined jobs.

The behavior of the foreman then became part of a vicious circle of job segregation by reducing the job content and thereby further limiting the learning and growth potentials of the operators. As the first level of management was in this way lowering itself in order to complete the tasks within its particular area of command, so each higher level was correspondingly pulled down to fill out what was then lacking in control and coordination. The adverse consequences of such work organization at the floor level will easily affect all levels of management, a fact typically found in large organizations. Even at Hunsfos, these tendencies were evident. By filling in for their subordinates, the managers and foremen were subtly redefining their own jobs in a way that reinforced the tendencies of the men on the shop floor not to show more initiative than was demanded by the traditional job design. Thus, the vicious circle was established.

CONDITIONS FOR OPTIMUM CONTROL BY SELF-REGULATION

When the goals and purposes of an enterprise are operationalized on different levels in the organization, it is not arbitrary which of the factors—throughput, quality, material, labor, etc.—are given the highest priority in the ongoing optimization processes on each level. According to the theory of open systems, the choice of priorities will depend on conditions outside as well as inside the enterprise. Hence, at Hunsfos, we felt that key problems of optimization on the two lowest levels of the socio-technical system were the following:

1. *Process control* to achieve for each product a given set of quality specifications minimizing machine hours, cost of material, labor cost, etc. Among the cost factors, primary attention is usually paid to machine utilization.

2. *Production planning* to achieve optimum allocation of products and orders for market requirements as well as production costs. Whereas the individual customer would vary in terms of quality demands, time of delivery, etc., machine down-time would depend on the size of the orders, the production sequence of products, etc.

The two activities are obviously interdependent and complementary, yet the latter area potentially contains tasks for which a new type of supervision could develop.

For the process control function, this type of technology requires that it match an extended interdependency network, as well as meet the demands for immediate responses in the social system. This implies that the control sequences have to be explored in detail. Generally speaking, a self-regulating production system requires at least the following components:

1. *A production unit* that converts a specific input material into a specific output.
2. *An output standard* against which the output of the production unit can be judged at any time.
3. *A measuring device* that can detect deviations from the target output standard and feed the information back to a "brain" unit.
4. *A "brain" unit* that can translate the information received into a new set of operational instructions, appropriate to returning the production performance to the target, while also taking the momentary input characteristics into consideration.
5. *An operation unit* capable of carrying out the operational instructions.
6. *An input standard* (usually identical with the output standard of the preceding production unit) against which the input can be judged and a feedforward to the "brain" unit of information about momentary deviations.

Applied to man/machine systems, this classification implies that human elements to some extent will be part of the control sequence either by performing the component tasks or by transmitting information between the components. The effectiveness of the feedback loops will therefore depend on:

1. The properties of the components.
2. The transmission of information.

Firstly, considering the qualitative aspect of pulp production, we found that, among the output criteria most relevant to process control, only degree of digestion, brightness and tearing strength were measured systematically by the laboratory technicians. Cleanliness was judged subjectively from special test sheets, but factors such as pitch and homogeneity were too expensive or difficult for regular measuring. While there were no measurements on the quality of the input chips, information about pH value and percentage of sulphur dioxide in the acid were available. The use of standards and control limits were rarely based on statistical calculations. Because of the great variances observed in some of the quality measurements of individual batches, it was difficult to reveal long-term trends in the process control. The lack of feedback on this level reduced possibilities for continuous learning and control. With some improvements, we felt that these measurements might form the basis of a temporary bonus that would make potential group goals visible to the operators. Since the measurement requirements were insufficiently met for us to bring such aspects as throughput, yield, waste or material costs directly into the experiment, we shall only note in passing that the lack of measuring devices for dry weight and moisture content of the chips in the boilers restricted further learning among the boilermen.

Secondly, in order to keep the feedback loops as short as possible, we suggest that information and decisions be brought to the lowest organizational level for meeting the requirements for skill and responsibility, also that they kept within the fewest work roles that the constraints imposed by the technology and the means communication would allow for. Hence, the well-known benefits of specialization and centralization, which tend to extend the information flows across special barriers (work roles, skill differences, levels in the organization, etc.), must be weighted not only against the obvious costs, incurred by delays and misinterpretations of the information, but also against the loss of task motivation and job satisfaction that pertain to tasks of a substantial degree of wholeness (a strong *gestalt*) and allowing the men themselves a sufficient measure of control over the materials and processes (see the second section).

As a consequence, the segregation of individual operator jobs and the division of labor among operator, laboratory technicians, cleaners, maintenance men and the supervisory levels were not necessarily optimum in terms of the total control requirements of the chemical pulp department.

A practical example of an inadequate feedback loop was test sheets showing the degree of cleanliness of the unbleached pulp, against which the screening performance was judged. These sheets were prepared by the laboratory workers about one hour after the screening of a new batch had begun. Instead of returning these sheets immediately to the screener, who could then correct the ongoing process according to the information given, the sheets were formerly sent to the foreman and some of the supervisors in other departments. Since the foreman was frequently away from his office, the feedbacks to the operators were often delayed. This is a very obvious case, because there was neither a question of the workers' ability to interpret the information embodied in the test sheets nor any doubt that the other departments would also benefit by a change in this feedback procedure. The critical factor was the speed of the feedback.

Considering the technical means of communication, it appeared that telephones were missing at some critical points and that the system of written information could be improved upon.

Finally, since it was evident that optimum conditions for control could be achieved only if the flow of information matched the technical interdependencies of the process, the actual communication network among operators was analysed before and after the experiment (see summary of analyses and results).

PROGRAM FOR REDESIGN OF JOBS

Based on the previous analysis, it was assumed that an optimum socio-technical system in the chemical pulp department could be achieved only if:

1. The men as a group took greater responsibility for the operation of the department as a whole.
2. They were enabled and initially encouraged to increase their understanding and control of the processes.

Consequently, increased autonomy for extended groups (across shifts) was a plausible name for the principle forming the basis of the experiment. The method of introducing change was to be step-by-step problem solving by small groups consisting of a representative from the workers, supervisors and management. Among the prerequisites for the development of partly autonomous work groups were:

1. Specification of the group's boundaries in relation to the environment (adjacent units).
2. Clarification and definition of what had to be measured in terms of quality and quantity of raw materials and services both received and delivered by the group as well as specification of quality control limits for the various criteria.
3. A proper incentive, such as a bonus, which could stimulate the groups to cooperate.

The following specific measures were to be introduced in order to support the group arrangement:

1. Training the operators to make them as far as possible qualified for all tasks within the department.
2. Allocation of a special repairman to the operator group to cope with smaller breakdowns requiring immediate attention.
3. Setting up an information center on the shop floor where measurements and other information were quickly available so that everyone would be aware of the current situation in the department. (If necessary, statistical methods would have to be employed.)
4. Arranging suitable conditions for department employees to meet in smaller or larger groups when necessary.
5. Installation of telephones in each department section.
6. Electing a group representative on each shift to facilitate communications.

THE PROCESS OF CHANGE

The changes suggested in the program were accepted by the management and by the majority of the workers in the department.

Gradually, but not without resistance on the part of some of the men concerned, the various measures were introduced with support from top management and from the union. In addition, operator training was linked to job rotation for the assistants, attempts were made to retrain the foremen and certain technical improvements were introduced in the bleaching. At the same time, the initiative in the socio-technical change process in the department was transferrèd from the research team to a project action committee (with one representative each for management, for the foremen and for the operators), then to the department management. Finally, by January 1966, with the introduction of a marginal group bonus paid on cleanliness, tearing strength, degree of digestion and brightness, the new basis for operator participation was established.

The subsequent years of 1966 and 1967 can (in terms of our dependent variable, the level of personal participation) be divided for analytical purposes into a search, a growth and a stagnation phase. Hence, abnormal variances in the timber inputs initiated a search among the men for new means of process control.

With a return to normal inputs before the summer 1966, the results of the above effects, combined with the effects of the change in job design, had made the men experience a situation that allowed them to exercise more discretion. In 1967, however, the project did not get the necessary attention from the management, which at that time had to concentrate their efforts on market problems and a technical reconstruction program. As will be seen, pulp quality reached a peak in the growth phase and thereafter stabilized at a higher level than before the experiment. Space allows only for a brief summary of the key points in the analysis and the major conclusions.

SUMMARY OF ANALYSES AND RESULTS

The experiment was designed in such a way that pulp quality as measured by the bonus would be the best single index of operator performance. It is agreed within the company that a general improvement in pulp qualities has been achieved (Table 1). This applies to the bleached pulps in particular. In line with this, the number of extremely bad batches have also been reduced during the experiment. For the majority of the individual quality variables (for each pulp), there appears to be some correspondence between quality achieved and the change in the conditions for operator participation.

This broad picture of the bonus trend is confirmed by the more detailed breakdown on pulp qualities.

Before inferring too much from these broad indices, we had to explore whether:

1. The improved quality was achieved at excessive costs.
2. The improved quality was due to improved performance on the group level.
3. There was some evidence that the men took a greater interest in their work.
4. The improvement could have occurred without the men changing their approach to the job.
5. The men themselves perceived the new situation as favorable.

Taking these points in turn:

1. There is no evidence that quality has been achieved at the expense of an increased consumption of material resources. The major costs (fibre, yield, chemicals and machine utilization) that had shown decreasing trends before the experiment, continued to fall during the experiment (Table 2). There is, in fact, some indication that the experiment may have contributed to an increase in yield. It was agreed that manpower should be kept constant during the experiment.

2. The improved control of pulp quality can to a large extent be ascribed to the men who as a group assumed greater responsibility.

   (a) The quality development of the main product (fir pulp), which goes through all steps in the process, also the bleaching, shows a clear improvement in cleanliness and tearing strength (Table 3). At the same time, the changes in the kappa number show that the boilermen have changed their strategy from overcooking to undercooking, whereas the changes in brightness shows that the bleachers have moved from underbleaching to overbleaching (Englestad, Emery and Thorsrud, 1969).

   The terms underbleaching and overbleaching are to be understood as relative to the given standards for kappa number and brightness, respectively. Nevertheless, these standards are arbitrary ones based on current knowledge and judgment about what would be required to achieve a given pulp quality with the available raw materials, technical equipment and labor force.

   A detailed analysis of the situation revealed that the trends in pulp quality indicated could be explained only if the operators, on the basis of the new conditions established, had to some extent changed their attitudes towards the task and their way of working. From previously seeking to optimize within their own delineated work area, therefore, it appeared to be a change in orientation towards optimizing on department level, which required an increasing awareness of the technical interdependencies between the part-processes (for example, the removal of lignin in cooking and bleaching, respectively). In other words, the operators now tended to take responsibility as a group.

   This conclusion was supported by measurable changes in the pattern of communications and the increased problem-solving activities in the work groups.

TABLE 2 MEASURES OF COST OF VARIOUS MATERIALS BEFORE AND DURING THE EXPERIMENT

Materials	Nine-month period before experiment	Twelve-month period during experiment	Percentage improvement
Magnesium oxide per ton of pulp	106·0	91·0	14·0
Chlorine per ton of pulp	87·3	73·5	15·8
Sulphur dioxide per ton of pulp	128·0	123·0	3·9
Pulp yield per m³ timber	100·0	103·8	3·8

TABLE 3 BONUS AS A PERCENTAGE OF THE THEORETICAL MAXIMUM FOR PURITY AND TEARING STRENGTH

Quality dimension	Type of wood	Phase		
		Search	Growth	Stagnation
Cleanliness	Fir	42	61	60
(spots)	Hardwood	45	53	53
	Spruce	3	21	10
Tearing	Fir	63	90	71
strength	Hardwood	76	96	93

(b) Analysis of the communication data shows that the flows of information after the experiment match the technical interdependencies in the process more closely than before (Engelstad, Emery and Thorsrud, 1969). At the same time, the men as a group have attained a higher level of autonomy. It also appears that the assistant operators have now become better integrated into the groups. Table 4 shows that the increased interaction in 1967 in all essentials refers to the substantial growth in inter-operator communication (+70 per cent).

(c) Concrete examples of operator participation in problem solving and decision making within the department during the experiments also indicate that the men have increased their capability to operate as a team.

3. The operators have, during the period of the experiment, contributed a number of suggestions for improvement of the technical equipment and the working condition in general, demonstrating an interest in the job that they previously had not shown (Table 5). At the same time, the operators have become more interested in problems of process control, timber utilization and costs.

TABLE 4 NUMBER OF CONTACTS PER SHIFT BEFORE AND AFTER THE EXPERIMENT

Contact	1965	1967	Difference, per cent	1965, per cent	1967, per cent
Operator/operator	26•0	44•1	+70	25	34
Laboratory technician/ operator	37•7	37•7	0	36	30
Foreman/operator	34•6	39•4	+14	33	31
Foreman/laboratory technician	7•6	6•7	+13	7	5
Total	105•9	127•9	+21	101	100

TABLE 5 NUMBER OF SUGGESTIONS ADVANCED AND ACCEPTED IN THE OPERATOR MEETINGS*

Date of meetings	Shifts	Acid	Boiling	Screening	Bleaching	Total
15th March 1966	3 + 4	5	5	11	3	24
25th March 1966 (additional)	1 + 2	1	9	3	3	16
August 1966	1 + 2 + 3 + 4	2	4	3	4	13
Total		8	18	17	10	53

*As a comparison, the company suggestion scheme had produced approximately one suggestion per year in the chemical pulp department for the period 1958–64.

4. Obviously, factors other than those included in the experimental design may have contributed to those improvements. It is unlikely, however, that the improved performance gained in the department during the experiment can be assigned to unilateral management actions (regardless of operator response) either in terms of the technical improvements introduced or in terms of the directives given. Indications of this were lack of pressure from the men before the experiment for improvements in equipment or instrumentation and the fact that, when management's major concern in the summer of 1966 turned to input costs, this had no effect on the strategies being followed by the operators in the department. As far as our evidence goes, the improved control, the increase in operator suggestions and other changes in group activities were primarily due to the voluntary efforts of the men.

5. No doubt the experiment as it developed in 1966 caused many operators to build up considerable expectations, and the feelings of disappointment that

were brought out in some of the interviews clearly refer back to the fact that the project was in 1967 only half-heartedly followed up in the department because of other priorities. Unfortunately, at this crucial point in the experiment, new measures necessary to sustain growth in the desired direction, that many had hoped for, were not introduced. In accordance with the logic of systems, it is unlikely that changes in a part will be sustained over an extended period if the changes are not reciprocated by sufficient adjustments in the total system (Angyal, 1941, pp. 243–61). Within areas where permanent learning has taken place or new technological conditions have been established, however, the socio-technical system in the department appears to have reached a new level of functioning. This applies to pulp quality, operator skill and the degree of flexibility in the shift teams.

FURTHER DEVELOPMENTS IN THE COMPANY

The preconditions for a work group or department to assume the increased responsibility conveyed by a higher level of group autonomy are that (a) critical variances in the process can be brought under control, and (b) the change in job design and operator roles is sufficiently supported by adjustments in tasks and roles of the foreman and of the management. Changes in tasks and roles on department level, however, in the long run require adjustments on company level as well. In practice, this implies that the new principles of job design must be integrated into the objectives, policy and style of management, to guide the activities at all levels in the organization. In principle, a part of a system influences other parts only through its effects on the total system.

Accordingly, during the autumn of 1966 and the spring of 1967, experiences from the chemical pulp department produced discussions of company policies among the top management. It was decided to follow up the project within the company with a new experiment in the papermill, where a team of operators would run two of the papermachines without shift foremen. The changes in job design that were introduced in 1968 have otherwise mainly corresponded to those in the chemical pulp department, but the initiative in the change process has consistently been carried by the parties concerned through a temporary project action committee. The first six months' agreement about experimentation was extended for another six months. Nine months after the jobs had been redesigned, one could ascertain definite growth in commitment to the new way of working among operators and management. The operating team had then showed that they were able to utilize their machinery in a very flexible way, even without shift supervision, and the productivity trend proved very satisfactory.

Finally, by 1969, the company had decided on a three-year plan for redesigning the organization that will include:

1. Comprehensive operator training for multiple skills and increased technical insight.

2. Doing away with shift supervision of the old type. (By 1964, it had been an explicit policy to strengthen the hand of the foreman.)
3. The introduction of a management philosophy that encourages local problem-solving activities.

In particular, on the basis of what we have seen in the fourth field experiment at Norsk Hydro, we believe that this way of working will lead to a self-sustaining learning process that will improve the reliability of the human component in the process of control as a whole.

Appendix 1

Psychological Job Requirements

1. The need for the content of a job to be reasonably demanding in terms other than sheer endurance, yet providing a minimum of variety (not necessarily novelty).
2. The need for being able to learn on the job (which implies standards and knowledge of results) and go on learning. Again, it is a question of neither too much nor too little.
3. The need for some minimum area of decision-making that the individual can call his own.
4. The need for some minimum degree of social support and recognition in the work place.
5. The need to be able to relate what one does and what one produces to one's social life.
6. The need to feel that the job leads to some sort of desirable future.

REFERENCES

Angyal, A. (1941) *Foundations for a Science Personality*. Harvard Unviersity Press.

Box, G. E. P. (1957) "Evolutionary Operation—A Method for Increasing Industrial Productivity." *Applied Statistics*, vol. 6, no. 1, pp. 3–22.

Emery, F. E. (1959) *Characteristics of Socio-Technical Systems*. Tavistock Institute, doc. 527.

Emery, F. E., ed. (1969) *Systems Thinking*. Penguin Books.

Engelstad, P. H., Emery, F. E., and Thorsrud, E. (1969) *The Hunsfos Experiment*. Work Research Institute, Oslo, mimeographed.

Guest, R. H. (1957) "Job Enlargement: A Revolution in Job Design." *Personnel Administration*, vol. 20, March/April, pp. 12–15.

Herbst, P. G. (1962) *Autonomous Group Functioning*. Tavistock.

Rice, A. K. (1958) *Productivity and Social Organization: The Ahmedabad Experiment*. Tavistock.

Thorsrud, E., and Emery, F. E. (1969) *Mot on ny Bedriftsorganisasjon*. Tanum, Forlag, Oslo.

Trist, E. L., Higgin, G. W., Murray, H., and Pollock, A. B. (1963) *Organisational Choice*. Tavistock.

Walker, C. M. (1950) "The Problem of the Repetitive Job." *Harvard Business Review*, vol. 28, no. 3, pp. 54–8.

Appendix 2

FIGURE 1   Matrix of Variance

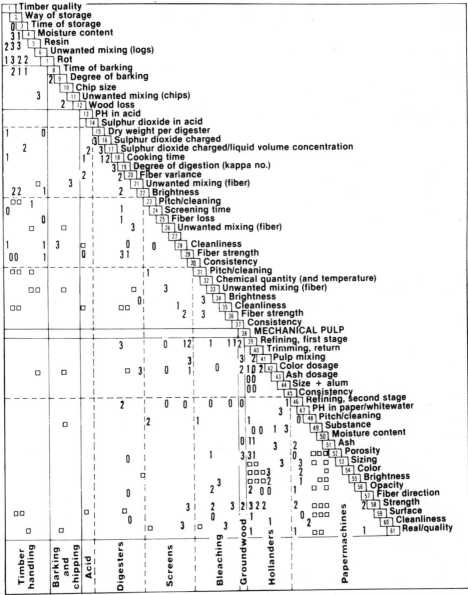

Meaning of variances

0- of theoretical interest only
1- of little practical importance
2- of medium practical importance
3- of great practical importance

☐ : variance control designed into technical system, human intervention excluded
or
☐ : indirect dependence, intervening variable controls variance transmission

20
A Measure
of Work-Group Autonomy
Jon Gulowsen

THE BACKGROUND OF THE INVESTIGATION

When social scientists entered the Norwegian debate on industrial democracy, one of their first conclusions was that the kind of influence that employees could get through representation on the boards of directors of companies would not, in itself, change the quality of working life significantly for the ordinary worker. Emery and Thorsrud (1969) argued that the basis of participation should permit every employee to develop himself through his work and to take on responsibility. Other kinds of participation would be of little importance if this process did not occur.

Having reached this conclusion, the researchers began looking for job designs and work organizations making it more likely that human resources could develop in an industry. The issue of autonomous work-groups arose. The Tavistock Institute, London, had reported experiments in the British coal mines, where the workers had organized themselves into composite work-groups and taken responsibility for production (Herbst, 1962; Trist et al., 1963).

This form of work organization had positive consequences for the workers' self-development, for general satisfaction in the workplace, and for productivity. The findings in the coal mines were backed up by results from the United States (Davis, 1966) and India (Rice, 1958).

In fact, the miners and the other workers studied had developed ways of work organization that illustrated what democracy in the work-place might look like. With this as background, a team working at the Norwegian Work Research Institutes concentrated its attention on the concept of autonomous work-groups. The team started experiments in industrial plants where it tried to set up autonomous work-groups. At the same time, the team studied existing work-groups that were autonomous in some respects. The investigation considered the following questions:

1. Are there any structural dependencies between areas where work-groups can have autonomy and where they cannot?
2. What conditions must be satisfied if groups are to have autonomy? The research team was primarily interested in conditions imposed by technology, geography, wage systems, and local culture.

Excerpts from Jon Gulowsen. "A Measure of Work Group Autonomy." (Selvystyrte Arbeidsgruper). Oslo: Tanum Press, 1971. Translated by author.

3. Is the idea of autonomous work-groups in harmony with Norwegian work culture? It was assumed that ways of work contrary to local customs probably could never obtain any significant diffusion in industry.

This article will only treat the first issue, the others having been reported elsewhere (Gulowsen, 1971).

No precise conceptual framework had been formulated when the case studies were made. However, the choice of case studies was not made completely without guidelines. The research team chose to study groups with some kind of joint payment, and in some cases, groups having a composite work organization, since it was believed that these factors contributed to the emergence of work-group autonomy.

Some central variables, such as group size and working relationships within the groups, were not treated in this study. Neither were power relations in the organization and competence among the group members. Furthermore, all the groups operated within comparatively simple technologies, where innovations were not particularly dramatic. Finally, the empirical material includes only eight case studies, of which only four were performed by the author. For these reasons, this study should be regarded as indicative rather than definitive.

CRITERIA OF AUTONOMY

The criteria of autonomy were developed on a theoretical basis independent of, but following the collection of, the data for all the case studies. The criteria were not based on the empirical material in the cases, but were concerned with the "what, where, when, who, and how" of the groups' functions. Excluded were decisions regarding determination of norms, policy and doctrines, although such decisions would have central importance, e.g. in religious or political groups. Under these restrictions, the following criteria of autonomy were developed:

1. *The group can influence the formulation of its goals, including:*
   (a) *qualitative aspects* (in other words, what the group shall produce), *and*
   (b) *quantitative aspects*. Included in the quantitative aspects of production are two issues. The first is the influence of the group on production volume; the second is the influence of the group on the terms of payment and other sanctions: e.g. through direct negotiations between the group and the company management. It is suggested that Criterion 1(b) is satisfied only if the group can influence both issues. This presupposes that both parties enter into negotiations on equal terms.
2. *Provided that established goals governing relationships to the super-ordinate system are satisfied, the group can govern its own performance in the following ways:*
   (a) *The group can decide where to work*. This criterion is relevant only if it is possible to move both raw materials, means of production, and products; therefore, a social scientist, for example, has possibilities

for autonomy that are excluded for a coal miner. None of the case studies covered here can be measured against this criterion.

(b) *The group can decide when to work*. This criterion includes two issues. The first concerns the timing of different tasks, which is in fact a question of plans and methods and will be treated under Criterion 3. The second concerns the limitation of working hours. It is suggested that Criterion 2(b) is satisfied in any one of the following cases:

(i) if the group can limit working hours for the group as a whole;

(ii) if the group can decide whether any of its members may leave work during the regular working hours;

(iii) if the group decides if and when its members may work overtime.

(c) *The group can decide which other activities it wishes to engage in*. This criterion is satisfied if the work-group can leave work or take breaks on its own recognizance. It is also satisfied if the group members may do personal work or other tasks as long as they have satisfied the established goals of production.

3. *The group makes the necessary decisions in connection with the choice of the production method*. (Whether or not the individual worker may decide on his own work methods is a question of individual autonomy and is dealt with in Criterion 7.) It is suggested that Criterion 3 is satisfied if the work-group has total responsibility for the means of production, and the environment only performs boundary control. The simplest way to operationalize this criterion is as follows:

(a) there exist obvious alternative methods;

(b) outsiders do not interfere in the choice of method.

The criterion is irrelevant if (a) is not satisfied.

4. *The group makes its own internal distribution of tasks*. As was the case for Criterion 3, this criterion is satisfied if:

(a) there exist alternative task distributions (technological constraints and formal requirements may limit the possibilities);

(b) outsiders do not interfere in the decision process.

The criterion is irrelevant if (a) is not satisfied.

5. *The group decides on its own membership*. Three important categories of choice are possible:

(a) the group selects and appoints new members;

(b) the group expels unwanted members;

(c) management chooses members, and the group has no means of sanctioning the choice.

It is suggested that the criterion is satisfied if either (a) or (b) describes the procedure. Whether the decisions are made in plenum or, for example, by a local shop steward is unimportant in this context.

6. *The group makes its own decisions with respect to two crucial matters of leadership:*

(a)*The group decides whether it wants to have a leader with respect to internal questions, and – if it does – who this leader shall be.*
(b) *The group decides whether it wants a leader for the purpose of regulating boundary conditions, and—if it does—who this leader shall be.*

Criteria 6(a) and 6(b) are operational in their existing format, and referred tests of satisfaction are not necessary.

Criteria 1–6 concern decisions on the group level. But there are also other kinds of decisions within work-groups. The individual worker can to some extent make decisions that concern himself and his own work situation. Therefore, the concept of autonomy is also relevant at the level of the individual. Particularly with respect to the choice of production methods, it is convenient to distinguish between the level of the individual and the level of the work-group. It therefore seems useful to add a seventh criterion of autonomy, although this one cannot be immediately compared with the others:

7. *The group members decide how the work operations shall be performed.*
There are three important possibilities:
(a) The worker determines his own method; the criterion is satisfied.
(b) Some other person — for instance, a foreman or planner — decides; the criterion is not satisfied.
(c) Technology leaves no important choices. This situation was well illustrated by Charles Chaplin in *Modern Times*. In this case, the criterion is considered to be irrelevant.

THE CASE STUDIES

The empirical material includes case studies of eight work-groups. Four of the case studies were performed by the author. The other four have been described in previous literature: the coal mining group (Herbst, 1962), two groups of lime-workers (Hegland and Nylehn, 1968), and the groups in an electrical panel-heater production department (Ødegaard, 1967; Qvale, 1968). Detailed treatment is given here only of those groups not described fully in other sources. The groups are considered in the order of their respective autonomy, as revealed by subsequent analysis.

The Logging Group
Together with the introduction of new and highly mechanized equipment in 1962, a new type of organization was established for a five-man logging crew at Meråker Brug. The group consisted of three *loggers* equipped with motorsaws and axes. Their job was to fell trees and remove their branches. Further, there was a *driver* who used a specialized tractor equipped with a powerful winch. The tractor, which could penetrate almost any kind of terrain, collected from eight to twenty

logs at a time with the winch and a cable, and pulled them from the cutting area to the production area. The fifth man in the group, the *cutter,* worked in the production area cutting logs to proper lengths. He sorted out the different sizes and placed them in different stacks using a motorsaw and a tractor with stacking equipment.

The logging crew worked in areas which are distant (two to five miles) from Meråker and quite separated from other crews. The cutting areas where the group worked were usually so large that the distance between the members of the group prevented cooperation with each other. The only exception was that the driver periodically had contact with each of the workers. However, the group had lunch together and travelled to and from work together.

The group was responsible to a forest inspector and a forest guard, who were both responsible for much larger areas. Thus, they had contact with the group only a few times a week. However, these were the two who determined the extent of the cutting areas for the group. The boundaries were always clear, and it was never difficult for the group to decide which trees to cut.

The group was paid at a joint piece-rate which was equally shared. The payment calculations were based on the quantity of timber cut of different qualities and the price per cubic foot of each quality. The piece-rates were negotiated beforehand between the group and the management. The quantity of the production was measured by officially appointed persons. These people measured the size of the logs after they were cut and sorted in the production area.

There were always negotiations about the payment terms before the group started working in a particular area. The results of these negotiations were valid as a contract between the group and the management as long as the group worked within the given area. This period usually lasted from five to seven weeks. The rates of payment within an area were primarily dependent on the quality of the forest and how well the ground was suited for transport of timber. When working conditions changed abruptly and unexpectedly while the group was in an area (for instance after an early or heavy snowfall), new negotiations were started to develop a fair pay-rate for the group.

This group never formally or informally appointed a leader; group members, therefore, usually acted jointly during the payment negotiations. It only happened once that the group and management could not agree on terms. Their respective unions then took over the negotiations and found an agreement acceptable to both parties.

Although the logging crew consisted of workers with clearly defined and non-overlapping tasks, it was still almost completely autonomous. When at work, it was almost totally independent of the management. Every man knew his job, and the management never interfered with the work. For example, the workers themselves decided whether to cut off branches with axe or motorsaw, and how best to transport the logs from the cutting area to the central area. Finally the group carried out an important change in work method without consulting the management, gathering felled trees in the cutting area in a more comfortable, but less efficient, way than that originally planned.

The group determined its own working hours. Management kept no records of working hours or absence, and the workers themselves decided when to start and when to finish work. As an example of their autonomy, the group ceased to work on Saturdays without asking management.

The group also had influence over its own composition. When the group originally started to work in 1962, all the candidates were asked if they were willing to accept the new kind of work organization. Each time new employees were engaged, management first selected a candidate, and then the group members were asked if they were willing to accept him. One of the reasons why this worked is possibly that Meråker is a comparatively small community. Therefore the group members were likely to know the different qualities of a candidate, and were able to judge whether he would fit into the group or not.

There is one factor that must not be overlooked when we try to understand what made the group so autonomous. Probably the most important reason is that loggers have by tradition been accustomed to autonomous work. Formerly, a logger often worked alone all day, and his work consisted of more operations than the work of any of the men in the group at Meråker. As a result, the loggers seem to have less autonomy and less composite jobs when they work in the group than they had had when each worked alone. Autonomy, thus, to some extent, was moved from the individual to the group, and the technological changes made the different tasks less differentiated.

The Coal-Mining Group and the Electrical Panel-Heater Group

The study in the coal mines was made in England in the early 1950s (see Herbst, 1962). The group in the electrical panel-heater department is much more recent (1967-68), and reflects the experience of a group established in close cooperation with the research workers in the Norwegian participation experiment (Ødegaard, 1967; Qvale, 1968). Nevertheless, the analysis of the coal mining group and of the workers in the electrical panel-heater department showed that these groups had generally the same kinds of autonomy as did the logging group, although their decision-making processes, of course, were adapted to their different situations.

Alfa Lime Works: The Oven Group and Quarry Group

The Alfa Lime Works, which produces calcinated or burnt lime for industrial purposes, employed a total of about twenty workers. Within this body of workers there were two groups, one comprising three quarriers and the other comprising four workers stationed near the lime-kiln (oven). Each of these groups was autonomous within certain fields.

The members of the two groups, together with a worker who was in charge of transport between the groups, were paid according to a joint piece-rate system. The system included sanctions to be used against those who did not conform to the regular working hours. However it did not include the level of the piece rate. This was settled between the management and the national union.

The production planning was done during daily morning meetings between the manager and the workers. These meetings included discussions of what kind of maintenance and cleaning jobs workers should do if the work load allowed it.

The technology was very simple, and the questions regarding method seldom seemed to cause any problems. However, there was no doubt that the groups and the group members had complete control in this field. They also determined how the different tasks should be divided among the members.

Neither of the groups had chosen any leader. The group of quarriers had a *pro forma* leader — a post required by the national safety regulations — but his leadership did not go beyond the question of safety.

The group members were themselves responsible for the recruitment of new members.

The Rail-Spring Group

In an isolated corner of the implement department at Christiania Spigerverk, a group of four men made rail springs. These rail springs were used by the Norwegian State Railways to fix the tracks to the sleepers. The springs had been made in the same way using the same machinery for more than ten years.

Since the demand for the springs was quite large, it was possible to maintain a fairly steady production load most of the time. However, at times it was necessary to cut back production from the usual two shifts to one shift for periods of up to a few months. This was the situation at the time of the investigation.

Rail springs were made from steel plates fabricated in another department, which were delivered to the group in large quantities. The task of the group was first to shape the springs by punching, forming, and cutting operations. The springs were then automatically hardened and annealed. Finally they were inspected and packed ready to be delivered to the customer.

The work area of the group consisted of a corner of a large production bay. The major mechanical equipment belonging to the group consisted of two punch presses with heating furnaces, one cutting machine, and an automatic hardening and annealing furnace.

Two men operated each of the punch presses, one operated the cutting machine, and the fourth man inspected and packed. The punch press operators alternated working so that one man punched while the other filled his furnace with steel plates and regulated the heating. Following forming, the cutting machine operator cut off one end of the spring and placed it on the hardening and annealing furnace conveyor. Finally, the springs were inspected for a critical dimension and the acceptable pieces were packed.

The production was frequently interrupted, usually because of mechanical trouble in one of the furnaces. Quite often one of the steel plates became stuck because of uneven edges or because of errors in the feeding equipment. Then the worker operating that furnace tried to remedy the error himself, while the worker on the identical machine immediately took over the production. As a result, errors of this kind did not necessarily cause a slow-down in production. Other errors such as complete breakdown in one of the heating elements, or mechanical breakdown in one of the punch presses, made it necessary to get aid from a repairman, who was assigned to provide immediate help to the group when needed.

As a consequence, the group, to a very high degree, was dependent on a repairman, and the formal organization therefore built up in such a way that there was contact between the group and one special repairman below the foreman level. His connection with the group was so strong that he had to leave whatever job he was on when the group called for his help. It is estimated that the repairman spent from 25 per cent to 50 per cent of his time with the group.

The repairman often needed help to do his work, and the group itself decided how to organize this. Each week one group member was responsible for calling on and helping the repairman when necessary. The same man was responsible no matter which unit broke down, so when he was absent, the other workers rearranged themselves to carry on the complete production cycle. (This meant that one of the two punch presses would always be unattended in the case of larger repair jobs.) The group completely adjusted itself to those variations that cause changes in the production capacity. However, if there was complete breakdown, then the necessary changes in manning were taken care of by management.

The workers formed their own work pattern and established a completely composite organization. All workers managed all the tasks, and there was complete job rotation with circulation every hour. Job rotation was introduced by the workers because, they argued, it made the work less monotonous. The workers themselves decided when, in case of mechanical breakdown, it was necessary to cut down the manpower from four to three workers, and made necessary changes without any orders.

As previously mentioned, one of the group members inspected each of the rail springs before packing to check if a critical measurement on the spring was within the desired range. On-going quality control inspection also took place. Every hour a quality control inspector, whose work area covered the entire implement department, thoroughly inspected a sample of five randomly selected springs. The inspection results were used as a basis for adjusting the punching equipment and the conditions in the hardening and annealing furnaces and not to accept or reject the product.

Since the repairman was the one who actually adjusted the punching equipment and thus in effect controlled many of the variables affecting the quality of the product, the work-group was almost without influence upon the quality of the springs. The work-group controlled most of the variables which determined the quantity of springs produced, while the quality control inspector and the repairman controlled the variables determining the quality of the product.

This was in harmony with the wage system. Payment was by group bonus based on quantity of output, which was controlled by the work-group. On the other hand, the quality, which the group could not influence, did not affect payment.

The production unit operated by the rail-spring group was characterized by unusually stable and indisputable boundary conditions. Their tasks included a complete production cycle. This was probably the main reason why the group was so little dependent on external leadership. In fact, although the group formally shared a foreman with other workers, they contacted him at most once a week. The foreman never involved himself in the work, but tried to regulate the external conditions to the benefit of the group. The group had no formal or informal internal leader, but seemed to manage internal questions together.

The group had less direct influence on recruitment than the logging crew. Nevertheless, they once demanded that the management discharge a group member whom the rest of the group found uncooperative. Although the group was very hesitant to do this, it shows that they had sufficient indirect participatory influence to avoid unwanted members. It is important in this context that the labour turnover was very low.

The group had very little autonomy outside the area indicated. Technology determined the tasks and work methods to such an extent that choice between alternative work methods seems irrelevant. The working hours had been agreed upon between the company and the trade union leaving no choice for any work-group in the company. Finally, management had the right to move people whenever they found that the production or the economic situation made it necessary.

The Ferro-Alloy Group

The author also studied four work-groups around an electrical furnace making ferro-alloys. For the most part, these groups had autonomy and lacked autonomy in the same areas as did the rail-spring group, and it is unnecessary to describe them fully here. They are included in the matrix analysis, below.

The Galvanizing Group

The galvanizing group, also in the Christiania Spigerverk, was most typical of the groups reported for industrial organizations. Most readers will easily be able to think of groups with as little autonomy. Detailed description will therefore not be given, but only a suggestion about how the decisions were made in this group according to the criteria of autonomy.

Working hours and piece-rates were negotiated between the company and the local union. Production plans were determined by the planning department so the group could only make changes within the schedule of one shift. Depending on the workload, management could decide if it was necessary to increase or decrease the manpower, and who should be moved from one job to the other.

The work method was as often as not determined by the foreman. However, on night-shifts, the group had some influence on these questions. Internal leadership in the group was also decided on by the management. Thus all that was left entirely to the group members was to determine how each one of them should do his own job. The foreman never seemed to interfere in this decision.

ANALYSIS

Analysis of the data followed completion of the case studies and development of the criteria of autonomy. Primary interest was placed in possible structural relationships between the criteria of autonomy. The Guttman Scaling Technique was found suitable (Guttman, 1944), but before a matrix could be established, a few questions regarding the coding of the material had to be settled.

Decisions Made at Different System Levels

When comparing different units, it is important to make sure that the units really are comparable. For example, the two groups engaged in lime production made some decisions within their respective groups, while others were made at the morning meetings, where the local manager was also present. It is of course possible to treat the morning meeting as a group, but one can clearly see that this group is not immediately comparable with the other groups. It might therefore look as if the morning meetings had comparatively little autonomy. To avoid this problem, the individual groups have been chosen as the units of analysis. Each of these groups is considered to be autonomous in those areas in which it has been able to actively influence the decisions at the morning meetings.

Measurement Scale

It was convenient to use a scale with the following values when coding the material:

+ The group or individual members within the group make the decisions either without interference or in cooperation with outsiders. In the latter case, it is presupposed that the group has a right to have a say.
0 The question is irrelevant. Nobody makes the actual decision.
− The group has no right to have a say in the decision-making process.

The Matrix

Once these rule were established, a matrix could be set up with the different groups along the one axis, and the criteria of autonomy along the other.

The criterion regarding the groups' right to determine where to work (2a) proved to be irrelevant for all the groups. It was therefore not included in the following analysis.

Sorting the groups according to how many criteria of autonomy they satisfied, and sorting the criteria of autonomy according to how many groups satisfied them, the following matrix was generated.

The matrix shows that the criteria of autonomy, according to these data, form a Guttman scale. According to Guttman, if this scale were not purely accidental, one should, probably be able to find some underlying variable. In order to find such a variable, consequences of decisions were studied.

In many cases, a fairly obvious underlying variable might be that the consequences of a decision were either "great" or "small." This variable, however, is insufficiently precise to offer much additional meaning or illumination for the investigator. Therefore, it was decided to look at two somewhat richer aspects of decisions. Since consequences of decisions may last for long or short periods, it was natural to look first at the time span. How long does it take before an actual decision does not represent an important limitation for the system any longer? Second, since decisions may have impact on different system levels, the level of the system on which the decision had impact could be used as another variable.

FIGURE 1   Matrix

Criteria of Autonomy

Groups	The group has influence on its qualitative goals	The group has influence on its quantitative goals	The group decides on questions of external leadership	The group decides what additional tasks to take on	The group decides when it will work	The group decides on questions of production method	The group determines the internal distribution of tasks	The group decides on questions of recruitment	The group decides on questions of internal leadership	The group members determine their individual production methods
	1a	1b	6b	2c	2b	3	4	5	6a	7
The logging group	−	+	+	+	+	+	+	+	+	+
The coal-mining group	−	+	+	+	+	+	+	+	+	+
The electrical panel-heater group	−	+	+	+	+	+	+	+	+	+
Alfa Lime Works, oven group	−	−	−	+	+	+	+	+	+	+
Alfa Lime Works, quarrier group	−	−	−	+	+	+	+	+	+	+
The rail-spring group	−	−	−	−	−	○	+	+	+	+
The ferro-alloy group	−	−	−	−	−	−	+	+	+	+
The galvanizing group	−	−	−	−	−	−	−	−	−	+

Both the time span of the consequences of the decisions and the system level could be considered underlying variables according to these data. These conclusions are more precisely stated below.

CONCLUSIONS AND HYPOTHESES

The analysis shows that the criteria of autonomy are ordered along a Guttman scale. This suggests the conclusion that autonomy is a one-dimensional property within work-groups. It therefore becomes realistic to talk about degree of autonomy. In spite of the fact that the data point toward a clear conclusion, however, the reader is reminded that the empirical material is somewhat scanty and that other dimensions such as group size, group competence and the kind of task have not been brought into consideration. On this tentative basis, the following hypotheses are proposed:

Hypothesis 1
Autonomy, as defined here, is a one-dimensional property. The different criteria of autonomy have a specific order, as shown in the matrix. This order may be termed the scale of autonomy. In order to reach a certain level on this scale, a group must satisfy all the criteria that precede it on the scale of autonomy.

Why is the property of autonomy one-dimensional? Two reasons exist which are probably mutually interdependent. They concern the time span and the level of decision making.

Hypothesis 2
Once a group has made a decision, it has committed itself on shorter or longer terms. A group cannot make decisions that bring it into a long-term commitment unless it also makes the decisions that commit it on shorter terms.

Hypothesis 3
Decisions are made on different system levels. No group can make decisions about questions on higher system levels unless it also makes the decisions on the lower system levels.

Hypotheses 2 and 3 will not both be correct unless there is a one-to-one correspondence between the system level of the decisions and the time-span of its consequences. The limitations of the data available in the case materials make it impossible to test these relationships empirically. If these hypotheses prove to be correct, they will obviously have impact on the development of shop-floor democracy.

One final consequence can be mentioned since it is heavily backed by other data found in the case studies. It seems beyond doubt that external conditions such as technology and layout, or payment, or planning systems will have impact on how a work-group will behave and what kinds of responsibility it can take on. Some of these external conditions seem to limit a group's possibility for having certain kinds of autonomy.

It is probable that autonomy with respect to decisions high on the scale presupposes autonomy with respect to all the decisions lower on the scale. This means that if one of the kinds of autonomy low on the scale is dependent on certain external conditions, all kinds of autonomy that are higher on the scale are equally dependent on those same conditions. To illustrate this, the hypotheses give us reason to believe that control or planning systems that leave no room for individual workers to make decisions about their own work methods will leave no room for any kind of group autonomy.

In conclusion, there seems to be a very important difference between the three most autonomous work groups and the other groups. The loggers, the coal miners and the groups in the electrical panel-heater department work on time limited contracts, which impose equal obligations on the management and on the groups. These contracts last for periods from one to three months. Within these periods management has no right permitting it to interfere with what the groups are doing, as long as the groups are producing according to the contract. As for the other groups, it is beyond doubt that their autonomy relies completely on the attitudes of the management. After the case studies were made, the research team observed that some groups lost their autonomy through changes in work supervision.

It is therefore suggested that the term ''autonomous work-group'' be reserved for groups that negotiate and operate under contracts which impose obligations on both parties for a certain time period. Other groups may be called ''relatively autonomous.''

REFERENCES

Davis, L. E. (1966) "The Design of Jobs." *Industrial Relations,* vol. 6, pp. 21-45.

Emery, F. E., and Thorsrud, E. (1969) *Form and Content in Industrial Democracy.* Tavistock.

Gulowsen, J. (1971) *Selvstyrte Arbeidsgrupper,* Tanum, Oslo.

Guttman, L. A. (1944) "A Basis for Scaling Qualitative Data." *American Sociological Review,* vol. 40.

Hegland, T. J., and Nylehn, B. (1968) "Adjustment of Work Organizations." In *Contributions to the Theory of Organizations.* Munksgaard, Copenhagen.

Herbst, P. G. (1962) *Autonomous Group Functioning.* Tavistock.

Qvale, T. U. (1968) *"Etterstudier ved N O B Ø Fabrikker."* Institute of Industrial and Social Research, Trondheim, Norway.

Rice, A. K. (1958) *Productivity and Social Organization: The Ahmedabad Experiment.* Tavistock.

Ødegaard, L. A. (1967) *"Feltforsok ved N O B Ø Fabrikker."* Institute of Industrial and Social Research, Trondheim, Norway.

Trist, E. L., Higgin, G. W., Murray, H., and Pollock, A. B. (1963) *Organizational Choice.* Tavistock.

21
An Experiment
in Work Satisfaction
Lars E. Björk

The woes of mass production are familiar, and I shall review them only briefly. The principles are job simplification, repetition and close control. The worker is viewed as one more interchangeable part, programmed to perform a small task that is precisely specified on the basis of time and motion studies. He is assumed to be a passive element in the production process, motivated primarily by his economic needs and characterized primarily by a predictable degree of strength, agility and perseverance; innovation and dealing with variations in the flow of production are considered beyond his scope and are left to specialists. In order to energize and coordinate some dozens or hundreds of atomized human "parts" in a plant, a rigorous and highly detailed control system is called into play, exemplified in its most extreme form by the balanced, intricately interwoven network of conveyors that constitutes an automobile assembly line.

Mass production has had its advantages, better pay and a proliferation of consumer goods among others. In the 1960s, however, particularly in the affluent societies of northern Europe and the U.S., its disadvantages were increasingly perceived, first by workers and their unions and then by industry. The jobs were dull and tiring and destructive of the worker's self-esteem. Things got worse as monotony and exhaustion led to resentment and sloppy work; the response — simpler jobs, tighter control and more speed — made for further monotony, exhaustion and resentment. Turnover and absenteeism became major problems. The assembly line and the minute subdivision of labor made companies particularly vulnerable: the absence of only a few men could jeopardize production, and the line itself was inflexible in the presence of variations in demand or in the delivery of parts.

All of this was accentuated in Sweden. An implicit respect for engineering and engineers, a passion for efficiency and hard work, a highly competitive situation in industry and the persistence of piecework pay along with highly rationalized mass-production methods — all combined to heighten the pace of production and the consequent stress on the worker. Perhaps even more important, these developments in industry flew in the face of contemporary changes in Swedish society as a whole. Increased equality had become a primary goal. More young people

Excerpts from Lars E. Björk. "An Experiment in Work Satisfaction." *Scientific American*, Vol. 232, 1975, pp. 17-23.

were staying in school longer, and the educational system itself was dropping its old authoritarian methods and emphasizing initiative, a critical attitude toward authority and mutual cooperation in small groups. The unions, the powerful metalworkers' union in particular, responded to their members' demand for better working conditions and specifically for more direct influence over their own situation on the shop floor as a necessary step toward industrial democracy. Moreover, by the end of the 1960s many industries simply found themselves unable to recruit enough new workers, to keep those they had recruited from quitting and to keep those who stayed with them on the job every day. Turnover climbed as high as a third of the payroll per year for some companies; maintaining a full crew, at an estimated average replacement cost of $2,000 per man, became prohibitively expensive, and with almost full employment in Sweden it was often impossible.

The upshot was that many companies began to wonder if there was not a better way to design jobs and organize the flow of work. They were ripe for the ideas being articulated in Sweden by a number of social scientists, including Bertil Gardell and Reine Hansson, who were criticizing the increasing impoverishment of work and who felt that more satisfactory methods could be developed based on different assumptions about the nature of man, of workers and of work-places. Human beings are not passive, according to such critics, but alive and curious. They learn, reason, evaluate and strive toward goals. When workers go home, they are grown-up men and women; regarding them as grown-ups on the job changes one's view of what they can do and of the principles of work organization. People need not be motivated by piecework rates; they can be self-propelling, motivated by the task as well as by pay. They can work in autonomous small groups shaped to fit the job. The groups can solve problems, learn from the problem solving and derive satisfaction from it. Instead of specifying each task in detail management can simply specify such essentials as quantity, quality and cost, what Philip G. Herbst of the Tavistock Institute of Human Relations in London called "minimum critical specifications." There need be no prescription of just how each job should be done; after a period of learning the workers will find the best solutions on their own, and they will be solutions based on how people really function and what the immediate shop-floor conditions really are. Technology is admittedly a limiting factor in any choice among various organizational possibilities. The model of man that is postulated by the people who make such choices, however, is even more limiting. In other words, given a specific technology there is more than one organizational choice, and the choice can take social requirements into account along with the workers' right to organize their work and design their own jobs.[. . .]

In 1969 . . . URAF*. . .sponsored six independent research projects on various aspects of industrial democracy. One of the projects, on work organization and job design, was initiated by our research group at the Swedish Council for Personnel Administration.[. . .]

[Editors' note: Development Council for Collaborative Questions, jointly sponsored by Confederations of Employers and Unions.]

When the URAF project came along, our group had just spent a year investigating organization and motivation in Department 698 of the Sickla Works, near Stockholm, of Atlas Copco Mining and Construction Technique, Inc. We had been interested in particular in how the motivation of the workers, who were engaged in the final assembly of rock-drilling machines, was affected by job design and work organization. The department had recently been reorganized and rationalized on the basis of time and motion studies. Its personnel, picked for their experience, skill and diligence, had more than met the goals set for the rationalized department, which involved a 25 percent increase in productivity. With the approval of Atlas Copco and the local chapter of the metalworkers' union, we sought a grant from a public foundation funded by the Swedish national bank and organized our new research project during the summer of 1969.

Together with management and the unions, we set up a development group as the decision-making body for the experiment. It consisted at first of representatives of management and the several unions in the plant and three researchers: Peter Hellberg, an industrial engineer, Reine Hansson, a psychologist, and myself, a social psychologist. There were two unusual things about our basic agreement. One was that the overall objective for the project would be to increase work satisfaction among the employees; productivity was not named as a primary goal, although management had made it clear that the current level should at least be maintained. The second was that in order to equalize the distribution of power each party in the development group was given the right to veto any action it interpreted as a threat to its interests. The objective of increased work satisfaction was intended to be achieved by changes aimed at giving the worker more opportunity to influence his own job, to take on responsibility, to solve problems and to advance his own development in the job. We were interested in learning whether such changes could in turn affect motivation to work and productivity. We assumed, however, that changes in these factors could not be measured precisely, as in a stimulus-and-response experiment in a laboratory; rather, we looked on the potential changes as elements in a slow and irreversible process.

The development group decided on a preliminary study that would begin with a survey and analysis of the department and end with proposals for change. We set up a working group (one man from management, one from the blue-collar union and two researchers) to meet weekly and carry out the study. Our analysis made it clear that the social system in Department 698 had become "hung up" on the technological system in ways that contributed neither to fulfilling the unit's objectives nor to the workers' satisfaction.

The department consisted of 12 men and a foreman. The input to the department consisted of the component parts of the rock drills, which came from elsewhere in the plant or were obtained outside. The department's products were some 40 different drill models, mostly variations on six basic types, together with spare parts. Production figures for each item were set by a planning department on the basis of actual orders and expected demand; the year was divided into eight six-week planning cycles (with a four-week vacation in July).

The department operated on a traditional "one man, one machine" basis. Each of the 12 workers had one of the following tasks: degreasing the incoming parts in a washing machine, grinding and honing the air-throttle elements, preassembly, assembly, testing, painting and packing. There were two floaters: an "instructor" and an adjuster who between them handled quality control, rigged machine tools for new products, checked on unsatisfactory components and corrected errors in assembly. Most of the workers knew only their own regular job and perhaps one or two of the easier other tasks. The foreman directed the work and was also busy adjusting the complicated pay systems. These were of several kinds. The washer, grinders and assemblers, constituting a team, received piecework pay based on the department's output but at various base-rate levels; the tester and the painter were on individual piece rates, again at two different levels. The adjuster and the instructor were paid by the month. The pay levels were decided on the basis of time and motion studies, time studies alone or subjective evaluation by the foreman. There was a great deal of concern and mutual suspicion with regard to rates of pay, and an informal status hierarchy had developed based on skill, job difficulty and pay levels. The two workers on the assembly line felt themselves most exploited: underpaid and bound to one location and to a flow of work they could not control.

The analytical phase had been conducted primarily by the researchers. As we entered the stage of working out changes early in 1970 a need was felt for more participation by the workers in the department. The development group proposed that both it and the working group be expanded to include the foreman and two of the workers. The workers agreed and chose their own representatives. This in effect represented the experiment's first increase in worker autonomy. Through discussions in the working group and through a series of individual interviews we held with all the workers (interviews that were repeated at intervals throughout the experimental period), we went through each job in the department. Each employee discussed his own job and suggested improvements in its design. Most of the suggestions involved small changes, aimed primarily at equalizing the various tasks and their rates of pay.

One major change was suggested by almost every worker, though. It was to do away with the conveyor-belt assembly line and substitute a large table on which the drills could be assembled at the men's own pace and in their own way. The company agreed to try it, and after some delay a specially built table designed by the workers was installed and several lots of drills were assembled on it. Rather surprisingly the drills were assembled as quickly as they had been along the production line, even without a breaking-in period. The table made for freer and less monotonous work. On the other hand, it was hard to handle the heavy steel components and move them around and to keep track of the many small parts on the table. Slowly a new point of view developed among the workers. The conveyor belt was seen not as simply a source of unvarying stress but as a tool: it could be used as a means of transportation, with its speed controlled by the workers themselves as they assembled drills on benches alongside the belt in the new ways they had developed by working around the table. Elements of the belt were brought back, having taken on a new meaning for the workers as a result of their own active experimentation; the belt technology could be useful to them because they had broken up the highly specified organizational pattern it had previously entailed.

The experience with the table served also to show the workers that management would allow them to work out and test innovations they themselves suggested.

Meanwhile, however, the experiment had run into trouble over wages. The men were uneasy about the economic consequences of the experiment, fearing their pay might suffer in the long run as production methods changed. They asked for some guarantee that the proposals they made would not lead to lower piece rates and thus in effect a speed-up. Management proposed a new system under which 80 percent of their average current earnings would be guaranteed, with the remainder depending on production. The workers considered that worse than either straight piecework or a straight monthly wage and said no, and the working group suspended its activities. After the July vacation there was another unsuccessful proposal from management. At that point the union, anxious lest the entire experiment be ended by the wage problem, stepped in and played a more active role. After some negotiations the workers got their guarantee: Regardless of the level of production, their earnings would not, for the duration of the experiment, fall below their previous average pay.

Once the wage question was resolved it took less than a month for the working group to formulate a set of principles for changes in organization, largely on the basis of ideas developed at four spontaneous meetings of all the members of Department 698. The proposals were not specified in detail but rather outlined some possible and permissible areas of change. When the guidelines came before the development group in November, the management representatives asked for more precision. That was hardly possible, they were told, since the whole idea was to let the systems change in pace with the employees' experience and not to establish detailed job specifications. A series of negotiations reached a new agreement on wages, and after that, in February of 1971, the development group approved the guidelines and a formal one-year experimental period began.

The basic idea was that the workers in the department would constitute a single team, with equal pay. The team would be split up into groups of from two to four men, and each group would move through the department, carrying out the entire sequence of operations for a single lot, or batch, of drills. The allocation of individual tasks within each group would be left up to the group to decide, as would the exact method of performing each operation. It was to be more than job rotation among previously designed jobs, since the old designs could be scrapped in favor of whatever methods the men found most convenient and satisfying. The wage agreement provided for continuation of the existing guaranteed hourly rate and also an incentive system: a small hourly increment for each percentage point by which the team as a whole exceeded its established production level.

Things began slowly. When there was plenty of time, the foreman would let from two to four men take a drill lot through the entire production process. More and more of the men learned new jobs, and they sorted themselves into permanent groups that gradually came to handle all production. This meant not only the assembly process but also managing the flow of goods through the department. In consultation with the foreman the groups decided, on the basis of delivery schedules and production goals, which lots of drills to process.

It was not an easy period. The workers were going through a time of intense learning, not only of new operations but also of new social relations: group cooperation in place of the individualistic and even antagonistic relations that had been shaped by the old one-man, one-machine organization. The mood was often one of irritability and tension as the men pressed to maintain the rate of production, partly for fear of losing their guaranteed earnings and partly to show that they could keep pace while working in their own way. At the end of the first six months management was pleased with the level of production but disappointed to see so little obvious change in production technique. The large changes in the patterns of work and social relations that the men were experiencing were not easily perceived by management.

Meanwhile two new conference groups, one for planning and one for rationalization, were established so that the men could deal directly with matters that had previously been handled by specialized management departments. The planning group consisted of two workers, the foreman and a representative of the planning department. It met once a week to discuss current production, establish priorities and deal with changes in parts or products. The rationalization group, consisting of two workers, the foreman and production engineers from the rationalization department, met about once a month so that the men could take part in any new technological developments. In these groups the specialists no longer prescribed the workers' actions but rather served their needs by supplying technical know-how and information.

During the second half-year of the experiment the department settled into a new steady state. There were fewer conflicts among the workers, who increasingly concerted their efforts and took on responsibility for the department's objectives and for one another. The foreman, who had been uncertain of his role at first, became more comfortable with his changed status. No longer required to maintain close control of every operation, he too was able to move to a higher level of competence, attending to budgetary and personnel matters and laying out machine tools and systems for assembling new models.

At a meeting of the development group early in 1972 the experiment was formally ended. In effect it was declared a success: management wanted the new system to continue as the ordinary way of doing things in Department 698. The other parties agreed. The working group was disbanded and the development group gave itself the assignment of evaluating the project.

That is not an easy thing to do. The most readily quantifiable change is in productivity, which is measured in Department 698 as the ratio between the man-hours allotted for a certain amount of production and the man-hours actually worked. Productivity has increased about 5 percent, but to report that figure is not to give the whole story. What seems more important is that a considerable amount of learning has taken place, with consequent benefits for long-term productivity. The men know one another's jobs and are anxious to cooperate, and so they can fill in when someone is absent. If several workers are off the floor simultaneously (at a meeting, for example), there is simply one less group in action, whereas the conventional in-line assembly process would have been seriously disrupted; the group system provides what the Tavistock theorists call "redundancy in function." Because the men are more oriented toward mutual goals and much more informed about the flow of materials and the logic of production schedules, they are better able to cope with variations in deliveries and with rush orders. The entire operation has become more flexible.

Work satisfaction is even harder to measure than productivity. Absenteeism and turnover, its traditional indicators, were low before the experiment began and have not changed. Perhaps the most obvious sign of increased satisfaction is the fact that none of the men wanted to go back to the old system. Satisfaction is subjective, however, and means different things to different people. What the former assembly-line workers wanted most, for example, was freedom from the line; they got it, and they were pleased. In our interviews most of the men mention the opportunity to perform different operations as the best result of the experiment: "It makes the job more pleasant." Many of them say the mood of the department has changed for the better, something they had not expected: "We've got calmer. It's not as stressful as it was before." They like laying out jobs in their own way: "Makes you feel like you're your own boss." There were exceptions, however. One man told us: "I'd rather work alone than in a group. Then you worry about yourself and you don't have to depend on all the bull all over the department."

As for the workers' power to exert influence, that has manifestly expanded. The experiment was in effect a lesson in wielding influence. The workers' very reluctance to make suggestions at first made their influence felt. In the course of the experimental year it was the workers who increasingly influenced the design of their own jobs and then the movement of material through the department. Behavioral scientists often say that once a need is filled it no longer motivates an individual's actions, and we saw that illustrated in the department. When the men had got themselves an acceptable degree of influence in one area, they refocused on the next most important question and thus worked themselves from one issue to another. Their aspirations kept rising: "In the future we want to be in on decisions on the department's budget."

The concept of responsibility broadened during the experiment from individual concern for product quantity and quality to group responsibility for the entire department's production flow. The men assumed that taking on such responsibility was a prerequisite for continuation of the experiment and for an increase in their influence. It involved taking the initiative to keep production moving: "We take a lot of responsibility now. We untangle pileups ourselves." Social responsibility has also broadened. The men help one another with new jobs: "We have to be more considerate of each other now. Before the experiment we didn't have any desire to get together. Everyone worked for himself."

The entire experiment was also an exercise in problem solving, with the request for, and the modification of, the assembly table being perhaps the most obvious example. During the year all the workers were drawn into the solving of practical problems of job design and work organization. Once they had all learned one another's jobs and once the new organization had become set, however, there seemed to be no problems left to solve. Several of the men expressed a desire to keep making new changes and came to feel that their work situation had once again become monotonous. This raises a question about experiments such as ours: Does the active period of change arouse interest and expectations that bring on a kind of relapse into boredom? In Department 698 there is still one good outlet for problem solving, the rationalization conference group, which continues to deal with production technique and changes in the department. Its activities directly involve only two of the workers at a time, however.

As we analyzed the experiment we came to see it as a learning process not only for individuals but also for groups and for the major parties involved. The experiment freed the workers to change their own situation, but experience showed that the freedom to change was utilized only as the workers learned more about their situation. We had assumed that the conditions that would fundamentally affect changes in influence, responsibility and problem solving were management's traditional control mechanisms: work organization, job design, wages, supervision, planning and so on. This turned out to be true on the whole, but we found that the links among those mechanisms were also important. In other words, one cannot change a control mechanism such as wages without considering the effect of the change on organization, job design, planning and so forth. Those relationships also must be learned, by the researchers, the workers and the management. Values and attitudes are deeply involved here. In many cases we found management had little understanding of how a control mechanism was perceived by the workers.

The fact that the experiment involved so much learning is perhaps the best explanation of why it took almost three years. Considering the amount of learning that went on at various levels, it was really not such a long time. One does not introduce a new way of working as one installs a new tool or even a new conveyor belt; behavior cannot be changed overnight by the promulgation of new rules. Actually the aim was quite different: to unfreeze the production technology and the grip it had on the social system and the people.

Two questions that need to be raised about an experiment of this kind have to do with reliability and diffusion. How much can be proved by an experiment involving 12 men? Not much, if the object is to measure a lot of factors before and after the experiment and see how they differed — to collect, in other words, what in a social context are incorrectly called "results." What we sought to do, however, was to understand the how and why of the differences, and in an effort to do that we followed the entire process of change, starting a year and a half before the experiment began and conducting our last interviews a year after it ended. Through our continuous contact with management, the unions and the individual workers we have been able to check dubious data in a way that is not possible in a large before-and-after survey. Our examination of the process of change has primarily confirmed the predictions we made, admittedly from a definite point of view: an assumption that people are capable of controlling their work situation. What we learned about the process of change seems to us to "prove" that our initial assumptions were correct, but there should be additional evidence as the outcome of other URAF experiments becomes known.

Finally, does the experiment say anything about what can happen in the future and what can happen beyond the walls of Department 698? For the process of change to continue there will have to be changes elsewhere in the company. Horizontal diffusion is not important in this case, but the supervisory layers above the assembly department will have to modify their planning and control functions if the men in the department are to gain increased influence and autonomy. Any further diffusion through industry will depend heavily on the attitudes of the major labor-market organizations. As of now the position of the Swedish Employers' Confederation has been to promote practical cooperation at the local level between workers and management in a plant and not to talk about increasing influence. The Confederation of Trade Unions, on the other hand, is anxious to obtain legislation that will secure the worker's right to increased influence by law, even in situations where local cooperation breaks down in conflict. Broad diffusion of the new ideas will also depend, as the beginnings of change did in the 1960s, on the changing values of Swedish society as a whole.

In time perhaps such words as "experiment" and "pilot project" — which imply that one wants to leave the doors open for retrogression, to be able to sneak back to the old way if things go wrong — will seem old-fashioned. We may come to think of the delegation of power and influence to the worker as being quite normal and undramatic.

Part 6

FUTURE OF JOB DESIGN

Introduction

22.
Job Design and Industrial Democracy (1976)
Joep F. Bolweg

23.
Job Design:
Future Directions (1977)
Louis E. Davis

INTRODUCTION

This concluding section ends on two notes. The first is that job design is a major means for enhancing the quality of life at the workplace and for changing relations at work so as to move toward democratizing the workplace. The second is that for the purposes of new design and redesign, jobs are neither conceptually nor operationally useful entities. Focusing on jobs, as an organizational unit, risks accepting the status quo of existing organization structure and management methods which limit the opportunities for work reform. Focusing on jobs also restricts the solution space or opportunities to examine a great number of relationships and issues that affect the performance of jobs and the quality of jobs.

Taking the earliest national development, that of Norway, Bolweg (reading 22) relates the Norwegian experience with work reform — in its larger context as industrial democracy — to similar developments in other industrialized countries. Job design–work democratization is related to changes in industrial relations and to meeting changes in the social environment of organizations.

In the closing paper Davis (reading 23) reviews recent conceptual and practical changes and concludes that job design independent of organization design, has no future. This position is bolstered by recent new plant–new organization designs. Only as an outcome of organization design or redesign can the structure and content of jobs effectively influence organizational effectiveness and quality of working life.

22
Job Design and
Industrial Democracy
Joep F. Bolweg

All these developments [work reform experiments] could leave one with the false impression that a general consensus exists about the necessity of these attempts to create more interesting and challenging work. On the contrary there are a number of serious controversies and some difficulty to reconcile empirical social science findings in this area. First there is the consistent reporting of generally high job satisfaction among the work forces of the industrialized countries (Barbash, 1974). For the U.S. a recent monograph by the Department of Labor analyzing longitudinal data concluded that there is no conclusive evidence of a dramatic decline in job satisfaction. This study showed that between 1958 and 1973 the percentage of satisfied workers in the U.S. labor force fluctuated between 81% and 92% (U.S. Department of Labor, 1974). A 1972 representative sample of 2262 LO members in Norway also showed a high percentage of satisfied workers. In this survey 95% of the respondents were very satisfied or satisfied, 12% were neither satisfied nor dissatisfied, while only 3% were dissatisfied or very dissatisfied (Karlsen, 1972, 41). Fein (1973) concludes from these satisfaction percentages that there is no urgent need for job redesign.

Those supporting job redesign reject this argument and counter job satisfaction studies with empirical studies showing high alienation among certain groups of

Excerpts from Joep F. Bolweg. *Job Design and Industrial Democracy: The Case of Norway.* Martinus-Nijhoff (Leiden), 1976, Chapter 6, pp. 110–136.

industrial workers (Sheppard and Herrick, 1972; H.E.W., 1973). They reject Fein's interpretation of the findings of job satisfaction studies and postulate adaptive worker responses to work, the high degree of ego involvement in work, and the lack of alternative experiences for workers which could change their current expectations as the explanations for the reported high job satisfaction (Cherns and Davis, 1975). Despite high job satisfaction only a few in Western Europe would reject the following analysis by a well known French sociologist: "Nobody wants to be an industrial worker . . . if you are a young man and go to work in an industry you are considered a marginal man. . . . The industrial culture is disappearing . . . When people have choice they move from the industrial organization to the tertiary system" (Quoted in Barbash, 1974). The question remains however whether or not high percentages of satisfied workers are a sufficient reason to retain the existing forms of work organization?

A second related discussion centers around the interpretation of the behavioral indices of job satisfaction. Increased management concern is reported about rising absenteeism and turnover. This concern is supported by national statistics of rising quit rates and absenteeism in a number of industrialized countries (O.E.C.D., 1973). In addition some Norwegian and Swedish employers are facing recruitment problems for unattractive jobs. Do the quit rates and absenteeism statistics reflect the need for job redesign? No, concludes a recent U.S. study which confirmed increased absenteeism and turnover (Flanagan et al., 1974) because the increases can be satisfactorily explained by changes in the demographic composition of the labor force. The proportion of the work force of groups with high quit and absentee rates (women, blacks, and young workers) has risen.

A third controversy centers around the interpretation of the dominant worker attitude to work. Studies by Goldthorpe and his associates (1969) and the reanalysis by Fein (1973) of the H.E.W. data, support, for blue collar workers at least, the existence of a predominant instrumental attitude to work. Goldthorpe et al. (1969, 38-39) discount the importance of work itself for the workers and state: "The primary meaning of work is as a means to an end, or, ends, external to the work situation; that is, work is regarded as a means necessary to support a valued way of life of which work itself is not an integral part." The U.S. unionist Winpisinger (1973) underscores this conclusion in a more blunt manner: "If you want to enrich the job, enrich the pay check." Proponents of job redesign do not question Goldthorpe's findings but argue that it is exactly the lack of any intrinsically satisfying work experiences that contributes to these instrumental attitudes. Only experiences with more challenging and interesting work will cultivate a taste for it. Some support for this argument was provided in the analysis of the Norwegian experiments.*

Finally, a lack of consensus exists whether or not fragmented and specialized work has an impact upon personal characteristics and activities outside the place of work. Kohn and Schooler (1973) in a very careful analysis report the following relationship between the extent to which a worker controls his job and certain

---

*Editor's Note: Reviewed in Chapter 1 of Joep F. Bolweg, *Job Design and Industrial Democracy.*

personal characteristics: "The evidence constantly suggests that although men undoubtedly do choose and mold their jobs to fit their personal requirements, it is not likely that these processes alone can sufficiently explain occupational conditions and psychological functioning" (Kohn and Schooler, 1973). Meissner (1971) finds support for the position that workers in highly specialized jobs are less active in their leisure activities than those which have less specialized jobs. His research clearly points to a carry-over effect from work experience to leisure activities. The opposing view with respect to the impact of work on the worker and his leisure activities is that leisure activities adequately compensate for the strain, stress, or lack of challenge on the job. Work is not very central to the life interests of the workers. The central life interest of workers is centered around his non-work activities. The latter reflects Wilensky's (1960) compensatory hypothesis, which involves "explosive compensation for the deadening rhythms of factory life." The spillover hypothesis refers to the situation where mental stultification produced by work permeates leisure. Parker (1972) reports empirical studies supporting both hypotheses.

Scepticism and concern is also generally found among trade union leaders, with the possible exception of Norwegian and Swedish unionists, who fear that ameliorating the quality of working life is another underhanded means to improve productivity and weaken the benefits the unions have won on behalf of their members. Unionists fear that job redesign is a new manipulative tool to get more work out of workers without appropriate remuneration; that it is designed to deflect workers from making wage demands by increasing intrinsic rewards in work; that job redesign is an attempt to reduce worker attachment to their unions by making them more satisfied; or that it is designed to generate the illusion of greater worker control at the same time as reducing the substance by giving workers a greater say over unimportant decisions, thereby deflecting their attention from the bigger and more important decisions.

There is little doubt that increased productivity and cost reduction are the underlying interests of management in job redesign and the quality of working life. Adequate worker control in the redesign phases can sufficiently counterbalance this management interest however. The management interest in the productivity aspects of job redesign points to the necessity of differentiation between the job redesign principles as proposed in the quality of working life literature and the practical implementation of these principles at the company level.[. . .]

This brief presentation of the opposing views with respect to the necessity of job redesign gives an impression of the unclear picture which presents itself to policy makers in this area. It also reflects an inherent weakness of social science research which leaves its findings open to so many different interpretations. The use of different research paradigms, e.g. the job satisfaction and alienation paradigms, leads to seemingly opposing interpretations with respect to the necessity of job redesign. Job satisfaction research is interpreted as evidence that there is no problem in this area (Fein, 1973), while alienation research findings (H.E.W., 1973) can be interpreted as pointing to a clear need for changes in our organizational structures. An inherent weakness of the descriptive social science studies is its reliance upon data from existing organizations. This in itself is a strong argument in favor of longterm, carefully monitored experimentation in organizational and job redesign. Whether or not to support job redesign experiments is basically a political decision based upon a subjective value assessment whether industrial and service sector jobs need improvements or not.

In this study the endorsement of job redesign experiments has been obvious. This does not imply however "the prospect that work can be self-actualizing for everybody, or almost everybody" (Barbash, 1974). Endorsement of the new job design principles means that efforts should be made to make work as attractive and challenging as practically possible. Working out of necessity in a somewhat more intrinsically satisfying manner has been proven possible in an increasing number of different organizational circumstances. Unnecessary polarization, which is particularly evident in the U.S., France, and Belgium, hampers the chances for new experiments in redesigning jobs.

One area of the quality of working life discussion which is unnecessarily polarized is the question raised earlier: what is the "true" worker interest in work? A simple solution to the controversy could be that both pay and interesting work are important to the worker. The experiments reported so far do not suggest any necessary trade-off between pay and more interesting work. The Norwegian projects even suggest that the outcome of job redesign can be both slightly increased pay and somewhat more interesting work. The findings of Daniel seem to support the thesis that workers are interested in both pay and interesting work; but that their relevance is not the same in different contexts (Daniel, 1970; Daniel and McIntosh, 1972). Daniel develops a contingency model of worker interest and finds subsequent support for it in his studies of productivity bargaining in a number of British companies. Workers, following Daniel's argument, have different sets of priorities that relate to different situations and contexts. He distinguishes between two major contexts: the negotiation context and the operating context (the day-to-day work situation). In the negotiation context, which includes both the job searching process and collective bargaining, the level of income is the dominating worker interest. In these situations considerations of job satisfaction and interesting work are irrelevant. The worker is here only interested in making the best financial deal for himself. In the case of collective bargaining, the interests more closely related to the nature of work become only prevalent *after* the agreement is settled.[. . .]

Emery and Thorsrud's (1969) developmental model of industrial democracy is based on similar learning premises. The experiments in Norway provide very limited support for the theory that increased autonomy at the shop floor will lead to increased worker involvement in broader company affairs.

What the experiments showed more clearly was: 1. that increased autonomy at the shop floor combined with other changes in the work organization were evaluated positively by the workers despite initial resistance against such changes (the "experience hypothesis"); 2. that changes beyond the immediate job redesign are severely constrained by the larger organization. No continuous change process developed in the Norwegian companies; the projects stagnated after a certain period of time. This stagnation or the lack of continuity seems to be a general characteristic of such experiments in job design (Van der Does, 1973).

The recently started experiments in a number of Norwegian companies probably will reach a similar stagnation phase in particular where the goals of recent experiments are more limited: to increase productivity and improve the work situation in order to attract sufficient labor. Management in these companies does not envision any overall organizational change process to occur. In this respect the latest experiments in Norway resemble the developments in Sweden. It is clear that in most of those experiments the four conditions for industrial democracy are not met. A Swedish LO official with special responsibilities in the area of job redesign complained that most companies are interested only in limited forms of reorganization: "When it comes to more far-reaching expansion of the independence and competence of workers within companies, there is not so much interest" (Janerius, quoted in Jenkins, 1974).[. . .]

This body of literature and the experiences from the Norwegian field projects indicate that there are indeed individual differences with respect to desire for and responses to more interesting and demanding work. Older workers and also young woman workers sometimes resist changes in job design. Some workers prefer a simple routine task, which can be performed automatically and almost unconsciously, and leaves them free to talk, gossip, and daydream. This is sometimes preferred over a more complex task that requires full attention. These preferences and individual differences should be respected as far as possible in job redesign projects.

The stringent labor market in Norway has been mentioned several times as the reason for the current interest in management circles in job redesign. The developments in the other industrialized countries of Western Europe, with unusually high unemployment rates (4%-5%), suggest that national aggregate unemployment is less important in triggering job redesign experiments than labor shortages in certain segments of the labor market. In addition to segmental labor shortages the industrialized countries of Western Europe are faced with increasing problems with respect to the substantial numbers of foreign workers from Southern Europe and North Africa. This results in a situation where both high unemployment and large numbers of foreign workers coincide. In the Netherlands in November 1974 there were 165,000 people registered as unemployed while at the same time 80,000 foreign workers were employed. In Dutch government circles job redesign is being considered as one possible method to reduce both unemployment and the number of foreign workers. Making jobs more attractive could theoretically reduce the number of nationals unemployed.

Another context in which job redesign can be considered is the decentralizing trend in Western European industrial relations and the suggested decrease in legitimacy of the established management and union institutions at the company level. Schregle (1974) and Dufty (1973) agree on a decentralizing trend in collective bargaining, while Kassalow (1974) cites increased industrial unrest at the shop floor levels as an indicator of a need for change in the established management and union practices. Whether the downward trend in collective bargaining is a result of increased shop floor demands for a role in the rule determining processes or a response to certain macroeconomic developments (differential industry and company growth rates under high inflation conditions) is hard to establish.

The return in Norway in 1974 to industry bargaining without a national framework agreement is best explained by the macroeconomic factors. The change in worker attitudes is another hard to ascertain trend. The exact causes for the increased rejection of traditional legitimate decisions are difficult to identify but increased levels of education, full employment, increased affluence, and modern social welfare provisions are generally cited as underlying the changes in worker attitudes (O.E.C.D., 1974). If the current hierarchical organization structures with their differentiated material and psychological reward systems become less generally accepted, new organizational designs must be found which do have some necessary degree of legitimacy. In this context the participative design process (Emery and Emery, 1974) of new forms of work organization reflects the historical trend from unilateral to bilateral legitimization procedures in industrial relations. In a democratic society "management's unilateral right to manage" becomes more and more an empty slogan. Any right that management has in a democratic society must depend on the consent of that society and in particular on the consent of those managed. This consent will depend on the extent to which unilateral management decisions are considered legitimate by the workers. Job redesign is possibly also a response to a decrease in legitimacy ascribed to unilateral management decisions in certain areas. Dufty suggests an increasing managerial acceptance of the idea "that the only way for management to retain control is to share it" (Dufty, 1973).

A final perspective from which job redesign and work democratization can be analyzed is the one suggested by Strauss and Rosenstein (1970). They argue that "participation" is partly a symbolic reconciliation between contradictory managerial and union ideologies rather than an organizational solution to any real life problems. The start of the Norwegian Cooperation Project partly motivated by a desire of the NAF to stall on the introduction of a board representation system, provides some support for Strauss and Rosenstein's argument. The more recent job redesign projects are of a very concrete nature and a response to practical management problems. The relationship of these projects to industrial democracy is therefore indeed merely a symbolic one.

[. . .] The start of the Norwegian Cooperation Project was a function of a particular historical, socio-political, and economic national context. A late and balanced industrialization process had facilitated the growth of a stable industrial relations system in Norway. The Norwegian trade unions attained a high degree of organization; Kassalow (1974) estimated that about 65% of the Norwegian labor force belongs to a trade union, and their strong ties to the Labor Party resulted in a societal power position which is comparable to that of the employers' interests. The Labor Party represents and integrates the Norwegian working class in the power centers of the nation.

This socio-political context provided the background setting of an industrial democracy debate in the late 1950s and early 1960s. The labor movement demanded more industrial democracy but did not have its demands very well defined. The employers' organization was afraid of the possibility that a scheme providing for worker representation on the board of directors would be legally imposed on Norwegian companies. Thorsrud's intervention in which he advocated industrial democracy through job redesign was well received. In his proposals Thorsrud linked the notion of industrial democracy, with its roots in socialist thought, to the Tavistock ideas of increased individual learning through more worker autonomy and responsibility at the shop floor level. Both LO and NAF, obviously for different individual reasons, decided to support experiments in job redesign. A few years later the government also gave its financial support to the experiments.

The Norwegian experiments in job design show great similarity to the current developments in most industrialized countries under the labels of the humanization of work, and the quality of working life. The essence of these developments is the question whether or not through certain forms of job complication the highly simplified industrial and white collar jobs can be improved in terms of greater worker autonomy and job satisfaction while at least maintaining current levels of productivity and efficiency.

The support of the government and national labor and employers' organizations in Norway legitimized the job design notions of the researchers involved in the early experiments. Later experiments show that this national institutional support might be a necessary condition to start experimentation in an organized manner; however this support does not determine whether or not an individual experiment is successful in terms of starting a democratizing process within a company.

The initiative to start a job redesign experiment is predominantly a management initiative. Management reacts to particular problems which are often related to the difficulties in attracting, maintaining and disciplining the necessary company labor force. A stringent labor market is the underlying cause of many of these managerial problems in Norway. This results in the paradoxical situation where increased industrial democracy should be the outcome of a management initiated and controlled job redesign program. A unilateral management introduction of a new work organization at the shop floor, which is basically the method followed in job enrichment in the U.S., cannot be defined as contributing to industrial democracy. The boundaries of this type of democracy are well indicated by the following quote from an U.S. worker involved in an organizational change project: "You can make any decision as long as it agrees with management" (Quoted in Elden, 1974). In this type of project the four necessary conditions in order for job redesign to contribute to industrial democracy are not met. The projects are generally successful in terms of increased productivity and increased job satisfaction. The number of Norwegian companies where further democratization took place is probably limited to 7, this despite the supportive institutional environment.

A considerable gap exists between the theories and strategies for organizational democratization as presented in the literature and the manner in which they are implemented. The managerial control of the organization's hierarchy makes democratization difficult in particular because job redesign is characteristically not defined by management in terms of democracy but in terms of lower total production cost. If the immediate management problem is solved no motivation remains on the initiating and controlling side to continue the change process. The local union generally perceives job redesign also as a tool to attain its traditional objectives. The job redesign strategies which potentially could alter the traditional principles of organizational control through hierarchy and technology are redefined by management and the local union as just another means to achieve their traditional goals. These goals for management are cost reduction, higher productivity, and maintaining its position of power; for the union these goals are higher wages, better working conditions, and securing a stronger position inside the enterprise. Job redesign, as a form of direct worker participation, is perceived by management as a form of democracy which is preferred over the more formalized and institutionalized forms of representation of the worker interest. This could be one possible reason why local unions generally have not yet defined job redesign and improvement of individual jobs as an autonomous union bargaining goal. The existing managerial prerogative in the direction and organization of work has not yet been radically challenged by the unions. This challenge is necessary if workers themselves are going to influence the design of their work to any significant extent.

The organizational realities described here do not preclude the possibility that redesigned jobs provide the workers with more intrinsic satisfaction. A more challenging job, more variety, and increased autonomy and responsibility are changes to be positively evaluated in themselves. The start of a continuous democratization process can hardly be expected given current organizational conditions. Democratization has taken place in individual departments of companies; however diffusion into the larger organization has seldom taken place. The experimental department usually remains a "foreign body" in a larger organization operating under different organizational principles.

The main contribution to industrial democracy by Einar Thorsrud and his collaborators has been his advocacy and partial implementation of opening up the job redesign process itself to workers and their representatives. The process of change and the changes in job design which result, are of coordinate importance. The experiments in Norway have shown that workers initially may resist changes in their jobs. However, after having experienced the redesigned work organization, they do not want to return to the old situation. Changes in job design have, in all cases, been accompanied by concomitant changes in the wage rate and wage system. In the successful cases a shelter agreement, which guarantees certain management and worker rights, has been agreed upon between management and the union, while in a later phase of the experiments changes in the work-effort bargain were referred to collective bargaining. Most unions have been able to renegotiate the wage system as a result of the introduction of new forms of work organization. At the national level LO and the national unions have not been successful in integrating job design and work democratization into their daily policies.

Potentially, work democratization through job redesign can fill the gap left by the existing representative approaches to increase industrial democracy. Their representative nature inherently restricts the direct impact of those approaches on the shop floor. Representation is no alternative to active shop floor participation. Work democratization through job design is an essential element in the package approach towards industrial democracy. The Cooperation Project has shown that in a rather restricted number of companies (7), job redesign did indeed contribute to industrial democracy as defined earlier. The Cooperation Project also contributed to refinements of the socio-technical model, to a deepening insight into organizational change processes, to the identification of the importance of the change process itself, and to a better understanding of the difficult role of the social scientist as consultant. In Norway the Project led to a sharp decline in the use of time and motion studies, stimulated the introduction of fixed wage systems with predominantly small group bonuses and initiated the start of organizational change projects in the educational system and the important shipping industry. The Project also triggered experiments in Sweden (e.g. Volvo and Saab-Scania) and Denmark.

The complexity of the Norwegian Cooperation Project makes a simple concluding evaluation impossible. The developments as they present themselves today are ambiguous. The question whether or not job redesign has contributed to industrial democracy is difficult to answer. On the whole the Norwegian experience is not too positive from an industrial democracy perspective. On the other hand a rather small number of companies has progressed in a direction which seems to support the underlying theoretical notions of Einar Thorsrud and his collaborators. This ambivalence could be substantially reduced if the parties involved — employers, unions, workers, and researchers — make their objectives more explicit. The resulting clarity will facilitate the understanding of similar organizational change projects. It will also clarify whether or not the social scientist plays a "democratizing" or merely a "cost reducing–productivity enhancing" role.[. . .]

REFERENCES

Barbash, J. (1974) *Job Satisfaction Attitude Surveys*. Paris: O.E.C.D.
Cherns, A. B. and Davis, L. E. (1975) Assessment of the State of the Art. In L. E. Davis and A. B. Cherns, eds. *The Quality of Working Life*. New York: Free Press.
Daniel, W. W. (1970) *Beyond the Wage Bargain*. London: MacDonald.
Daniel, W.W. and McIntosh, N. (1972) *The Right to Manage?* London: MacDonald.
Dufty, N.F. (1973) *Changes in Labour-Management Relations in the Enterprise*. Paris: O.E.C.D.
Elden, M. (1974) *The Anatomy of Autonomy: A View from the Inside*. Oslo: AFI.
Emery, F.E. and Emery, M. (1974) *Participative Design*. Oslo: AFI.
Emery, F. E. and Thorsrud, E. (1969)*Form and Content in Industrial Democracy*. London: Tavistock.
Fein, M. "The Real Needs and Goals of Blue Collar Workers." *The Conference Board Record,* February 1973, 26-33.
Flanagan, R. J., Strauss, G., and Ulman, L., "Worker Discontent and Workplace Behavior." *Industrial Relations,* 1974, 13(2), 101-123.
Goldthorpe, J. H., Lockwood, D., Bechhofer, F., and Platt, J. (1969)*The Affluent Worker in the Class Structure*. Cambridge: University Press.

H.E.W. Task Force Report on *Work in America*. Cambridge: MIT Press, 1973.

Jenkins, D. (1974) *Industrial Democracy in Europe*. Geneva: Business International.

Karlsen, J. E. (1972) *Arbeidsmiljo og arbeidsskader*. Oslo: L.O.

Kassalow, E. M. "Conflict and Cooperation in Europe's Industrial Relations." *Industrial Relations*, 1974, 13, 156-163.

Kohn, M. and Schooler, C. "Occupational Experience and Psychological Functioning: An Assessment of Reciprocal Effects." *American Sociological Review*, 1973, 38, 97-118.

Meissner, M. "The Long Arm of the Job: A Study of Work and Leisure." *Industrial Relations*, 1971, 10, 239-260.

O.E.C.D. (1973a) *Absenteeism and Staff Turnover*. Report on a meeting of management experts. Paris: O.E.C.D.

O.E.C.D. (1974b) *Work In a Changing Industrial Society*. Paris: O.E.C.D.

Parker, S. (1972) *The Future of Work and Leisure*. London: Paladin.

Pateman, C. (1970) *Participation and Democratic Theory*. London: Cambridge University Press.

Schregle, J. "Labor Relations in Western Europe: Some Topical Issues." *International Labour Review*, 1974, 109(1), 1-22.

Sheppard, H. L. and Herrick, N. Q. (1972) *Where Have All the Robots Gone?* New York: Free Press.

Strauss, G. and Rosenstein, E. "Workers' Participation: A Critical View." *Industrial Relations*, 1970, 9, 197-214.

U.S. Department of Labor. "Job Satisfaction: Is There a Trend?" Manpower Research monograph No. 30, 1974.

Van der Does de Willebois, J. L. "On the Quality of Working Life." In W. Albeda, ed. (1973) *Participation in Management*. Rotterdam, University Press.

Wilensky, H. "Work Careers and Social Integration." *International Social Science Journal*, 1960, 12, 543-574.

Winpisinger, W. "Job Satisfaction: A Union Response." *AFL-CIO Federationist*, 1973, 80(2), 3-10.

23
Job Design:
Future Directions
Louis E. Davis

At present most people engaged in sociotechnical, systems-based organization and job design activities are acquiring most of their learning from action research and from case studies of changes made in organizations and in jobs. The utility, difficulties and limitations of these methods of acquiring knowledge have been explored at some length by Davis and Cherns (1975) and by Clark (1975). While there is a need to extend as well as to refine and strengthen these methods so as to increase the rate at which reliable knowledge can be accumulated, action research studies are providing leads that need to be pursued by discipline-based researchers.

The action research mode of direct engagement with organizations to create new forms of working — providing enhanced relationships between people and work — derives from two central facts about life in the workplace. Both of these points add complications and cast doubt on what we already have accepted as reliable knowledge. First, in advanced industrial societies, most, if not all, organizations, processes and jobs are inventions which are under constant modification; they are man-made and are based on the existing world view or culture (assumptions about what will be successful and about the perceived environment). Any research that treats organizations and jobs as natural entities will tend to provide misleading results. Second, what is being studied or measured is often the consequence of the "iron law of adaptation" or the "self-fulfilling prophecy," particularly in studies of job satisfaction. The "law of adaptation" states that people act out the roles required of them and, to a large extent, adapt, accommodate or adjust to the circumstances invented by others. People make the best of the situation, particularly when it does yield material rewards and when other alternatives are either not available or are not attainable. Having made the bargain and accepted the various costs to self and family, the situation becomes "normal" or the expected one by those affected. The widespread resigned acceptance in advanced industrial societies of the belief that one must endure a poor quality of life at the workplace as a cost of acquiring its material rewards is one such example.

If we wish to learn how people adapt to narrow, restricting work lives and its costs, then researchers should go on studying existing organizations, technology and jobs. However, if we wish to learn how organizations can meet the needs of

Excerpts from Louis E. Davis. "Job Design: Overview and Future Direction." *Journal of Contemporary Business*, Vol. 6 (1977), No. 2, pp. 85-102.

society and the needs of their members, effectively, how human aspirations and potential may be fulfilled, how innovation takes place and how social responsibility evolves, then researchers must avoid the trap of the "iron law of adaptation." At present this sets another task for the researcher which requires that person first to develop organization structures, technology and jobs that are based on different concepts which have the joint goals of effectiveness and high quality of working life.

Such engagements reinforce the reality of people's relationships to work, leading to the recognition that this is a systemic relationship consisting of people, technical processes and the machine artifacts having multiple objectives, satisfying multiple needs and being embedded in changing environments. Such recognition clearly requires research to proceed on a systemic basis, focusing on work systems that seek to respond to the environmental forces impinging on the organization. This requires taking into account all aspects of the work system and its environment. It is not possible to predict what will be learned or how valid the learning will be if research proceeds by piecemeal examination of favorite relationships (whether these be person-machine, motivation, enriched or enlarged tasks, autonomy, rewards or shared-power).

DEVELOPMENTS OF THE 1970s

Developments in the 1970s continue to undermine the viability of jobs (person-task units) as basic organizational units. This is brought about in part by the continuation, quite unabated, of the intrusion of social, technological, political and economic environments into organizations. Additionally, the place of employment is seen by the U.S. society as the place for carrying out deep changes in its social behavior; in the work organization, changes are being required in response to affirmative action regulations in support of the Equal Employment Opportunity Act. The special aspect of the environmental intrusions is that in addition to a high and increasing rate of change, actions and institutions in the different environments are interacting, developing an environmental texture identified as turbulent by Emery and Trist (1965). Survival strategies in turbulent environments place a premium on organizational cooperation and adaptability, further straining the utility of the concept of the person-job as a basic organizational unit.

The design of Volvo's Kalmar automobile assembly plant is a prime illustration of the theoretical reasons that undermine the concept of the person-job as a basic organizational unit; also, our own design experiences with three new plants and their organizations structures added to the theoretical base. These designs represent a practical application of a theoretical development of the mid-1960s. The Kalmar plant assembles automobiles without a fixed assembly line, using carriers to transport frames and bodies as they are completed and employing an organization consisting of semiautonomous work teams. The design breaks with the traditional practice of industrial organization based on scientific management, that is, whether in a production station or on an assembly line, it must be possible for each individual worker to be held responsible by an external supervisor. The traditional organizational unit specified by F. W. Taylor as the building block of organization under scientific management is the individually supervised person-task unit.[. . .]

Carrying these developments further in our continuing new plant-organization designs, the concept of the open sociotechnical system unit as a "unit of design" is now taking on more specific characteristics. The concept being tested in new organization designs as the basic organization unit is the self-maintaining organizational unit. As the name implies, it is an organizational unit of one or more people and the relevant technical system, information system, authority structure and internal requisite variety of competences. It is so bounded technically and organizationally that its members, once accepting targets or goals, have the means, resources, competences and authority to achieve the goals without external coercion, given reasonable rewards to themselves. Experiences over the last 5 years of implementing such designs have shown that semiautonomous groups of five to twenty members have better achieved mutual goals than they individually had been capable of when each person was under supervisory control. Such experiences indicate why there is a changing emphasis to semiautonomous groups and to roles for group members as areas of research and practical concern. The continuing emphasis of the concept of jobs, job enlargement, job enrichment, all based on the one person-one task unit, undoubtedly will continue. However, it will grow increasingly dysfunctional since it is based on an underlying concept actually contrary to that just described.

FUTURE DIRECTION

What began as job design 25 years ago, comfortably based on the concept of the one man-one task unit of organization, is being transmuted to work organization (as system) design and to role design for its members. Some of the reasons lie in theoretical and conceptual developments, and others lie in the changed world in which organizations and their members find themselves. The evolving turbulent texture of organizational environments raises questions about the survival of organizations, in turn giving emphasis to cooperation and adaptability as a strategy, since planning frequently becomes a trap in such environments.

A cooperative adaptive strategy gives rise to a focus on items such as task integration, composite self-directing groups, wide competence and work authority, which clashes with the one person-one task concept of a basic organizational unit. The latter concept requires for organizational functioning extensive rules and external controls, like those in bureaucracy and scientific management models of organization. One may say that bureaucracy and scientific management require the one person-one task unit and postulate it as an organizational construct. In operation, bureaucratic-scientific management organizations are based firmly on the one person-one task behaviors on the part of organizational components and their members.

The changes in the environments of organizations, the changes in values and expectations of those who work and the growth of the workplace as a crossroads for societal concerns, such as equal employment opportunity, environmental protection and occupational safety and health, have contributed to further moving away from a focus on the job (person-task unit) as a basis for meaningfully attacking the concern about the content of the relationship between people and organizations. By the end of the 1960s, concern had shifted to the structure of work organizations. Now in the mid-1970s, concern is focused on (1) the design and development of viable organizations that can maintain themselves in ways which support and enhance the societies of which they are a part and (2) the design and development of roles that promote and support organization members as healthy, whole, responsive and adaptive human beings. Viability means that organizations can develop the capacity continuously to meet the rapidly changing and growing demands from their economic, social and technological environments, as well as from the growing and changing demands of their members who increasingly question the very basis of their relationship to the organization.

The achievements of the growing number of new plant-organization designs based on the self-maintaining organization unit and reinforced by the search for organizational and job forms that support organization survival, indicate increasing future research interest in the characteristics and behaviors of such units. Not only does the self-maintaining organizational unit provide a new and alternative principle of organization design, but also it requires a new basis for management. Relatively little is known about managing autonomous or semiautonomous groups with requirements for "boundary protection," goal agreement or resource provision, for example. Research on requirements for managing such groups also will grow.

Existing knowledge of small groups is useful, but inadequate for design, operation and management of self-maintaining organizational units. Many successful groups are larger than those to which small-group theory directs itself. Further, as segments of organizations, such groups have multiple goals—some in conflict with others—and multiple needs to satisfy, ranging from maintaining the organization to providing a future for each member. Some research, though it is not sufficiently extensive, has been undertaken. The center of the future trend of research and application will be on self-maintaining organizational units and related research on role design and development. Such self-maintaining organizational units that have been created and have performed successfully are based on the concepts that the work to be done belongs to the group as a whole, which assigns tasks to its members based on competence and exigencies of the situation. Among members of such organizational units, a popular term used in their discussions is the "work assignment for today," reflecting the fact that they have no fixed jobs but, rather, that they have a role to fulfill whose specific tasks may change from one time period to another. In these instances, compared to conventional organizational designs, the roles are quite expanded, including, for example, task assignment which formerly was the responsibility of job designers. Research on characteristics and behaviors of such roles will be strongly increased.

Additionally, and particularly in relation to issues of organizational survival, research on the discretionary aspects of roles as compared to the prescribed aspects will increase. Treating discretionary tasks as part of the "informal organization" is growing increasingly less useful. This is particularly true in high technology or continuous process technology since organizational success or survival depends strongly on commitment to discretionary tasks. Under the stochastic character of high technology, organizational adaptability may exist only in the appropriately designed roles. Parenthetically, the one person-one task concept was developed under conditions of deterministic technology with its known, steady divisible and predictable character.*

Last, future research will need to focus intently on work organization structures to provide future knowledge of requirements for boundaries of organizational units and of alternative organizational forms that are neither bureaucratic nor coercive. Additionally, organizational design guides or principles derived from experience with designing evolving alternative organizational forms congruent with self-maintaining organizational units raises a new issue. Central now is the issue of whether organizations are overdesigned, as they appear to be in conventional bureaucratic organizations when compared to the evolving alternative forms. Suggested here is the principle of minimal critical specification. Further research and development of the process of design is required. Again, here we are vastly more knowledgeable about organizational analysis than we are of design.

In conclusion, new and alternative forms of organizations are evolving which provide remarkably good performance results. The design of jobs as a specific activity is absent in such developments. What people do, how they are rewarded, how they deal with futures, how they satisfy needs and adapt to future requirements are being determined on a wider scale that brings together more requirements as a part of the organization design process.

REFERENCES

Clark, Alfred W., ed. (1976) *Experimenting with Organization Life.* New York: Plenum.
Davis, Louis E. and Cherns, Albert B., eds. (1975)*The Quality of Working Life, Cases and Commentary.* New York: Free Press.
Emery, Fred E. and Trist, Eric L. (1965) "The Causal Texture of Organizational Environments," *Human Relations,* vol. 18, pp. 21–32.

---

*Editors' note: These concepts are elaborated upon in reading 12.

FURTHER READING

Work and Society

Bell, D. (1956) *Work and Its Discontents*. Boston: Beacon Press.
Bell, D. (1973) *The Coming of Post-Industrial Society*. New York: Basic Books.
Biderman, A. D. and Drury, T. F. (1976) *Measuring Work Quality for Social Reporting*. New York: Halsted Press.
Crozier, M. (1965) *The Bureaucratic Phenomenon*. London: Tavistock.
Csikszentmihalyi, M. (1976) *Beyond Boredom and Anxiety*. San Francisco: Jossey–Bass.
Department of Health, Education, and Welfare. (1972) *Work in America*. Cambridge, Mass.: M.I.T. Press.
Dubin, R., ed. (1976) *Handbook of Work, Organizations, and Society*. Chicago: Rand-McNally.
Hirsch, F. (1977) *Social Limits to Growth*. Cambridge, Mass.: Harvard University Press.
Hopwood, A. (1977) *Toward Assessing the Economic Costs and Benefits of New Forms of Work Organization*. Geneva: ILO.
Kanter, R. M. (1977) *Men and Women of the Corporation*. New York: Basic Books.
Pirsig, R. (1975) *Zen and the Art of Motorcycle Maintenance*. New York: Random House.
Rosow, J. R. (1974) *The Worker and the Job*. Englewood Cliffs, N.J.: Prentice-Hall.
Sheppard, H. L. and Herrick, N. Q. (1972) *Where Have All the Robots Gone?* New York: Free Press.
Terkel, S. (1975) *Working*. New York: Pantheon.
Yankelovich, D. (1975) *The New Morality*. New York: McGraw-Hill.

Effects of Technology and Automation on Jobs and Workers

Blauner, R. (1964) *Alienation and Freedom*. Chicago: University of Chicago Press.
Caplan, R. D., Cobb, S., French, J., Jr., Harrison, R., and Pinneau, S., Jr. (1975) *Job Demands and Worker Health*. Washington: U.S. Government Printing Office.
Gardell, B. *Alienation and Mental Health in the Modern Industrial Environment*. Proceedings from World Health Organization Symposium: Society, Stress and Disease, no. 1, Stockholm, April, 1970.
Meissner, M. (1969) *Technology and the Worker*. San Francisco: Chandler.
Schumaker, E. F. (1975) *Small Is Beautiful*. New York: Harper-Colophon Books.
Taylor, J. C. (1971) *Technology and Planned Organizational Change*. Ann Arbor, Mich.: Institute for Social Research.
Walker, C. R. and Guest, R. H. (1952) *The Man on the Assembly Line*. Cambridge, Mass.: Harvard University Press.
Walker, C. R. and Guest, R. H. (1957) *The Foreman on the Assembly Line*. Cambridge, Mass.: Harvard University Press.

Current Developments

Clark, P. (1972) *Action Research and Organizational Change*. London: Harper and Row.
Davis, L. E. and Cherns, A. B., eds. (1975) *The Quality of Working Life* (Volumes I and II). New York: Free Press.
Dickson, P. (1975) *The Future of the Workplace*. New York: Weybright and Talley.

Ford, R. N. (1969) *Motivation through the Work Itself*. New York: American Management Association.
Herzberg, F. (1976) *The Managerial Choice*. New York: Dow-Jones.
Hill, P. (1976) *Towards a New Philosophy of Management*. London: Gower Press.
Jenkins, D. (1975) *Job Reform in Sweden*. Stockholm: Swedish Employers' Confederation.
Klein, L. (1976) *New Forms of Work Organization*. Cambridge, England: Cambridge University Press.
Lindestolm, R. and Norstedt, J. (1975) *The Volvo Report*. Stockholm: Swedish Employers' Confederation.
O'Toole, J., ed. (1974) *Work and the Quality of Life*. Cambridge, Mass.: M.I.T. Press.
Warr, P., ed. (1976) *Personal Goals and Work Design*. New York: Wiley.
Warr, P. and Wall, T. (1975) *Work and Well-Being*. Harmondsworth, England: Penguin.

Sociotechnical Systems

Clark, A. W., ed. (1976) *Experimenting with Organizational Life: The Action-Research Approach*. London: Plenum Press.
Clark, P. (1972) *Organization Design*. London: Tavistock.
Cummings, T. G. and Srivastra, S. (1977) *The Management of Work: A Sociotechnical Systems Approach*. Kent, Ohio: Kent State University Press.
DeGreene, K. B. (1973) *Sociotechnical Systems*. Englewood Cliffs, N.J.: Prentice-Hall.
Emery, F. E., ed. (1969) *Systems Thinking*. Harmondsworth, England: Penguin.
Emery, F. E. (1977) *Futures We're In*. Leiden, The Netherlands: Martinus-Nijhoff.
Emery, F. E. and Trist, E. L. (1973) *Towards a Social Ecology*. New York: Plenum Press.
Herbst, P. G. (1974) *Socio-Technical Design*. London: Tavistock.
Herbst, P. G. (1976) *Alternatives to Hierarchies*. Leiden, The Netherlands: Martinus-Nijhoff.
Katz, D. and Kahn, R. L. (1966) *The Social Psychology of Organizations*. New York: Wiley.
Miller, E. J. and Rice, A. K. (1967) *Systems of Organization*. London: Tavistock.
Mumford, E. and Sackman, H., eds. (1975) *Human Choice and Computers*. Amsterdam: North Holland Publishing.
Schon, D. (1971) *Beyond the Stable State*. New York: Norton.
Trist, E., Higgin, G., Murray, H., and Pollack, A. (1963) *Organizational Choice*. London: Tavistock.

INDUSTRIAL DEMOCRACY

Adizes, I. (1971) *Industrial Democracy, Yugoslav Style*. New York: Free Press.
Bolweg, J. F. (1976) *Job Design and Industrial Democracy: The Case of Norway*. Leiden, The Netherlands: Martinus-Nijhoff.
Emery, F. E. and Thorsrud, E. (1969) *Form and Content in Industrial Democracy*. London: Tavistock.
Hunnius, D., Garson, G. D., and Case, J., eds. (1973) *Workers' Control*. New York: Vintage.
Jaques, E. (1951) *The Changing Culture of a Factory*. London: Tavistock.
Jenkins, D. (1973) *Job Power*. Garden City, New York: Doubleday.
Pateman, C. (1970) *Participation in Democratic Theory*. Cambridge, England: Cambridge University Press.

INDEX